JUDICIAL FACTORS

JUDICIAL FACTORS

by

N. M. L. WALKER

C.B.E., LL.D.

Advocate

Published under the auspices of

THE SCOTTISH UNIVERSITIES LAW INSTITUTE

EDINBURGH

W. GREEN & SON LTD.

1974

First published in 1974

© 1974. The Scottish Universities Law Institute

ISBN 0 414 00662 7

PREFACE

THIS is the second of two volumes which together will cover the field of Trusts, Trustees, Executors and Judicial Factors. It is much the shorter of the two and as it was completed first it is being published now in advance of Professor W. A. Wilson's larger volume on Trusts, Trustees and Executors which, although with the printers, will not be published for some months. There are a few cross-references to Professor Wilson's work.

Sheriff Thoms' book on Judicial Factors was published well over a century ago. In 1881 Fraser brought out a second edition, recast and largely rewritten. Irons in 1908 followed Fraser's scheme, but for the reasons explained on page 9 its basis disappeared with the passing of the 1889 Act. I have therefore recast again, which has involved complete rewriting.

The appendix contains only three items, an excerpt from the Distribution of Business Act 1857, the Act of Sederunt of February 13, 1730 (both to an uncertain extent superseded and no longer published in the Parliament House Book), and, by courtesy of the Commercial Union Assurance Company Limited, a form of bond of caution in use in the Court of Session.

The Pupils Protection Act 1849 and the Distribution of Business Act 1857 are cited throughout by these, their familiar, titles, but under the Short Titles Act they may be cited as the Judicial Factors Act 1849 and the Court of Session Act 1857.

I acknowledge the help of Mr. David Maxwell Q.C., Sheriff P. G. B. McNeil, Mr. I. D. Macphail, advocate, Professor A. J. McDonald, Mr. J. A. C. Weir, Sheriff-Clerk of Fife, and particularly that of Mr. John Anderson, the Accountant of Court, with whom I have been in constant communication. Mr. John Blackie prepared the Table of Cases and the Table of Statutes.

N. M. L. W.

St. Andrews.
April 1974.

v

CONTENTS

TABLE OF CASES

TABLE OF STATUTES

CHAPTER I

INTRODUCTORY

Nature of the office

A judicial factor is an officer appointed by a competent court to administer property in accordance with the law applicable to his office and on his own responsibility.[1] An interlocutor appointing a factor and " purposely contrived to screen " him " by the authority of the court in all his proceedings " was strongly disapproved from the Bench.[2] He is the officer of the court and does not become identical with the owner, if any, of the estate. But he is under obligation to account to the owner and therefore it is competent to arrest in his hands in security of a debt due by the owner.[3]

Certain duties are imposed on a judicial factor by statute and Act of Sederunt, and his other duties arise from the particular purpose for which he has been appointed. On appointment he is granted " the usual powers," *i.e.* those normally necessary for the performance of his duties, the Trusts (Scotland) Act 1921, as amended,[4] confers on him additional powers and, possibly, privileges, and the court will grant him special powers if it is satisfied that he requires them. Descriptions of a judicial factor as the " servant " or " agent " of the court may be misleading. The judge who appoints him is not responsible for his remuneration or his actings, and the bond of caution is not a fidelity bond for the protection of the judge, nor as a general rule does a factor carry out the instruction or directions of the court. If he makes an unauthorised investment or an improper payment from income the court as judge enforces the law against him by requiring him to restore any money lost. But when the court fixes or increases the amount paid for maintenance of a ward or as an allowance to a third party,[5] it may be regarded as intervening as master or principal.

It follows from the nature of the office that the court will not appoint more than one factor to administer the same property.[6] The appointment being to administer property, there must be property of an appreciable

---

[1] *Drew* (1867) 5 M. 892; *Mathieson* (1857) 19 D. 917.
[2] *Craigie* (1758) Mor. 7455.
[3] *Mitchell* v. *Scott* (1881) 8 R. 875. The factor was called in the action, but he had ceased to hold office when decree was granted and no decree passed against him. The report does not disclose the terms of the schedule of arrestment, but presumably the arrestment was in the hands of the factor as factor of sums for which he was bound to account to the *absens*. See *Gracie* v. *Gracie*, 1910 S.C. 899.
[4] Trusts (Scotland) Act 1961, s. 4; Trustee Investments Act 1961, s. 10.
[5] See Chap. XVI.
[6] *Watson* (1839) 1 D. 543; *Sloan* (1844) 7 D. 227. The appointment of several factors *loco tutoris* to the same pupils was probably made *per incuriam*: *Wood* (1849) 11 D. 1494. See also *Speirs* (O.H.) 1946 S.L.T. 203.

1

amount [7] or, at least in the case of an *incapax*, a claim which may be enforced. [8] A factor has as such no power over the person of the ward, [9] but custody of a pupil may be awarded to a factor *loco tutoris*. [10]

A factor occupies a fiduciary position in relation to the estate. [11] Accordingly he is not entitled to remuneration apart from his commission, [12] if he uses estate funds for his own purposes any profit belongs to the estate, [13] and, though a transaction between him as factor and himself in another capacity may not now be reducible, [14] he will have to make good any loss. [15]

The appointment does not stop diligence against the estate except where it has been sequestrated for the benefit of creditors. [16]

While the grounds for making or refusing an appointment are dealt with in the particular chapters, the general rule is that the court will refuse to appoint if the purpose of the application is to resolve a dispute which would be more appropriately settled in an action, [17] and if the pleadings raise such questions the usual course is to sist the petition to allow an action to be raised. [18]

English law differs so greatly that it would be unwise to rely on English authority. A legal estate in land cannot be vested in an infant [19]; a father is at common law guardian only of the person of his infant child [20]; and the property of persons of infirm mind is usually administered by the Court of Protection. [21] An *obiter dictum* of Lord Chancellor Cottenham, based on English law and represented in the rubric as a decision of the House of Lords, [22] completely altered the law as to the power of a judicial factor to elect between legal rights and testamentary provisions. [23]

Statutory definitions

The Pupils Protection Act 1849 [24] provides that in that Act, unless there be something in the subject or context repugnant to such construction, " judicial factor " shall mean factor *loco tutoris*, factor *loco absentis* and curator *bonis*. The Judicial Factors (Scotland) Act 1889, by section 6,

---

[7] *Dunbar* (1848) 10 D. 866.
[8] *Moodie* v. *Dempster*, 1931 S.C. 553 at p. 555.
[9] *Dick* v. *Douglas*, 1924 S.C. 787.
[10] *Gulland* v. *Henderson* (1878) 5 R. 768.
[11] Gloag, *Contract* (2nd ed.), p. 508.
[12] *Mitchell* v. *Burness* (1878) 5 R. 1124; *Kennedy* v. *Rutherglen* (1860) 22 D. 567.
[13] *Guthrie* v. *Fairweather* (1853) 16 D. 214.
[14] Trusts (Scotland) Act 1961, s. 2.
[15] Gloag, *Contract* (2nd ed.), p. 510; *Dunn* v. *Chambers* (1897) 25 R. 247.
[16] *Ferguson* v. *Murray* (1853) 15 D. 682.
[17] *Simeone* (O.H.) 1950 S.L.T. 399; *Williamson* (O.H.) (1900) 8 S.L.T. 195.
[18] *Blake's Trs.* v. *Jolly* (O.H.) 1920 1 S.L.T. 304. See also *Church of Scotland Trust* v. *O'Donoghue*, 1951 S.C. 85.
[19] *Halsbury's Laws of England* (3rd ed.), Vol. 32, p. 389.
[20] *Ibid.*, Vol. 21, p. 203.
[21] *Ibid.*, Vol. 29, pp. 566, 592.
[22] *Turnbull* v. *Cowan* (1848) 6 Bell's App. 222.
[23] *Skinner's Curator Bonis* (1903) 5 F. 914, discussed at p. 112. The analogous case of a trust is referred to in *Ewing* v. *Orr Ewing* (1883) L.R. 9 App.Cas. 34, by Lord Blackburn, whose speech is printed in (1884) 11 R. at p. 613.
[24] s. 1.

subjected to the provisions of the 1849 Act " all other factors and persons
. . . appointed by the Court of Session . . . or by any of the sheriffs . . . to
hold, administer or protect any property or funds belonging to persons
or estates in Scotland." The words " appointed by . . . Scotland " must
qualify factors, and the effect was to extend the definition of the 1849 Act
to include all judicial factors.[25] The word " persons " would include
others besides judicial factors. Executors-dative and trustees appointed
by the court are therefore expressly excepted.[26] An interim manager [27]
might be included.

The Trusts (Scotland) Amendment Act 1884, which extended provisions
of the Trusts Acts to judicial factors, defined " judicial factor " to mean
any person judicially appointed factor upon a trust estate or upon an
estate of a person incapable of managing his own affairs, factor *loco
tutoris*, factor *loco absentis* and curator *bonis*. This definition was repeated
in the Trusts (Scotland) Act 1921,[28] and it was not till 1925 that it appeared
of what widely differing interpretations it was capable.[29] In 1961 a new
definition was substituted, *viz.* " any person holding a judicial appointment
as factor or curator on another person's estate." [30] " Curator on another
person's estate " appears to mean curator *bonis*.

The Rules of Court 1965 [31] provide that the expression " judicial
factor " includes curator *bonis*, factor *loco tutoris*, factor *loco absentis*
and factor on trust or other estates, and also includes guardians where
caution is required. The inclusion of the words " or other estates "
widens the definition so as to meet the Lord President's doubt.[32]

Origin of the office

Before the Union extraordinary remedies were provided by the Privy
Council.[33] It authorised an applicant to take charge of the person and
property of his imbecile brother [34]; on the resignation of curators it made
new appointments [35]; it appointed an interim tutor to act until a tutor-
dative was granted.[36] But even at that time the Court of Session was in
use to sequestrate rents and appoint a factor. This it did when a minor's
estate was in danger of dilapidation,[37] when there was a competition
of maills and duties [38] and where the estate was insolvent.[39] When the

---

[25] *Aitken* (1893) 21 R. 62.
[26] *Accountant of Court*, 1907 S.C. 909 at p. 911.
[27] *Gibson* v. *Clark* (1895) 23 R. 294.
[28] s. 2.
[29] *Lowe's Judicial Factor*, 1925 S.C. 11; *Leslie's Judicial Factor*, 1925 S.C. 464.
[30] Trusts (Scotland) Act 1961, s. 3.
[31] Rule 199.
[32] *Leslie's Judicial Factor*, 1925 S.C. 464 at p. 469.
[33] *Bryce* v. *Graham* (1828) 6 S. 425, interlocutor at p. 430; Kames, *Historical Law Tracts* (1758), p. 325.
[34] Campbell (1638) R.P.C. (2nd series), VII, 62.
[35] Innes of Cokstown (1635) R.P.C. (2nd series), VI, 61.
[36] Cleghorn (1689) R.P.C. (3rd series), XIV, 61.
[37] Hamilton (1676) R.P.C. (3rd series), IV, 542. This is the only class of judicial factor mentioned by Stair (IV, 50, 27).
[38] *Law* v. *Lundie* (1624) Mor. 14339.
[39] *Creditors of Broomhall* (1702) Mor. 14341.

Privy Council was abolished in 1707 the gap in respect of these remedies was filled by the Court of Session acting under the *nobile officium*.[40] So great was the number of applications that it was found necessary in 1730 to pass an Act of Sederunt to regulate the duties of judicial factors.

The first Lord President Clyde enumerated eight classes of judicial factor, though he did not regard his list as exhaustive.[41] Some of these had a statutory origin in the nineteenth century, but the more common arose from the exercise of the *nobile officium* in circumstances where the law gave no remedy, *e.g.* where no tutor had been, or could be, appointed, or where an action of choosing curators or a cognition of the insane was impossible, or where the trustees had been removed.[42] Since common law appointments involved the exercise of the *nobile officium* they were originally made by the whole court or, later, by the Inner House, and when jurisdiction was transferred to the Outer House,[43] this was described by Lord Deas as a statutory delegation to a Lord Ordinary of the power to exercise the *nobile officium*.[44] Legislation was consistent with this view until 1948,[45] but the Rules of Court of that year and of 1965 appeared to assume, until the amendment of the latter,[46] that the Lords Ordinary were exercising, not the *nobile officium*, but an independent statutory jurisdiction.[47]

Sequestration of the estate

Sequestration on the strictest definition is a judicial order having a purely negative effect, *viz.* the removal of property from the control of its possessor, and Stair treated it as a species of arrestment. But both he and Erskine define it so as to include the positive element of appointment of an administrator by the court. By sequestration " not only the subject is arrested . . . without the access of either party contending . . . but likewise the custody of the thing controverted is intrusted, by an act and commission of the Lords, to persons nominated by them." [48] " Sequestration . . . is a judicial act . . . whereby the management of the subject sequestrated is taken from the former possessor and is intrusted to the care of a factor . . . named by the court." [49]

If some person is already holding and administering the estate, the result of merely appointing a factor will be that there will be " two powers in action at the same time." [50] Sequestration is one method of avoiding

---

[40] *Bryce* v. *Graham*; Kames, *ut supra.*
[41] *Leslie's Judicial Factor*, 1925 S.C. 464 at p. 469.
[42] *Wotherspoon* (1775) Mor. 7450.
[43] Distribution of Business Act 1857, s. 4.
[44] *Campbell* v. *Grant* (1869) 8 M. 227 at p. 232. See also *Carmont*, 1922 S.C. 686.
[45] *Smith's Trustees*, 1939 S.C. 489.
[46] A.S. January 30, 1970, s. 1.
[47] See p. 125.
[48] Stair IV, 50, 27.
[49] Ersk. II, 12, 55. See also *Smith* v. *Smith* (1892) 20 R. 27, Lord Young at p. 28, Bell's Comm. (7th ed.) II, 244 and *Goudy on Bankruptcy* (4th ed.), p. 113.
[50] *Shand* (1862) 24 D. 829 at p. 832, where a sole trustee was required to resign before an appointment was made.

this result. Where a partner craved the appointment of a factor on the partnership estate the Lord Ordinary required him to amend by inserting a crave for sequestration.[51] He illustrated the point from a trust, observing that the absence of sequestration might lead to awkward questions between the trustees, whose management had not been formally suspended, and the factor. Another case applied to both trust and partnership. Partners had appointed a trustee to wind up the estate, and one of them applied for the removal of the trustee and the appointment of a factor. The court allowed the petition to be amended by adding a crave for sequestration, and then removed the trustee (which restored the powers of the partners), sequestrated the estate (which removed it from their control) and appointed a factor.[52] But it cannot be said that these principles have been consistently adhered to.[53] The same principle applies to executries.[54]

The question does not affect factors *loco tutoris* or *loco absentis* or factors on intestate estates or lapsed trusts,[55] since there is no person able to administer the estate and therefore no risk of conflict of powers. But it does arise in theory in the case of a curator *bonis*, who is appointed on the estate of a person who has not been cognosced or in any other way expressly pronounced by a court to be incapable of managing his own affairs, or of a minor, who, subject to conditions, has power to manage his own affairs. The anomaly of such appointments has not escaped notice,[56] but the question of sequestration does not seem to have been raised. In practice they are made without sequestration. The appointment of a curator *bonis* to an alleged *incapax*, while it lasts, has the same effect as a cognition, and is conclusive of incapacity.[57]

The factory

The appointment of a factor creates a " factory," which continues until it is recalled, even if the factor dies or is removed or his appointment is recalled. The Pupils Protection Act 1849, s. 17, treats the factory as subsisting though the factors change. The effect, so far as resumption of control by the previous administrator is concerned, is the same as if the estate had been sequestrated. A factor was appointed to receive the revenues of a railway company under the company's private Act and the Companies Clauses (Scotland) Act 1845, but died. It was held that, although only the Inner House had power to make the first appointment, the Lord Ordinary on the Bills could competently appoint a successor *ad interim*. This was on the ground that the original order continued in force. Two of the judges described it as a sequestration, but that word

---

[51] *Booth* v. *Mackinnon* (1908) 15 S.L.T. 848. See also *Dixon* v. *Dixon* (1831) 10 S. 178 and 209, (1832) 6 W. & S. 229.
[52] *Jackson* v. *Welch* (1865) 4 M. 177. See also *Carmont*, 1922 S.C. 686, where sequestration was granted after amendment.
[53] *Allan* v. *Gronmeyer* (1891) 18 R. 784; *Souter* v. *Finlay* (1890) 18 R. 86.
[54] *Birnie* v. *Christie* (1891) 19 R. 334, where the executry estate was sequestrated.
[55] But see McLaren, *Wills and Succession* (3rd ed.) II, 1278.
[56] see p. 15 (minors) and p. 22 (*incapaces*).
[57] *Mitchell & Baxter* v. *Cheyne* (1891) 19 R. 324 at p. 326.

does not occur in the Acts, which use language descriptive of an ordinary appointment of a factor.[58] This view was confirmed in a subsequent case. An *incapax* who was a beneficiary under a trust presented a petition for " recall of the curatory " on the ground that he had recovered. Pending these proceedings the curator *bonis* died, and the wife of the *incapax* applied for a new appointment. She stated that the trustees had been advised that the curator's death relieved the *incapax* from restraint in the management of his affairs and that they must now account to him. Lord Deas expressed strong doubt as to the soundness of this advice, and Lord Ivory said that the death of the curator did not alter the condition of the estate, meaning that it was still outwith the control of the *incapax*. Lord Curriehill was very doubtful of the competency of appointing a curator *bonis* without inquiry to a person who maintained that he was sane. Nevertheless the court appointed *de plano*.[59] In an application by the accountant for a rule under section 4 (7) of the Judicial Factors (Scotland) Act 1880 it appeared that some sheriffs held that, if a factor died, any petition for the appointment of a successor must be brought before the sheriff of the county where the ward was then resident, while others held that the new appointment should be made in the original petition in the court where the first appointment was made, even if the ward then resided elsewhere. The court ruled in favour of the second view. While this was done as matter of discretion on grounds of convenience, the judges regarded the new appointment as an incident in a " subsisting factory " or pending process.[60] Although interlocutors have not been consistent,[61] and language is not always precise,[62] the accepted view appears to be that the factory may subsist although the appointment of the factor is terminated.[63] Therefore if the need for a factor is over, recall of both factory and appointment should be craved; otherwise a crave for recall of the appointment should be followed by a crave for the appointment of a successor.[64]

Legislation

The Acts of Sederunt dated July 31, 1690, December 25, 1708, November 22, 1711, and July 31, 1717, applied to factors appointed to ingather sequestrated rents. The first two imposed liability for interest on rents recovered or, after a year, on rents which ought to have been recovered. The third required the lodging of an inventory, and the fourth prohibited a factor from buying in debts or receiving gratuities from a creditor. The Act of Sederunt of February 13, 1730, applied to all factors except such factors as were regulated by former Acts of Sederunt,[65] but, as it repeats

---

[58] *Primrose* v. *Caledonian Railway Co.* (1851) 13 D. 1214.

[59] *Forster* v. *Forster* (1859) 22 D. 15. *Beveridge* (1849) 12 D. 912, was not referred to.

[60] *Accountant of Court* (1893) 20 R. 573.

[61] *Sawyer* v. *Sloan* (1875) 3 R. 271: *A.B.* v. *C.B.*, 1929 S.L.T. 517, 1929 S.N. 85.

[62] In *Tweedie* (1886) 14 R. 212, the interlocutor recalled the appointment, but the judges spoke of recalling the curatory.

[63] Accountant's Notes. Contrast No. 34 (curator's recall, apparently a misprint for curatory's recall) with No. 35 (continuing factory).

[64] Accountant's Notes, No. 35.

[65] s. 12.

in substance [66] the Acts of 1690, 1708 and 1711, and the general law covers the provisions of the Act of 1717, these are now of no importance.

Much of the ground covered by the Act of Sederunt of February 13, 1730, is covered by subsequent legislation, particularly by the 1849 Act, extended by the 1889 Act, but no part of it has been expressly repealed, and to what extent, if any, it has been impliedly repealed does not appear to have been considered. It is probably a safe assumption that just as a statutory provision is impliedly repealed by a subsequent statutory provision repugnant to, or necessarily inconsistent with, it,[67] so is a provision of an Act of Sederunt. The provisions of the 1849 Act that a factor must lodge an inventory [68] and his annual account [69] with the Accountant of Court are inconsistent with the provisions of the Act of Sederunt that he shall lodge these in the hands of the clerk to the act appointing him, and the discretion as to penalty given by the statute [70] is inconsistent with the minimum penalty fixed by the Act of Sederunt. Sections 2 to 6 of the Act of Sederunt are therefore impliedly repealed. The power to grant tacks to continue for one year beyond the endurance of the factory is comprehended within the wider powers of the Trusts (Scotland) Acts,[71] and the power to remove a factor for failure in duty is repeated in the statute.[72] Sections 8 and 10 of the Act of Sederunt are therefore at least superseded. A factor must obviously make such payments as the court directs him to make. Section 9 of the Act of Sederunt is therefore otiose.[73] The remaining sections 1, 7, 11 and 12, appear to be still in force. The Act of Sederunt applied specifically only to factors *loco tutoris*, factors *loco absentis* and curators *bonis*, but, whether in terms of section 12 or as matter of practice,[74] it came to be applied to all judicial factors. The statute of 1849 applied to the same three classes of factor, but it was restricted to them.[75] The result was that from 1849 onwards these factors were regulated by the statute and all others by the Act of Sederunt.[76] This state of affairs came to an end with the passing of the 1889 Act, which brought all judicial factors under the 1849 Act.

The Trusts (Scotland) Amendment Act 1884 provided [77] that in it and previous Trusts Acts [78] " trustee " should include judicial factor, as

---

[66] s. 1.

[67] *Aberdeen Suburban Tramways Co.* v. *Magistrates of Aberdeen*, 1927 S.C. 683 at pp. 689, 692.

[68] ss. 3, 12.

[69] ss. 4, 11, 13.

[70] s. 6.

[71] 1921 Act, as amended by the Trusts (Scotland) Act 1961 and the Trustee Investments Act 1961.

[72] s. 6.

[73] It is also obscure and does not seem to have been considered in any reported case.

[74] *Thoms on Judicial Factors* (2nd ed.) p. 62.

[75] *Accountant of Court* v. *Morrison* (1857) 19 D. 504. See *Aitken* (1893) 21 R. 62, Lord Adam at p. 63.

[76] *Lowe* v. *Simpson* (1872) 11 M. 17; *Fisher* v. *Tod* (1865) 3 M. 889; *Nairne* (1863) 1 M. 515 (all trust estates); *Roxburgh* v. *Dryden* (1890) 17 R. 704 (intestate estate. The case began before the 1889 Act came into force, and the factor forfeited his commission presumably under the Act of Sederunt).

[77] s. 2.

[78] Trusts (Scotland) Acts 1861 to 1867.

there defined. The effect was to apply to some judicial factors some of the provisions relating to trustees. These and the amending Acts [79] were repealed and re-enacted in substance by the Trusts (Scotland) Act 1921, which has itself been amended. [80] Methods of completing title are affected by the Titles to Land Consolidation Act 1868, the Conveyancing Act 1874, the Conveyancing (Scotland) Act 1924 and the Conveyancing (Scotland) Act 1938.

This brief description of the legislation shows the importance of keeping in view the statute law applicable when a particular decision was given. [81] The court will not exercise the *nobile officium* on a matter covered by legislation. [82]

The Accountant of Court

Until 1849 there was no systematic control of judicial factors. Failure to lodge an inventory or the annual accounts required by the Act of Sederunt of 1730 might come to light years afterwards on a petition for removal or discharge. [83] Bonds of caution, inventories and accounts were kept in no central office, but were in charge of the clerk to the court which made the order, and if the court required a report it had to select an accountant in private practice. [84] The report of a Lord Ordinary illustrates the prevailing confusion, [85] and the court welcomed [86] the creation of the office of Accountant of the Court of Session. [87] In 1889 the office was combined with that of the Accountant in Bankruptcy [88] under the title of the Accountant of Court. [89] The Accountant now supervises all judicial factors, [90] and issues general notes for their guidance.

The Accountant's principal powers and duties are to receive the bond of caution and satisfy himself as to its form and due execution and as to the sufficiency of the cautioner, [91] and under the 1849 Act, now extended by the 1889 Act [92] to all judicial factors, to superintend the conduct of judicial factors, [93] to receive and adjust the inventory, [94] to receive and audit the annual accounts, [95] to fix the factor's commission, [96] to make

---

[79] Trusts (Scotland) Acts 1891, 1897 and 1898.
[80] Trusts (Scotland) Act 1861, ss. 3 and 4; Trustee Investments Act 1961, ss. 1 and 16 and Fifth Sched.
[81] *Cormack* v. *Simpson's Judicial Factor* (O.H.) 1960 S.L.T. 197. For illustrations in other spheres, see *Watson* v. *Duncan* (1879) 6 R. 1247 at p. 1250, and *Macleod* v. *Penman*, 1962 J.C. 31 at pp. 46 and 50.
[82] *Tennent's Judicial Factor* v. *Tennent*, 1954 S.C. 215 at p. 225; *Tod* v. *Marshall* (1895) 23 R. 36; *Mitchell Bequest Trustees*, 1959 S.C. 395.
[83] *Adamson* (1848) 10 D. 684. See Lord Jeffrey's remarks.
[84] *Aitken* (1893) 21 R. 62.
[85] *Simpson* v. *Doud* (1855) 17 D. 314 at pp. 316, 317.
[86] *Kerr's Trs.* v. *Moody* (1850) 12 D. 1041 at p. 1045.
[87] 1849 Act, s. 9.
[88] Bankruptcy (Scotland) Act 1856, s. 156.
[89] 1889 Act, s. 1.
[90] 1889 Act, s. 6: *Aitken* (1893) 21 R. 62.
[91] Rules of Court, 1965, r. 200 (e) (i).
[92] s. 6.
[93] s. 10.
[94] ss. 3, 12.
[95] ss. 4, 11, 13–17.   [96] s. 13.

requisitions and orders on the factor,[97] to report to the court any failure in duty by the factor,[98] to report to the Lord Advocate any malversation reasonably suspected,[99] to report to the court on applications for special powers [1] or for discharge [2] and other matters.[3] It is also his duty, if no one interested does so, to apply for the appointment of a successor to any factor who has died or ceased to act,[4] to make an annual report of all judicial factories,[5] and, if he discovers any diversity of practice in the sheriff courts which he thinks should be ended, to report to the First Division.[6] The records of his office are open to inspection, but may not be lent out without the authority of the court.[7] His fees are prescribed by Act of Sederunt.[8] In suitable cases factors obtain advice and assistance from the Accountant, for example where there is difficulty in recovering estate in England, and he has records of precedents which have not been reported. Where an important point is raised in a petition or note and there is no contradictor, it is proper for him to appear by counsel.[9]

Scheme of treatment

Judicial factors are appointed for many different purposes and in some cases under different titles. But they are all now comprehended under the same statutory definitions and subject to the same statutory and, to a great extent, common law rules, so that a decision given in relation to a factor of one class may be equally applicable to factors of other classes. The scheme of arrangement therefore presents a problem. The editor of the second edition of Thoms [10] solved it by dividing factors into two classes, those to whom the 1849 Act applied and those to whom it did not. He then went fully into one of each class and dealt with the remainder of that class by reference to it. Irons [11] followed Fraser's scheme, although its basis disappeared in 1889, when the 1849 Act was applied to all judicial factors. This involves many cross-references. In the hope of simplifying matters a chapter is here devoted to each class of judicial factor, but confined to questions peculiar to that class, and the chapters which follow take up the points common to all judicial factors. The final chapters deal with jurisdiction, procedure and the sheriff court.

---

[97] s. 19.
[98] s. 20.
[99] s. 21.
[1] s. 7.
[2] s. 34.
[3] *Brower's Exr.*, 1938 S.C. 451.
[4] 1889 Act, s. 10.
[5] 1849 Act, s. 18.
[6] 1880 Act, s. 4 (7); *Accountant of Court*, 1907 S.C. 909; *Accountant of Court* (1893) 20 R. 573.
[7] 1849 Act, s. 36.
[8] Act of Sederunt (Rules of Court Amendment No. 3) 1970.
[9] *Carmichael's Judicial Factor*, 1971 S.L.T. 336.
[10] Published in 1881. See the Preface.
[11] Published in 1908.

CHAPTER II

FACTOR LOCO TUTORIS

Introductory

The person and property of a pupil, *i.e.* a boy under fourteen or a girl under twelve, are under the control of the father.[1] On the death of the father control passes to the mother, either alone or along with tutors nominated by the father or by the court.[2] Failing the father and mother, the right passes first to tutors testamentar, *i.e.* tutors nominated by one or both parents,[3] next to the tutor-at-law, *viz.* the nearest agnate over eighteen,[4] and finally to the tutor-dative,[5] an office originally conferred by the King through the Exchequer and now by the Court of Session.[6] A local authority now has certain powers.[7] On the failure of all these the way is open for the appointment of a factor *loco tutoris*, whose powers, unlike those of a tutor, extend, except in special circumstances, to control only of the pupil's property.[8] But the court may also appoint where there is a tutor or a person in the position of tutor or entitled to that position, and it is usually in these cases that the question arises whether an appointment ought to be made.

Grounds for appointment

(a) *Father alive.* A father's position as administrator for his pupil and minor children is inseparable from the relation of parent and child, and the court cannot remove him from it. But it will in appropriate circumstances appoint a factor *loco tutoris*, or a curator *bonis*, to supersede the father in the exercise of his powers,[9] that is, except in special circumstances,[10] his powers relating to the child's property. One reason for doing so is that a conflict of interest has arisen between father and child.[11] A factor *loco tutoris* having been appointed because the father was abroad,

---

[1] This common law rule was overlooked by the framers of the Guardianship of Infants Acts 1886 and 1925.

[2] Guardianship of Infants Act, 1925, s. 4 (1).

[3] Guardianship of Infants Act 1925, s. 5. The father has the right at common law to nominate.

[4] Tutors Act 1474, as amended by Age of Majority (Scotland) Act 1969.

[5] *Trail* (1821) 1 S. 78.

[6] See *Wilson* (1857) 19 D. 286; *Urquhart* (1860) 22 D. 932.

[7] Social Welfare (Scotland) Act 1968, ss. 16, 17 and 18.

[8] Stair himself did not mention factors on the estates of pupils, and probably the court made no such appointments before the Union. The Act of Sederunt of February 13, 1730, however, narrates that the Lords have often been applied to for appointing factors on the estates of pupils not having tutors. The first reported use of the term factor *loco tutoris* appears to be in *Riddel* (1746) Mor. 16350.

[9] *Robertson* (1865) 3 M. 1077; *Shearer's Tutor*, 1924 S.C. 445 (this decision is no longer law; Guardianship of Infants Act 1925, s. 10).

[10] See Custody of pupils, *infra.*

[11] *Cochrane* (1891) 18 R. 456, where the petition was refused; *Mann* (1851) 14 D. 12, referred to in *Robertson* (1865) 3 M. 1077.

the court on his return refused to recall the appointment in respect of a conflict of interest.[12] The father's poverty alone is no ground for interfering with his right, except possibly to the extent of requiring him to find caution in respect of a particular fund,[13] but a factor was appointed where the father was in embarrassed circumstances and lived abroad.[14] The fact that the father is an undischarged bankrupt is not sufficient reason,[15] unless combined with other circumstances, e.g. that the father is occupying property belonging to the pupil and paying no rent [16] or has no fixed residence.[17] A factor *loco tutoris* was appointed where the father was insane,[18] and where the estate was small, another family was interested, and it was desirable to have one management.[19] Where decree of judicial separation or divorce is granted, the court may declare the guilty parent unfit to have custody of the children of the marriage, and that parent is not, on the death of the other parent, " entitled as of right " to the custody or guardianship of the children.[20] Since guardian means tutor [21] and the Acts describe the father as acting as tutor,[22] this appears to mean that a father against whom such a declaration has been made ceases to be entitled, on the death of the mother, to administer his pupil child's property.[23] If such a case arose, the father might perhaps be authorised by the court to administer, or a factor *loco tutoris* might be appointed.

(b) *Mother surviving father.* At common law the mother, as a general rule, had the right to custody of pupil children,[24] but she had no right to administer their property.[25] By statute she now becomes guardian, or tutor, on the father's death,[26] even if she has married again.[27] It is only if she resigns or declines the office [28] or has an adverse interest or a declaration as to her unfitness has been made [29] that a factor *loco tutoris* can be appointed.

(c) *Potential tutors alive.* A factor *loco tutoris* was appointed where

---

[12] *Macalister* v. *Crawford's Trustees* (O.H.) 1909, 1 S.L.T. 232.
[13] *Wardrop* v. *Gosling* (1869) 7 M. 532; *Stevenson's Trustees* v. *Drumbreck* (1857) 19 D. 462, (1861) 4. Macq. 86.
[14] *Moncreiff* (1891) 18 R. 1029 (narrative).
[15] *Walton* (1850) 12 D. 912; *Saunders* (1821) 1 S. 115.
[16] *Allan* (O.H.) (1895) 3 S.L.T. 87.
[17] *Johnstone* v. *Wilson* (1822) 1 S. 558, mentioned in *Robertson* (1865) 3 M. 1077.
[18] *Fleming* (1850) 13 D. 951.
[19] *McWhirter* (1852) 14 D. 761.
[20] Guardianship of Infants Act 1886, s. 7.
[21] *Ibid.*, s. 8.
[22] Guardianship of Infants Act 1925, s. 10.
[23] These Acts are " United Kingdom Acts," which means that they are framed under reference to English law with special provisions intended to make them intelligible and workable in Scotland. This method is unfortunate in relation to the administration of the property of pupils, since the common law of the two countries differs. In England a father is not at common law guardian of his pupil child's estate (*Webb* v. *Cleland's Trustees* (1904) 6 F. 274), and provisions that on the death of the mother the father shall be guardian and that he may by will appoint a guardian (1925 Act, ss. 4 (2), 5 (1)) are otiose in Scotland.
[24] *Borthwick* v. *Dundas* (1845) 8 D. 318.
[25] Such an idea was so foreign to Stair and Erskine that they did not even negative it.
[26] Guardianship of Infants Act 1925, s. 4 (1).
[27] *Campbell* v. *Macquay* (1888) 15 R. 784.
[28] *Willison* (1890) 18 R. 228.
[29] Guardianship of Infants Act 1886, s. 7.

the tutor nominate refused to act,[30] and where she was contumacious,[31] where the person entitled to be tutor-at-law refused to serve [32] or renounced after service [33] or was incapable,[34] and pending service by the tutor-at-law.[35] Hence the importance of intimation to potential tutors.[36]

(d) *Children nascituri.* It being impossible to appoint a factor *loco tutoris*, the difficulty is got over by appointing a judicial factor over the property to which the children, if born, will have a right.[37]

(e) *Illegitimacy.* Neither the father [38] nor the mother [39] has any control over the property of an illegitimate pupil, or any right to appoint a tutor, except over property left by him or her to the child.[40] It is therefore not very clear why it should have been necessary to aver in a petition for the appointment of a factor *loco tutoris* to an illegitimate pupil that his mother was dead and his father's whereabouts unknown,[41] or why it should be necessary to serve such a petition on the mother, the father being dead,[42] unless possibly the parents had a title to object to the nominee.

(f) *Adopted children.* Under section 13 of the Adoption Act 1958, all rights, duties, obligations and liabilities of the natural parents in relation to custody, maintenance and education of an infant (which includes a pupil),[43] including all rights to appoint a guardian, are extinguished and vest in the adopters. This transfers only the rights and duties of the parents *quoad* the personal welfare of the infant and their right to appoint a guardian, but leaves untouched the right of the father at common law and of the mother under statute [44] to administer the pupil's property. Any difficulties in practice might be resolved by the appointment of a factor *loco tutoris.*[45]

(g) *Sums decerned for.* On granting a decree for damages in an action of reparation in favour of a pupil child acting with the concurrence of a curator *ad litem* or in favour of a parent acting on behalf of a pupil child, the court may *de plano* appoint a factor to administer the money and give him powers to disburse capital and income and any other powers thought

---

[30] *Barwick* v. *Barwick* (1855) 17 D. 308; *Russell* (1855) 17 D. 1005.
[31] *Edgar* v. *Fisher's Trustees* (1893) 21 R. 325. The appointment was recalled: *Fisher* v. *Edgar* (1894) 21 R. 1076.
[32] *Black* (1839) 1 D. 676.
[33] *Munnoch* (1837) 15 S. 1267.
[34] *Macintyre* (1850) 13 D. 951.
[35] *Weir* v. *Prentice* (1829) 7 S. 805.
[36] *Russell* (1855) 17 D. 1005 (tutors nominate); *Fowlds* v. *Hodges* (1836) 15 S. 244 (nearest agnate).
[37] *Montignani* (1866) 4 M. 461; *Gowans; Prentice* (1849) 11 D. 1028; *Muller* v. *Dixon* (1854) 16 D. 536 (narrative).
[38] *Corrie* v. *Adair* (1860) 22 D. 897 at pp. 900, 902; *Clarke* v. *Carfin Coal Co.* (1891) 18 R. (H.L.) 63 at p. 68.
[39] *Brand* v. *Shaws* (1888) 16 R. 315.
[40] Bell, Prin. (10th ed.), s. 2071.
[41] *Davison* (1855) 17 D. 629.
[42] *Buckie* (1847) 9 D. 988.
[43] s. 57.
[44] Guardianship of Infants Act 1925, s. 4 (1).
[45] *Robertson* (1865) 3 M. 1077.

expedient.[46] This is a matter in the discretion of the court.[47] Where decree of divorce is granted and under arrangements for financial provision for children [48] the court decerns for payment of aliment to pupil children, it may appoint a factor *loco tutoris* to administer the sums decerned for.[49]

Parties

A petition may be presented by anyone who has an interest in the pupil or his estate. There does not seem to be any reported case where title has been challenged, and petitions have been entertained, though not always granted, at the instance of the father alone,[50] the mother alone,[51] a step-mother,[52] the next-of-kin,[53] step-brothers and step-sisters with concurrence of the next-of-kin,[54] trustees under obligation to make payments to the pupil,[55] persons liable to aliment him,[56] English guardians,[57] and a curator *ad litem*.[58] In the case of illegitimate pupils the petitions were presented by the paternal grandfather [59] and by persons who had maintained the pupil.[60]

The pupil's nearest of kin on both sides, if not concurring, should be called as respondents, and service made on them.[61] But such service may be dispensed with on any who is abroad or in minority.[62] Where testamentary trustees declined office and the testator's widow applied for a factor *loco tutoris*, intimation was ordered on the declining trustees.[63] The mother of an illegitimate pupil must be cited.[64]

Custody of pupils

A factor *loco tutoris* has in principle no right to custody. But if the parents, or the survivor, are unfit to have custody, the court may award it to a factor *loco tutoris* and may require him to submit a scheme for the pupil's upbringing.[65] The court has power to make an order for custody

---

[46] Rules of Court 1965, rr. 131–134; *Encyclopaedia of Scottish Legal Styles*, VI, Form 58.

[47] *Fairley* v. *Allan*, (O.H.) 1948 S.L.T. (Notes) 81; *Falconer* v. *Robertson*, (O.H.) 1949 S.L.T. (Notes) 57.

[48] Succession (Scotland) Act 1964, s. 26 (2).

[49] *Kynynmound* v. *Kynynmound*, May 27, 1965, unreported.

[50] *Cochrane* (1891) 18 R. 456; *Mann* (1851) 14 D. 310. See also *McWhirter* (1852) 14 D. 761.

[51] *Willison* (1890) 18 R. 228; *Lamb* (1857) 19 D. 699.

[52] *Raeburn* (1851) 14 D. 310.

[53] *Napier* (1851) 14 D. 10; *Macintyre* (1850) 13 D. 951.

[54] *Wood* (1849) 11 D. 1494.

[55] *Wardrop* v. *Gossling* (1869) 7 M. 532.

[56] *Black* (1839) 1 D. 676.

[57] *Viscountess Alford* (1851) 13 D. 950.

[58] *Thomson* (1841) 16 Fac. Dec. 1307.

[59] *Buckie* (1847) 9 D. 988.

[60] *Davison* (1855) 17 D. 629.

[61] *Logan* (1828) 6 S. 477; *Fowlds* v. *Hodges* (1836) 15 S. 244.

[62] *Carmichael* (1848) 10 D. 1286; *Macintyre* (1850) 13 D. 951.

[63] *Russell* (1855) 17 D. 1005.

[64] *Buckie* (1847) 9 D. 988.

[65] *Gulland* v. *Henderson* (1878) 5 R. 768; *Muir* v. *Kerr* (1868) 6 M. 268; *Denny* v. *Macnish* (1863) 1 M. 268. See also *Moncreiff* (1891) 18 R. 1029, and *Paul* (1838) 16 S. 822.

up to the age of sixteen,[66] but it may be necessary to consult the child's wishes on his attaining minority.[67]

Termination of factory

The factory terminates on service by the tutor-at-law,[68] or on the pupil's death. It also terminates on his attaining minority. If no curator is then appointed, the factor *loco tutoris* becomes curator *bonis*,[69] and, except for the change in the factor's title, the factory continues uninterrupted, that is to say the factor does not require a discharge *qua* factor *loco tutoris* and appointment as curator *bonis*. When the child had attained minority, the court recalled the appointment of factor *loco tutoris*, not the statutory appointment as curator *bonis*.[70]

---

[66] Custody of Children (Scotland) Act 1939, s. 1.
[67] *Morrison*, 1943 S.C. 481.
[68] *Young* v. *Rose* (1839) 1 D. 1242. See also *Weir* v. *Prentice* (1829) 7 S. 805, and *Ross* v. *Lockhart's Trustees* (1829) 3 W. & Sh. 481 (narrative, first paragraph).
[69] Judicial Factors (Scotland) Act 1889, s. 11.
[70] *Fisher* v. *Edgar* (1894) 21 R. 1076.

CHAPTER III

CURATOR BONIS TO MINOR

Anomalous nature of the office

A minor, *i.e.* a youth aged between fourteen and eighteen [1] or a girl aged between twelve and eighteen,[1] is not as such *incapax*, but is capable of acting alone with legal effect, under certain exceptions [2] and subject to his rights within the *quadriennium utile*, unless he has a curator or curators. A father is in effect curator to his minor children [3] and he is entitled to appoint curators to them by will.[4] If the father died without making any appointment, or the curators appointed by him failed, a minor had the privilege of choosing curators by action.[5] Curators do not oust the minor from control of his property, but their consent is necessary to give legal effect to his acts.[6] In other words, a curator acts with the minor, not for him, and so is not a judicial factor.[7]

Such being the legal *status* of a minor and the means available for supplementing it when necessary or desirable, it might be thought that in the case of a minor whose only disability is his nonage there is no room for the appointment to him of a curator *bonis*, seeing that the latter is a judicial factor,[8] acts therefore without the consent of the minor and supersedes him entirely in the management of his estate,[9] and may himself obtain special powers.[10] So impressed were Thoms and his editor with the anomalous nature of the office that several pages were devoted to an unsuccessful attempt to find for a curator *bonis* to a minor a position intermediate between a curator and a judicial factor.[11] Lord Pearson admitted his failure in the same quest.[12]

---

[1] Age of Majority (Scotland) Act 1969.

[2] The Succession (Scotland) Act 1964, s. 28, removes an exception.

[3] *Robertson* (1865) 3 M. 1077.

[4] Tutors and Curators Act 1696.

[5] Act 1555, c. 35 (now repealed); Tutors and Curators Act 1672. The action of choosing curators is no longer competent, but a minor may apply to the Court of Session to appoint curators to him: Administration of Justice (Scotland) Act 1933, s. 12.

[6] *O'Donnell* v. *Brownside Coal Co.*, 1934 S.C. 534 at pp. 543, 545, 547.

[7] In *Gilligan* v. *M'Culloch* (O.H.) (1900) 8 S.L.T. 187, the Lord Ordinary, incompetently it is thought, authorised the Accountant of Court to audit the accounts of a curator chosen by a minor. In the sequel (*Hutchison* (O.H.) (1908) 15 S.L.T. 1042) the Lord Ordinary, contrary to the view of the Accountant of Court and without delivering an opinion, authorised the curator to sell part of the minor's heritage, thus treating him as a judicial factor; *cf. Bird* (O.H.) (1908) 15 S.L.T. 1043.

[8] *Leslie's Judicial Factor*, 1925 S.C. 464 at p. 469; *Perry* (O.H.) (1903) 10 S.L.T. 536.

[9] *Mayne* (1853) 15 D. 554.

[10] *Semple* v. *Tennent* (1888) 15 R. 810.

[11] (2nd ed.) pp. 254–256, 267–271.

[12] *Perry* (O.H.) (1903) 10 S.L.T. 536. The crave discloses great doubts as to the function of a curator *bonis* to a minor. So in a lesser degree does the crave in *Waring* (O.H.) 1933 S.L.T. 190, 1933 S.N. 14.

A curator was included in the definition of trustee in the Trusts (Scotland) Amendment Act 1884 [13] and still is in the Trusts (Scotland) Act 1921.[14] He is now for the first time included in the definition of judicial factor,[15] but the whole phrase is " curator on another person's estate," and this probably means curator *bonis*. For a curator to a minor to do at his own hand any of the acts mentioned in section 4 of the 1921 Act would be clearly at variance with the terms and purposes of his appointment, *viz.* to act with the minor. Whether the court would entertain a petition by the curator under section 5 has not been considered.

Origin and development of the office

The office arose from difficulties in carrying out the procedure for choosing curators.[16] The Act of 1555 and the Tutors and Curators Act 1672, as interpreted,[17] required the minor to cite two of his next-of-kin on each side. Where this was impossible, either because the minor was illegitimate or because next-of-kin were not available, the court would either dispense with the citation of the next-of-kin and so enable the procedure to be carried through,[18] or it would itself appoint curators or curators *bonis*.[19] The latter practice developed in two ways.

First, where there were in the family both minor and pupil children the person appointed factor *loco tutoris* was frequently also appointed to protect the minors. In one case the appointment was of curators,[20] but in all the others it was of a curator *bonis*.[21] The practice was further extended to cases where there were only minors.[22] No explanation was ever given as to why curators were appointed in some cases and curators *bonis* in others, and one can only speculate that it depended on the crave. Indeed, the distinction came to be ignored,[23] and cases involving both offices were cited indiscriminately,[24] while the main argument of the First Division in their difference with the Second Division as to the necessity of an averment that the minor could not choose curators (about to be

---

[13] s. 2.
[14] s. 2.
[15] Trusts (Scotland) Act 1961, s. 3.
[16] No practice seems to have followed two isolated cases: *Bower* (1750) M. 8910 (interim pending choosing of curators); *Hay* v. *Grant* (1749) Mor. 8973 (for limited purpose).
[17] Ersk. I, 7, 11.
[18] *Kyle* (1861) 23 D. 1104, and cases there cited.
[19] *Young*, February 19, 1818, F.C., followed in *Wood* (1834) 12 S. 663; *Reid* (1839) 1 D. 1217; *Towton* (1847) 10 D. 225; *Ogilvy; McNeill* (1849) 11 D. 1029.
[20] *Wood* (1849) 11 D. 1494. A feature of this case is that the court appointed several curators, which was normal, and several factors *loco tutoris*, which was contrary to their own rulings: *Sloan* (1844) 7 D. 227; *Watson* (1839) 1 D. 543.
[21] *Johnstone* v. *Wilson* (1822) 1 S. 558; *Donaldson* v. *Kennedy* (1833) 11 S. 740; *Johnston* (1839) 1 D. 1030; *Dow* (1847) 10 D. 148; *Sutherland; Fleming* (1851) 13 D. 951; *McKinnon* (1851) 14 D. 12; *McWhirter* (1852) 14 D. 761; Contra *Whiteside* (1834) 12 S. 355, where the minors were told to choose curators. See also *Glassford* (1849) 11 D. 1030; *McLellan* (1847) 10 D. 148.
[22] *Webster* (1850) 12 D. 911; *Semple* v. *Tennent* (1888) 15 R. 810, where the crave was said to have been a mistake.
[23] In *Robertson* (1865) 3 M. 1077, the interlocutor uses both terms of the same person. Section 11 of the 1889 Act uses the term " curator *bonis*," while the side note has " curator."
[24] *Barron* (1854) 17 D. 61, citing *Macarthur*.

noticed) rested on the assumption that any appointment made would be of a curator *bonis*.[25] This became the normal appointment, and, although this has never been said, a feeling may have been growing that it is really more suitable that a boy of fifteen should have his property managed for him. The 1889 Act [26] provides that on a pupil attaining minority his factor *loco tutoris* becomes not his curator, but his curator *bonis*. The sheriff-substitute and the sheriff dismissed an unopposed application for the appointment of a curator *bonis* to a minor on the ground that as minors were not mentioned in the Act [27] they had no jurisdiction. The Division reversed, and the Lord President observed that, in accordance with the ordinary and proper use of the term, " curator *bonis* " is applicable to the factor appointed both in the case of minors and of the insane.[28] It may be, however, that Parliament did not intend to confer this drastic power on sheriffs, and that the omission of minors was deliberate.

Secondly, for a time the court refused to interfere, except where the same person was appointed curator *bonis* and factor *loco tutoris*,[29] unless it was shown that the minor could not choose curators.[30] The First Division maintained this attitude until 1853, but in 1857 the Second Division deliberately departed from it and appointed a curator *bonis* where no reason was given why the minor should not choose curators.[31] In the next reported cases, however, such an averment was made.[32] Present practice, which is unaffected by the abolition of the action of choosing curators, draws a distinction between cases where the curator *bonis* is also to be factor *loco tutoris* and where he is not. The averment is recommended in the latter case,[33] not in the former.[34]

Parties

Minors are presumed to be possessed of such a degree of judgment and discretion that guardians cannot be imposed on them against their wills.[35] The only exception is that a father may by will appoint curators.[36] A minor was free to choose curators or not as he wished.[35] Under the new procedure an application for the appointment of curators must be at the instance of the minor.[37] It might therefore be thought that *a fortiori* a petition for the appointment of a curator *bonis* to a minor based merely on the fact that he is a minor would be incompetent unless

---

[25] *Mayne* (1853) 15 D. 554.
[26] s. 11.
[27] Judicial Factors (Scotland) Act 1880, which extended to sheriffs the power to appoint factors *loco tutoris* and curators *bonis* to pupils or insane persons within their jursidiction.
[28] *Penny* v. *Scott* (1894) 22 R. 5.
[29] In the cases in note 30 there was no difficulty in choosing curators except in the last two.
[30] *Maclean* (1834) 12 S. 355; *Matthew* (1851) 14 D. 312; *Eaton* (1853) 2 Stu. 192.
[31] *Carter* (1857) 19 D. 286.
[32] *Hutchison* (O.H.) (1881) 18 S.L.R. 725; *Perry* (O.H.) (1903) 10 S.L.T. 536.
[33] *Encyclopaedia of Scottish Legal Styles*, VI, Form 57.
[34] *Ibid.* Form 56.
[35] Ersk. I, 7, 11.
[36] Tutors and Curators Act 1696.
[37] Administration of Justice (Scotland) Act 1933, s. 12.

at the instance of the minor himself. Nevertheless, curators *bonis* were appointed on the application of " relations," [38] and, although in a subsequent case the court insisted on a petition by the minors,[39] this was gone back on and an appointment was made on the petition of the mother,[40] and in three later cases the court entertained petitions at the instance of relations. In the first the Lord Ordinary had in view the serious result of granting the application, as his reference to *Mayne* [41] shows, and required that written consent by the minors be lodged before making the appointment.[42] In the second the minors opposed the petition, but the Lord Ordinary, instead of dismissing it as incompetent in the absence of consent, refused it on the ground that the minors could choose curators.[43] In the third, when it was argued for the minor that it was incompetent to appoint a curator *bonis* to her against her wishes, the Lord Ordinary did not decide the point, but gave effect to her opposition in another way.[44] These two cases have been taken to vouch the proposition that a curator *bonis* will never be appointed against the minor's wishes.[45]

If the father is alive, he must be a party either as petitioner with the minor or as respondent, since his position as administrator is affected. In other cases it would appear competent for the minor to petition alone without calling any respondent. If the minor wishes his property to be managed by a third party, that is his own affair. But since the matter is one of discretion, it is most unlikely that the court would appoint in such circumstances, and the practice is, if possible, to conjoin two of the next of kin on each side as petitioners (which saves expense) or to call them as respondents.[46] In case of difficulty the court might appoint a curator *ad litem*.[47]

Grounds for appointment

If the father has died without nominating curators, the court usually appoints, at least if no one will act as curator, provided that the minor consents and that no relevant objection is stated, *e.g.* to the person proposed for the office. A conflict of interest between the minor and the proposed curators might be a ground for appointing a curator *bonis*.[48]

If the father is alive strong ground must be shown for interfering with his right of administration.[49] A minor succeeded to property in England,

---

[38] *Johnstone* v. *Wilson* (1822) 1 S. 558; *Donaldson* v. *Kennedy* (1833) 11 S. 740 (appointment made in 1826).
[39] *Buchanan* (1854) 16 D. 717.
[40] *Galloway* (1855) 17 D. 321.
[41] (1853) 15 D. 554.
[42] *Hutchison* (O.H.) (1881) 18 S.L.R. 725.
[43] *Macdonald* (O.H.) (1896) 4 S.L.T. 4.
[44] *Hutcheon* v. *Alexander* (O.H.) (1909) 1 S.L.T. 71.
[45] Thomson and Middleton, *Manual of Court of Session Procedure*, p. 272.
[46] *Encyclopaedia of Scottish Legal Styles*, VI, Forms 56, 57.
[47] *Carter* (1857) 19 D. 286. The mother was petitioner with concurrence of the minors.
[48] See *McNeill* (1849) 11 D. 1029.
[49] *Robertson* (1865) 3 M. 1077. Where a father was in embarrassed circumstances trustees in paying money to him for his children required him to find caution, a course commended by the Court: *Stevenson's Trustees* v. *Dumbreck* (1857) 19 D. 462, (1861) 4 Macq. 87.

but the trustees declined to make payment because his father was bankrupt. On a petition by the minor with consent of his father the court appointed a curator *bonis* for the trust property only.[49] But in an earlier case where the father's affairs were embarrassed a general appointment was made with his consent.[50] A curator *bonis* was appointed against the father's wishes where he had misapplied the minor's property.[51]

Where decree for damages is granted to a minor or an extra-judicial settlement in his favour is made, the court may *de plano* appoint a factor to administer the money, give him powers to disburse capital and income and any other powers thought expedient, and also give directions as to payments.[52] The factory is part of the original process.[53] On granting decree of divorce and decerning for aliment in favour of a minor child [54] the court may appoint a curator *bonis* to administer the aliment. Adoption [55] does not deprive the father of his position at common law of administrator-in-law of his minor children *quoad* their property. Any difficulties arising from this situation might be avoided by the appointment of a curator *bonis*.[56]

Termination of curatory

The appointment comes to an end when the ward attains the age of eighteen.[57] Where a factor *loco tutoris* has become curator *bonis* by virtue of section 11 of the Judicial Factors Act 1889, he " shall continue the administration of the estate until the majority of the said minor or until he has himself chosen curators." In spite of the absolute terms of this provision the court as matter of discretion recalled [58] or refused to recall [59] the appointment of a factor *loco tutoris* who has become a curator *bonis*. In neither case did the respondent maintain that the court had no power to recall.

If the curator *bonis* has been appointed during minority, and therefore on the petition, or at least with the concurrence, of the minor, it might have been thought that the curatory cannot be maintained against his will and must be recalled on his petition. But this view cannot be reconciled with the decision in *Balfour Melville*.[60] That case was dealt with generally and without reference to section 11 of the 1889 Act, and the court refused the minor's application for recall on the ground that it was not satisfied with the proposals for managing his property. Lord McLaren

---

[49] *Glassford* (1849) 11 D. 1030.
[50] *McNab* v. *McNab* (1871) 10 M. 248.
[51] Rules of Court 1965, rr. 131–134; *Encyclopaedia of Scottish Legal Styles*, VI, Form 58. See *Fairley* v. *Allan* (O.H.) 1948 S.L.T. (Notes) 81; *Falconer* v. *Robertson* (O.H.) 1949 S.L.T. (Notes) 57.
[53] *McIntosh* v. *Wood*, 1970 S.C. 179.
[54] Succession (Scotland) Act 1964, s. 26 (2).
[55] Adoption Act 1958, s. 13. See p. 12.
[56] *Robertson* (1865) 3 M. 1077.
[57] Age of Majority (Scotland) Act 1969; *McIntosh* v. *Wood*, 1970 S.C. 179.
[58] *Fisher* v. *Edgar* (1894) 21 R. 1076.
[59] *Balfour Melville* (1903) 5 F. 347.
[60] (1903) 5 F. 347.

put it most specifically. " When the estate of the ward has been placed in the hands of the court, and an application is made to withdraw it, a public duty is cast on the court to see that the fund is not withdrawn except under a proper and effective scheme of administration." Subject to the observation that the point was not argued, this case is authority for holding that the minor has no absolute right to have the curatory recalled and that the court will recall only if satisfied that it is in his interest to do so.

Minority and lesion

While there is no reported decision that a transaction by a curator *bonis* is reducible on the grounds of minority and lesion, the proposition is supported by dictum and analogy. In expressing an opinion against empowering a factor *loco tutoris* to sell a pupil's heritage Lord President Hope observed that even if they granted the power the sale would be reducible on the ground of lesion,[61] and there is no distinction in this connection between a factor *loco tutoris* and a curator *bonis*. Each acts on behalf of his ward. An analogous case is an act done by tutors on behalf of a pupil, which is reducible on proof of lesion,[62] and where the court refused a judicial factor on a trust power to sell heritage destined to a minor, the opinion of the Lord President seems to mean that the minor could reduce the sale.[63] A minor may reduce even if he has acted with the consent of his curators.[64] The remedy of reduction is thus available to a minor or pupil not only against the weakness of judgment or levity of disposition incident to youth or the imprudence or negligence of his curators,[65] but also against the errors of his factor *loco tutoris* or curator *bonis*, an adult selected for his supposed integrity and capacity. Erksine [66] rejects the doctrine that a minor who acts with his curators has no right to restitution, but merely a remedy against them. He does however concede that in these circumstances there must be the clearest evidence of lesion, and this would apply with equal force to a transaction by a curator *bonis*.

---

[61] *Hammond* (1831) 10 S. 167.
[62] Ersk. I, 7, 34. See declaratory portion of the interlocutor reduced in *Vere* v. *Dale* (1804) M. 16389.
[63] *Auld* (1856) 18 D. 487.
[64] *Harkness* v. *Graham* (1833) 11 S. 760; Ersk. I, 7, 34.
[65] Ersk. I, 7, 36.
[66] I, 7, 34.

CHAPTER IV

CURATOR BONIS TO INCAPAX

Historical

The guardianship of the person and property of an insane person was originally vested in the Sovereign, who might, through the Exchequer, appoint a tutor-dative.[1] The gift may now be conferred by the Court of Session.[2] The law recognised two kinds of insanity, fatuity (or idiocy) and furiosity, and the usual mode of proof was by cognition by a jury presided over by the judge ordinary of the territory in which the person resided, in obedience to a brieve of fatuity or a brieve of furiosity from Chancery. This brieve, which might be purchased by any near relation,[3] directed the jury to find whether fatuity or furiosity existed and, if so, from what date, since no alienation of property after that date was valid.[4] Mackenzie's observation[5] that the Exchequer would not grant a tutory without cognition seems to be too absolute, since there are dicta to the opposite effect,[6] and tutors-dative have been appointed to persons not cognosced.[7] Under the Curators Act 1585, as interpreted,[8] the nearest male agnate aged twenty-five or over had the right to be served tutor-at-law[9] or curator-at-law[9] to a person cognosced as either fatuous or furious, and therefore the jury were required to name the qualified agnate. If the qualified agnate did not serve, a tutor-dative might be given,[10] but the tutory-dative fell on service by the qualified agnate.[11] No difficulty arises in regard to an insane pupil. His father,[12] or mother,[13] or testamentary tutors or a tutor-dative act for him in any event.[14] Where an *incapax* reached majority neither his father[15] nor any testamentary tutor[16]

---

[1] Stair I, 6, 11 and 25; *Bryce* v. *Grahame* (1828) 6 S. 425 at p. 433, (1828) 3 W. & Sh. 323.

[2] Court of Exchequer (Scotland) Act 1856, s. 19.

[3] *Larkin* v. *McGrady* (1874) 2 R. 170; *Bryce* v. *Grahame* (1828) 6 S. 425 at p. 429, (1828) 3 W. & Sh. 323. Lord McLaren overlooked these decisions: *A B* v. *C B* (1890) 18 R. 90 at p. 97, *sub nom. C B* v. *A B* (1891) 18 R. (H.L.) 40.

[4] Stair IV, 3, 7; Ersk. I, 7, 50.

[5] *Works* I, 215.

[6] *Bryce* v. *Grahame* (1828) 6 S. 425, Lord Mackenzie at p. 433, (1828) 3 W. & Sh. 323; *A B* v. *C B* (1890) 18 R. 90, Lord McLaren at p. 97, *sub nom. C B* v. *A B* (1891) 18 R. (H.L.) 40.

[7] *Stewart* v. *Spreul* (1663) Mor. 6279; *Dick* v. *Douglas*, 1924 S.C. 787, where, however, a curator *bonis* had already been appointed.

[8] Ersk. I, 7, 50.

[9] Both terms are used.

[10] *Larkin* v. *McGrady* (1874) 2 R. 170.

[11] *Colqhoun* v. *Wardrop* (1628) M. 6276; *Moncrieff* v. *Maxwell* (1710) Mor. 6286.

[12] Mackenzie, *Works* I, 297.

[13] Guardianship of Infants Act 1925, s. 4 (1).

[14] Stair I, 6, 25.

[15] On principle. See *Graham* (1881) 8 R. 996.

[16] Ersk. I, 7, 49. See *Bryce* v. *Grahame* (1828) 6 S. 425 at pp. 434, 435, (1828) 3 W. & Sh. 323.

could act for him until he had been cognosced, and the power of a tutor-dative would presumably cease unless insanity were proved. The period of minority does not seem to have been considered, probably because no one has cared to act as curator to a person known, or suspected, to be insane.

Since only a near relative might initiate a cognition, and no one could be compelled to do so, an insane person and his property would be unprotected, unless a tutor-dative were appointed. If no such appointment was made, the Privy Council gave a remedy. But after the Union and the abolition of the Privy Council the Court of Session was of necessity applied to, and it began a practice of appointing a curator *bonis* to administer the property, the appointment being regarded as a temporary one pending the service of a tutor.[17] Lord President Inglis observed that a tutor-at-law was suitable for an apparently permanent case of insanity and a curator *bonis* where there was a probability of recovery,[18] but this suggestion was inconsistent with the decision in *Bryce* v. *Grahame*,[17] where there was little chance of recovery, and has not been followed. Curators *bonis* are now appointed in all cases, and cognition, even under the simplified form introduced by section 101 of the Court of Session Act 1868, is never used.[19] The House of Lords questioned the power of the Court of Session, except as an interim expedient,[20] to appoint a curator *bonis* to a person whom no court had pronounced incapable of managing his own affairs and so depriving him of the management, but were somewhat reluctantly satisfied by the explanation of a majority of the whole court that the practice was justified by inveterate usage and necessity.[21] Some twenty years later Lord Justice-Clerk Hope again referred to the anomaly,[22] and it is noticed by Thoms.[23]

Grounds for appointment

The origin and justification of the office would confine it to cases of insanity, that is, to use the modern phrase, of " mental disorder," and the usual ground is that the person " is of unsound mind and incapable of managing his own affairs or of giving instructions for their management."[24] A local authority, when satisfied that any person in its area is " incapable, by reason of mental disorder,[25] of adequately managing and administering his property and affairs," that a curator *bonis* ought to be appointed, and that no arrangements have or are being made in that behalf, must apply

---

[17] *Bryce* v. *Grahame* (1828) 6 S. 425 (interlocutor), (1828) 3 W. & Sh. 323.
[18] *A B* v. *C B* (1890) 18 R. 90 at p. 95, *sub nom. C B* v. *A B* (1891) 18 R. (H.L.) 40. See also Bell, Prin. (10th ed.), para. 2121.
[19] The relative Rules of Court were omitted in 1965.
[20] See *Simpson* v. *Simpson* (1891) 18 R. 1207.
[21] *Bryce* v. *Grahame* (1828) 6 S. 425; (1828) 3 W. & Sh. 323.
[22] *Maconochie* (1857) 19 D. 366 at p. 376.
[23] *Judicial Factors* (2nd ed.), pp. 276, 278.
[24] *Brown* v. *Hackston* (O.H.) 1960 S.C. 27; *Encyclopaedia of Scottish Legal Styles*, V, Form 347.
[25] *i.e.* mental illness or mental deficiency, however caused or manifested: Mental Health (Scotland) Act 1960, s. 6.

for an appointment.[26] Insanity, or mental disorder, falls into two categories, imbecility or insane delusions, in fact the fatuity or the furiosity of the brieve.

Imbecility differs from mere facility. A petition based on averments of facility and undue influence was dismissed,[27] and on similar averments it was admitted that a curator *bonis* could not be asked for.[28] Where a person was in a condition of mental facility which incapacitated her from managing her own affairs, the Lord Ordinary refused to recall an appointment, but was doubtful whether the facts would have justified him in making one.[29] The distinction, however, is a narrow one, and appointments were made where the person was of weak mind and very apt to be misled,[30] and where his state of mind approached imbecility and rendered him liable to imposition or undue influence.[31]

Insane delusions or hallucinations unlikely to affect the person's management of his affairs are not a ground for appointment.[32] One question is as to an insane delusion relating to a person's nearest relations and its possible effect on his disposal of his property. In an application for recall of a curatory it was established that the ward could manage his business successfully, but that he still entertained an insane delusion as to the fidelity of his wife and the paternity of his daughter. In recalling the curatory the Lord Ordinary observed that the possibility of unfairness to his wife and daughter was no reason to continue the curatory and that the real question was whether the ward was suffering from insane delusions which might affect his disposal of his property to his own detriment.[33] The Lord Ordinary referred to *C B* v. *A B*,[34] but it is doubtful whether he attached sufficient importance to the speech of Lord Herschell, which was concurred in by Lord Watson and Lord Morris. In that case a man entertained insane delusions against his family and thought they were trying to poison him. One of the medical reports contained this passage: " If the management of his affairs includes a just and natural regard to the interests of his family, we do not consider he is worthy of being entrusted with their management, but we are not prepared to say that his mental condition incapacitates him from administering his affairs in other respects." When Lord Herschell observed that this obviously meant that C.B. was " suffering from insane delusions which might affect the disposal by him of his property and might lead him to employ it in a manner in which he would not employ it if he were sane," he must have meant the possible effect on the family, since that report referred to nothing else. The next report dealt mainly with the family, though it did in a hypo-

---

[26] *Ibid.* s. 91.
[27] *Calderwood* v. *Duncan* (O.H.) (1907) 15 S.L.T. 777. No medical certificates were produced.
[28] *Davie* v. *Hagart* (1894) 21 R. 1052.
[29] *A B* v. *A B's Curator Bonis* (O.H.) (1908) 16 S.L.T. 583.
[30] *Speirs* (1851) 14 D. 11.
[31] *Dewar* v. *Dewar* (1834) 12 S. 315.
[32] *Henderson* (1851) 14 D. 11.
[33] *A B* v. *C B* (O.H.) 1929 S.L.T. 517.
[34] (1891) 18 R. (H.L.) 40.

thetical way mention spiritualism. On these and earlier less detailed reports Lord Herschell thought the case for appointment clear. It seems obvious that if C.B. had bought himself an annuity, possibly increasing his income, and given the rest of his property to a spiritualist society or a cat and dog home he would employ his capital " in a manner in which he would not employ it if he were sane." If this interpretation is correct, some of the dicta in *Forsyth* [35] must be received with caution.

In spite of the origin of the office and at least one dictum that the court will not appoint a curator *bonis* except on proof of mental incapacity,[36] an appointment has been made to a person incapacitated by paralysis [37] or apoplexy [38] and was contemplated where the person was incapacitated by " disease." [39] It has also been made to a person who had been deaf and dumb since birth [40] and to one who was blind and deaf.[41] But in all cases the court must be satisfied that the handicap prevents the person from managing his affairs.[42]

An appointment was made pending a cognition,[43] and, at least as a general rule, should be made where a litigant becomes insane *pendente processu*.[44] In an action of divorce on the ground of incurable insanity a curator *ad litem* must be appointed.[45]

Evidence of incapacity

Normally the petition must be supported by two medical certificates,[46] which need no longer be on soul and conscience,[47] stating the date on which the person was last visited,[48] to the effect that he is through mental derangement incapable of managing his affairs or of giving instructions for their management.[49] If the person is an inmate of an asylum, one of the certificates must be by a doctor not connected with it.[50] But a petition will be entertained without certificates and inquiry allowed if the petitioner makes relevant averments of incapacity [51] and further avers that the alleged *incapax* or those in whose control he is have refused to allow him to be medically examined.[52] The same course was followed where owing

---

[35] (1862) 24 D. 1435. The ward's delusion was only the indirect cause of her dislike of her daughters.
[36] *Mackie* (1866) 5 M. 60 at p. 61.
[37] *Eddie* v. *MacBean's Curator Bonis* (1885) 12 R. 660 (narrative); *Howie* (1826) 5 S. 77.
[38] *Forster* (1848) 11 D. 1031 (narrative).
[39] *Cameron* (1849) 12 D. 912.
[40] *Blaikie* (1827) 5 S. 268.
[41] *Duncan* (O.H.) 1915, 2 S.L.T. 50; *Morrison* (1857) 19 D. 504; *Mark* (1845) 7 D. 882 (an exceptional case).
[42] *Kirkpatrick* (1853) 15 D. 734.
[43] *Simpson* v. *Simpson* (1891) 18 R. 1207.
[44] *Moodie* v. *Dempster*, 1931 S.C. 553.
[45] Divorce (Scotland) Act 1938, s. 3; *Ramsay* v. *Ramsay*, 1964 S.C. 289.
[46] *Robertson* (1853) 16 D. 317.
[47] Practice Note, June 6, 1968. As to certificates granted abroad, see *Dalrymple* v. *Ranken* (1836) 14 S. 1011.
[48] *Lord Advocate* (1860) 22 D. 555.
[49] See *e.g. Brown* v. *Hackston* (O.H.) 1960 S.C. 27.
[50] *Kennedy* (O.H.) (1901) 8 S.L.T. 388; *Knox* (O.H.) (1894) 2 S.L.T. 388.
[51] *Calderwood* v. *Duncan* (O.H.) (1907) 14 S.L.T. 777.
[52] *Davies* v. *Davies* (O.H.) 1928 S.L.T. 142; *Greig* (O.H.) 1923 S.L.T. 434. See also *Brown* v. *Hackston* (O.H.) 1960 S.C. 27.

to opposition the petitioner could produce only one certificate.[53] Where the alleged *incapax* is himself the petitioner the certificates must bear that he understands the effect of an appointment.[54] While it has been held that on the death of a curator *bonis* the court will not appoint a successor without proof of continued incapacity,[55] doubt is cast upon this by a subsequent decision.[56]

If the petition is opposed there must be inquiry,[57] provided that a relevant case is stated.[58] At one time a remit was made to the sheriff of the county where the person resided,[59] but the modern practice is to obtain a report from a doctor or doctors selected by the court.[60]

Parties

The alleged *incapax* himself may petition,[61] but the usual petitioners are relatives, wife,[62] father,[63] brother,[64] sisters,[65] step-brothers,[66] brothers-in-law and sisters-in-law (there being no known blood relations),[67] tutors of the children of a deceased daughter.[68] In the only reported case in which title was challenged that of cousins was sustained.[69] They had in fact an interest under the will of the mother of the alleged *incapax* if he died intestate without issue, but a pecuniary interest is unnecessary as the following cases show. Petitions were entertained at the instance of the person's solicitor,[70] and banker,[71] of a person with whom he had been residing,[72] of a factor *loco tutoris* on the *incapax* attaining minority,[73] of a curator-at-law,[74] of a curator *bonis* who retired,[75] and of the representatives of a deceased curator *bonis*.[76] Curators *bonis* have been appointed to the holders of offices on the petition of the Lord Advocate [77] and the heritors.[78] It is the duty of the local authority to apply if no one else does [79]

---

[53] *Leslie* (O.H.) (1895) 3 S.L.T. 128.
[54] *A B* (O.H.) (1908) 16 S.L.T. 557.
[55] *Beveridge* (1849) 12 D. 912.
[56] *Forster* (1859) 22 D. D. 15. In *Mackenzie* (1854) 16 D. 897, the question did not arise since the person had been cognosced.
[57] *Alston* v. *Alston* (1895) 23 R. 16.
[58] *Mackie* (1866) 5 M. 60.
[59] *Macfarlane* v. *Macfarlane* (1847) 10 D. 38, sequel to (1846) 9 D. 306.
[60] *Brown* v. *Hackston* (O.H.) 1960 S.C. 27; *Shand* v. *Shand* (O.H.) 1950 S.L.T. (Notes) 32 *C B* v. *A B* (1891) 18 R. (H.L.) 40.
[61] *A B* (O.H.) (1908) 16 S.L.T. 557, where certificates were lodged that the petitioner understood and approved of the application.
[62] *C B* v. *A B* (1891) 18 R. (H.L.) 40.
[63] *Kirkpatrick* (1853) 15 D. 734.
[64] *Graham* (1851) 13 D. 951.
[65] *Grierson* v. *Menteath* (1840) 2 D. 1234.
[66] *Gatherer* v. *Gatherer* (1852) 14 D. 1046.
[67] *Connon* (1848) 10 D. 1366; *Wright* (1849) 12 D. 911.
[68] *Calderwood* v. *Duncan* (O.H.) (1908) 16 S.L.T. 557. See also *Kirk* (1836) 14 S. 814.
[69] *Greig* (O.H.) 1923 S.L.T. 434.
[70] *Mason* (1852) 14 D. 761.
[71] *Johnstone* v. *Barbé* (O.H.) 1928 S.N. 86.
[72] *Bonar* (1851) 14 D. 10; *Macpherson* (1851) 13 D. 950.
[73] *Scott* (1855) 14 D. 362.
[74] *Mackenzie* (1854) 10 D. 897.
[75] *Halliday's Curator Bonis*, 1912 S.C. 509.
[76] *Ballingal* (1853) 15 D. 711.
[77] *Lord Advocate* (1860) 22 D. 555.
[78] *Ross* (1851) 13 D. 950.
[79] Mental Health (Scotland) Act 1960, s. 91

and of the Accountant of Court if a factor dies or has ceased to discharge his duties, and no one else applies.[80]

It was laid down apparently as an inflexible rule that service must be made on the alleged *incapax*,[81] but service is now dispensed with if the medical certificates bear that service would be dangerous to him.[82] It was also dispensed with when the person lived abroad and his condition was such that service would serve no useful purpose.[83] But personal service was made in Paris,[84] and an argument based on the need for haste [85] is weakened by the possibility of communication by air and of an *interim* appointment.[86] The nearest relatives should be parties, and if they do not concur in the petition [87] they must be called. But service on one of the next of kin who was insane and had no curator or curator *bonis* was dispensed with.[88]

Effect of appointment

Although the court makes no finding that the person is insane or otherwise incapable of managing his affairs, the interlocutor appointing the curator *bonis* has the same effect as a " proven " verdict of a jury in a cognition and is conclusive as to incapacity.[89] The *incapax* has no further control,[90] and it is not necessary to intimate to him a note by the curator *bonis* craving a special power.[91] There is no need to sequestrate the estate, and the appointment of the curator *bonis* is equivalent (after he has found caution) to service by the nearest agnate as tutor *quoad* property over which the *incapax* had control. So where an *incapax* was a beneficiary under a trust, the trustees continued to administer the trust, but a curator *bonis* had the management of funds in the hands of factors previously appointed by the *incapax*.[92] It is not clear what the court intended when it appointed a curator *bonis* with power to superintend trustees in the management of trust funds held for behoof of the *incapax*.[93] The right and duty of the curator *bonis* to administer the ward's moveable property in England are now statutory, subject to the condition that the English court has not exercised its powers under the Act,[94] and similar powers over moveables in Scotland are granted to receivers in England, if no

---

[80] Judicial Factors Act 1889, s. 10.
[81] *Lang* (1847) 10 D. 148.
[82] *McKechnie* (O.H.) (1890) 27 S.L.R. 261; Rules of Court 1965, r. 191 (*c*).
[83] *Buyers* (O.H.) 1910, 2 S.L.T. 201; *Allison* (O.H.) (1901) 8 S.L.T. 339.
[84] *Dalrymple* v. *Ranken* (1836) 14 S. 1011.
[85] As in *Allison* (*supra*).
[86] *Sharp* v. *McCall* (1860) 23 D. 38 at pp. 39 and 40.
[87] *Allan* (1852) 14 D. 486.
[88] *Hamilton* (O.H.) (1899) 7 S.L.T. 226.
[89] *Mitchell & Baxter* v. *Cheyne* (1891) 19 R. 324.
[90] *Lang* (1847) 10 D. 148. *Macgregor* (1848) 11 D. 285. In *Bryce* v. *Grahame* (1828) 6 S. 425, the petition was not served on Bryce.
[91] *Cameron's Curator Bonis* (O.H.) 1961 S.L.T. (Notes) 21.
[92] *Dick* (O.H.) (1901) 9 S.L.T. 177.
[93] *Robertson* v. *Lamb* (1829) 7 S. 573.
[94] Mental Health Act 1959, s. 117 (2).

curator *bonis* has been appointed.[95] Similar provisions apply to Northern Ireland.[96]

Although a curator *bonis* has no right to custody or control of the person of the *incapax*,[97] the court may grant this to him,[98] or a tutor-dative may be appointed, under reservation, if desirable, of the appointment of the curator *bonis*.[99] If the *incapax* is a trustee the curator *bonis* may be authorised to resign the office on his behalf,[1] and where the *incapax* was not a trustee, but her consent to sale of trust property was required the court authorised her curator *bonis* to give consent.[2]

Recall of curatory [3]

A curatory is recalled if the court is satisfied that the ward has recovered his capacity to manage his affairs. In every reported case with one exception, the petition has been presented by the ward, and medical certificates of his recovery have been produced.[4] An application by the ward for recall of the appointment only with a view to a new appointment is necessarily incompetent, since the ward *ex hypothesi* is still *incapax*.[5] A petitioner must call the curator *bonis* and, it is thought, those on whose application the appointment was made. Where there is no opposition, the court, if satisfied with the certificates, will recall.[6] If the petition is opposed, the practice is to remit to a doctor selected by the court.[7] The burden is on the petitioner to overcome the presumption of insanity created by the appointment of the curator *bonis*.[8] Recall was refused on a not proven finding [9] and granted on preponderating reports.[10] A curatory on the estate of a domiciled Englishwoman, which was all moveable, was recalled on the application of the committee appointed to her in England.[11] The curatory comes to an end on service by a tutor-at-law.

---

95 *Ibid.*, s. 117 (1).
96 Mental Health (Scotland) Act 1960, s. 93.
97 *Bryce* v. *Grahame* (1828) 6 S. 425 at pp. 436, 438, (1828) 3 W. & Sh. 323.
98 *Gardiner* (1869) 7 M. 1130.
99 *Dick* v. *Douglas*, 1924 S.C. 787. The reservation was of consent.
1 *Laidlaw* (1882) 10 R. 130.
2 *Cowan's Curator Bonis* (1902) 5 F. 19.
3 The distinction between recall of the curatory and recall of the appointment is not always observed in the interlocutors.
4 *A B* v. *C B* (O.H.) 1929 S.L.T. 517; *Inglis* v. *Inglis* (O.H.) 1927 S.N. 181; *A B* v. *A B's Curator Bonis* (O.H.) (1908) 16 S.L.T. 583; *Forsyth* (1862) 24 D. 1435.
5 *Mackenzie* (1845) 7 D. 283.
6 *Lawson* (1863) 2 M. 355; *Forster* (1848) 11 D. 1031.
7 *A B* v. *C B* (O.H.) 1929 S.L.T. 517; *Inglis* v. *Inglis* (O.H.) 1927 S.N. 181.
8 Bell, Prin. (10th ed.), para. 2103; Dickson, *Evidence* (3rd ed.), paras. 35, 114 (1). See *Forsyth* (1862) 24 D. 1435, Lord Deas at p. 1440.
9 *A B* v. *A B's Curator Bonis* (O.H.) (1908) 16 S.L.T. 583.
10 *A B* v. *C B* (O.H.) 1929 S.L.T. 517.
11 *Sawyer* v. *Sloan* (1875) 3 R. 217.

CHAPTER V

FACTOR LOCO ABSENTIS

Introductory

At least as early as the seventeenth century when a person who was abroad succeeded to property the court was in use to appoint a factor to manage the property until he returned or gave directions for its management.[1] But the earliest reported application for a factor to manage all the property of an *absens* was in 1708,[2] and the Act of Sederunt 1730 applied to such a factor.

Grounds for appointment

The broad ground is that a person has gone out of reach without appointing anyone to manage his affairs in his absence, and that it is necessary to protect his interests or those of third parties. Modern developments have in two ways greatly reduced the need for a judicial appointment. First, before the days of cable, wireless and air communication a person abroad might be said to be out of reach even if his address were known,[3] but nowadays a Lord Ordinary might well demur to making an appointment in such a case without ascertaining the wishes of the *absens*. Secondly, judicial appointments were made where the *absens* had disappeared many years before, and it was not known whether he was alive or dead.[4] Since the Presumption of Life Limitation Act 1891 empowers the court, on the application of anyone interested in an estate, to find that the *absens* died seven years after the date of his disappearance, a Lord Ordinary might be disinclined to make an appointment after seven years until satisfied that a petition under the Act was impossible. For practical purposes appointments are thus restricted to persons who have disappeared for less than seven years, and the only reported cases this century are in that category.[5]

Subject, however, to these changes, the older cases help to illustrate the situations in which an appointment will be made or refused. It was

---

[1] Stair IV, 50, 28 (4). Later instances are *Carmichael* (1700) Mor. 7454; *Gilchrist* (1752) M. 4070; *Paton* (1785) Mor. 4071.

[2] *Stuart* (1708) Mor. 7455. It was refused.

[3] The reports are not clear on this point, but illustrations may be *Knight* (1833) 11 S. 366, and *Brown* (1849) 11 D. 1027.

[4] *Kennedy* v. *McLean* (1851) 13 D. 705, where the instance ultimately approved included both the factor for, and the heirs of, the *absens* and thus provided for either eventuality. In *Barstow* v. *Cook* (1864) 24 D. 790, the court superseded consideration of claims in a multiplepoinding until satisfied that an *absens* was dead: (1874) 11 S.L.R. 363. In a later case where there was doubt as to whether the heir of an intestate was alive, the Lord Ordinary refused to appoint a factor *loco absentis*, and appointed a factor on the estate: *Gibson* (1882) 19 S.L.R. 605.

[5] *Lunan* v. *Macdonald* (O.H.) 1927 S.L.T. 661, 1927 S.N. 148; *Dobson* (O.H.) (1903) 11 S.L.T. 44.

refused where the *absens* had himself appointed factors and commissioners,[6] but a factor *loco absentis* might be appointed if the factors and commissioners were mismanaging.[7] Factors were appointed to a licensed grocer and hotel keeper who had disappeared [8] and to an *absens* who had succeeded to property,[9] but refused where his niece had entered into possession on the assumption that he was dead, on her finding caution for the rents.[10] It was also refused where the purpose was to raise an action to reduce a will and the court thought that the *absens* might not wish to challenge the will.[11] Appointments have been made at the instance of third parties where the *absens* was under obligation to grant a title [12] and where he was next heir of entail and intimation to him was necessary.[13]

Parties

An application may be presented by a wife [14] or a relative [15] who has at heart the interests of the *absens* and possibly also his own. It may also be presented by the third party whose interests require the appointment.[16] Respondents should be those who have an interest in the estate and to oppose, *e.g.* on the ground that the *absens* is dead [17] or that the appointment is unnecessary.[18]

Recall of factory

The factory terminates on the death, proved or presumed,[19] of the *absens*, or on his reappearance, though a temporary reappearance may not be enough,[20] or on his authorising someone to act for him [21] or undertaking the management himself.[22] Recall was refused where the *absens* had not been heard of for about fifteen years, but there was no other reason to suppose that he was dead.[23] In a doubtful case recall may be granted on caution being found.[24]

---

[6] *Steel* (O.H.) (1874) 11 S.L.R. 160; *Phaup* v. *Phaup* (1831) 9 S. 584.
[7] See *Sawers* v. *Sawers' Trustee* (1881) 19 S.L.R. 258.
[8] *Dobson* (O.H.) (1903) 11 S.L.T. 44.
[9] *Kennedy* v. *McLean* (1851) 13 D. 705; *Barstow* v. *Cook* (1862) 24 D. 790 (narrative).
[10] *Chambers* v. *Carruthers* (1849) 11 D. 1359.
[11] *Watson* (1864) 2 M. 1333.
[12] *Lunan* v. *Macdonald* (O.H.) 1927 S.L.T. 661, 1927 S.N. 148.
[13] *Knight* (1833) 11 S. 366. See also *White* v. *Stevenson* (1829) 7 S. 555.
[14] *Dobson* (O.H.) (1903) 11 S.L.T. 44; *Watson* (1864) 2 M. 1333.
[15] *Kennedy* v. *McLean* (1851) 13 D. 705.
[16] *Lunan* v. *Macdonald* (O.H.) 1927 S.L.T. 661, 1927 S.N. 148; *Knight* (1833) 11 S. 366; *Hope* (1850) 12 D. 912.
[17] *White* v. *Stevenson* (1829) 7 S. 555.
[18] *Chambers* v. *Carruthers* (1849) 11 D. 1359.
[19] *Barstow* v. *Cook* (1874) 11 S.L.R. 363; *Wardrop* v. *Wardrop* (1846) 18 S.J. 540; *Milne* v. *Wills* (1868) 40 S.J. 221. This may be done in a multiplepoinding: *Tait's Factor* v. *Meikle* (1890) 17 R. 1182.
[20] *Gowans* (O.H.) 1917, 2 S.L.T. 61.
[21] *Grant* v. *Cameron* (1835) 13 S. 966.
[22] *Gilchrist* (1752) M. 4070.
[23] *Reid* v. *Brown* (1834) 12 S. 278.
[24] *Milne* v. *Wills* (1868) 5 S.L.R. 189.

CHAPTER VI

FACTOR ON TRUST OR EXECUTRY ESTATE[1]

Appointment

Introductory

The court may appoint a judicial factor on a trust estate [2] where no trustees have been nominated, or those nominated have declined to accept office, or all the trustees fail or wish to resign, or it has removed the trustees or suspended their right to administer by sequestrating the estate. In all these cases except sequestration the court has statutory power to appoint new trustees. These powers are mentioned below in relation to the different situations, but since the appointment of a factor involves expense to the estate,[3] the court will probably appoint new trustees, if suitable persons are willing to act.

Failure of trustees

As a general rule the court will not make any appointment if some person has the power to nominate new trustees, *e.g.* a truster who retains a radical right, and is willing to do so. It refused to appoint new trustees on a marriage contract because the spouses had power to do so.[4] But it did appoint a judicial factor where there was a dispute between the spouses,[5] and in other cases where the reports disclose no special reason.[6] In all these cases the appeal was to the *nobile officium*. Since 1867 the court has had statutory power to appoint trustees,[7] but this does not affect the radical right of a truster,[8] and there is no reason to suppose that the court will exercise its statutory power if there is a person able and willing to appoint.

Where there was no one with power to nominate new trustees, the court at first appointed a judicial factor, whatever the wishes of the beneficiaries,[9] and a brief departure in favour of new trustees [10] was disapproved.[11] Whichever appointment was made, the court was at

---

[1] This chapter deals mainly with private trusts. Public and charitable trusts are mentioned briefly in the last paragraph. Executries raise similar questions to private trusts.

[2] As to the meaning of " trust estate " see *Leslie's Judicial Factor*, 1925 S.C. 464 at pp. 469, 470.

[3] See in a somewhat different connection *Yuill* v. *Ross* (1900) 3 F. 97 at pp. 98, 99.

[4] *Lindsay* v. *Lindsay* (1847) 9 D. 1297; *Tovey* v. *Tennant* (1854) 16 D. 866 (both referred to in *Newlands* v. *Miller* (1882) 9 R. 1104 at pp. 1113, 1114); *Dunlop* (1835) 13 S. 681.

[5] *Alcock* (1855) 17 D. 785.

[6] *MacGeorge* (1856) 18 D. 792; *Nicholson* (1850) 12 D. 911.

[7] Trusts (Scotland) Act 1867, s. 12, now Trusts (Scotland) Act 1921, s. 22.

[8] *Newlands* v. *Miller* (1882) 9 R. 1104; *Lord Glentanar* v. *Scottish Industrial Musical Association*, 1925 S.C. 226; McLaren, *Wills and Succession* (3rd ed.), II, p. 1273.

[9] *Grant* (1790) Mor. 7454; *Moir* (1826) 4 S. 801.

[10] *Melville* v. *Preston* (1838) 16 S. 457, (1841) 2 Rob. App. 45; *McAslan* (1841) 3 D. 1263; *Glasgow* (1844) 7 D. 178.

[11] *Watt* (1854) 16 D. 941.

that time exercising the *nobile officium*, and its reason for preferring a judicial factor was that it had more control over him.[12] The Trusts (Scotland) Act 1867 provided [13] that where trustees cannot be assumed under a trust deed the court may, on the application of any party having interest in the trust estate, appoint a trustee or trustees. Under this power the court appointed trustees where the truster failed to nominate,[14] where the trustees nominated all predeceased him [15] and where the last surviving trustee had died.[16] This statutory power renders the appointment of a judicial factor unnecessary, if not incompetent,[17] in a case of failure of trustees, where suitable persons acceptable to the beneficiaries are willing to hold office. Since such vacancies are usually accidental and do not arise out of disputes, it is not surprising that since 1867 there are few reported cases where the court has appointed a judicial factor on failure of trustees.[18] There is statutory power to appoint a factor on the estate of a deceased who has nominated no trustees or executors, or those nominated do not accept or do not act,[19] and where property is conveyed in liferent and fee and the fiars when the conveyance comes into operation are unborn or incapable of ascertainment.[20]

Trustees in office: general

A judicial factor, being an officer of the court, cannot share his responsibilities with a person who is not an officer of the court. Accordingly, a petition for the appointment of a factor *loco tutoris* to act jointly with the mother, who was guardian under the Guardianship of Infants Act 1925, was dismissed as incompetent,[21] and the court required a sole trustee to resign before it would appoint a factor.[22] The court may clear the way for the appointment of a factor either by removing the trustees or by suspending their right to administer by sequestrating the estate. This principle has, however, not always been recognised, and in several old cases the court appointed factors without superseding the trustees.[23] The results of this practice were disclosed in one case and discussed in another. In the first,[24] trustees were held entitled to give instructions to a person variously described as a curator *bonis* or a factor *loco tutoris*, but who, whatever his correct title, was an officer of the court and not the tool of a third party.[25] It is not surprising that Lord Glenlee doubted the

---

[12] *Kemp* (1848) 10 D. 1456; *Gemmill* (1846) 8 D. 942. See also *Melville* (1856) 18 D. 788.
[13] s. 12, now Trusts (Scotland) Act 1921, s. 22.
[14] *Auld* (O.H.) 1925 S.L.T. 83; *Patullo* (O.H.) (1908) 16 S.L.T. 637.
[15] *Graham* (1868) 6 M. 958.
[16] *Zoller* (1868) 6 M. 577.
[17] *Tod* v. *Marshall* (1895) 23 R. 36.
[18] *Leslie's Judicial Factor*, 1925 S.C. 464 (narrative), appears to be an example.
[19] Bankruptcy (Scotland) Act 1913, s. 163.
[20] Trusts (Scotland) Act 1921, s. 8 (2). See *Napier* v. *Napiers* (O.H.) 1963 S.L.T. 143.
[21] *Speirs* (O.H.) 1946 S.L.T. 203.
[22] *Shand* v. *Macdonald* (1862) 24 D. 829.
[23] *Goold* (1856) 18 D. 1318; *Halcomb* v. *Thoms* (1853) 15 D. 861; *Forbes* v. *Forbes* (1852) 14 D. 498; *Macarthur* v. *Gemmill* (1839) 1 D. 1174; *Adie* v. *Mitchell* (1835) 14 S. 185; *Laird* v. *Miln* (1833) 12 S. 187. See also *Taylor* v. *Taylor's Trustees* (1857) 19 D. 1097.
[24] *Cowan* v. *Crawford* (1837) 15 S. 398.   [25] *McCulloch* v. *McCulloch*, 1953 S.C. 189.

regularity of the appointment. In the second,[26] one trustee out of three
sued one of the other trustees for recovery of a debt due to the trust.
The report discloses no plea of no title to sue, but the Lord Ordinary
held that the pursuer had no title. The Division on the pursuer's application appointed a factor, deliberately without sequestrating the estate
(which prima facie would have destroyed the pursuer's title), sisted the
factor as party concurring, recalled the Lord Ordinary's interlocutor
and remitted to him to proceed, leaving it to the Lord Ordinary to decide
the effect, if any, of their interlocutors on the question of title. From the
opinions it appears that they regarded the factor as ousting the trustees
from the administration, so that the case, so far as it goes, is the opposite
of Cowan v. Crawford.[27]

Resignation of trustees

At common law a trustee who has accepted office has no power to
resign unless authorised to do so by the trust deed or by the court, or
disabled from acting by illness, absence or adverse interest and with
consent of those interested,[28] and a trustee who purports to resign without
power to do so remains responsible for the trust estate.[29] The Trusts
(Scotland) Act 1861 [30] empowered any gratuitous trustee to resign, and
the flaw in this legislation appeared almost at once, where a sole trustee
wished to resign. He met the difficulty by applying for the appointment of
a judicial factor, which was granted.[31] The Trusts (Scotland) Act 1867,
by section 10, provided that a sole trustee might not resign unless the court
had on his application appointed new trustees or a judicial factor. But
this did not meet every case. All the trustees under a marriage contract
resolved to resign, and, like the sole trustee in Shand v. Macdonald,[31]
though that case was not mentioned, they applied to the court for the
appointment of a judicial factor. The Lord Ordinary first appointed new
trustees and, on their declining office, appointed a judicial factor, continuing the cause for such further procedure as might be competent.[32]
The First Division adhered, the majority holding that the trustees had a
right to resign not affected by the statutory provision as to a sole trustee.[33]
They observed, however, that it would be inconsistent with the duty of
trustees to resign as a body, leaving no one to administer the trust, and
commended the action of the trustees in applying for a judicial factor.[34]
A subsequent case followed the same course.[35] The statutory power to

[26] Morison v. Gowans (1873) 1 R. 116.
[27] (1837) 15 S. 398.
[28] Maclean (1895) 22 R. 872; Hill v. Mitchell (1846) 9 D. 239.
[29] Logan v. Meiklejohn (1843) 5 D. 1066.
[30] s. 10.
[31] Shand v. Macdonald (1862) 24 D. 829.
[32] The further craves, for authority to resign and a judicial discharge, did not appear in
Shand, and were probably unnecessary. The petitioners had statutory power to resign
and would obtain a discharge from the judicial factor.
[33] Lord Deas reached the same result on a different ground, which he did not expand.
[34] Maxwell's Trustees v. Maxwell (1874) 2 R. 71.
[35] McConnell's Trustees (1897) 25 R. 330.

resign is thus qualified by the common law duty. The Trusts (Scotland) Act 1921,[36] with one small exception, repeats in substance the relevant portions of the Acts of 1861 [37] and 1867.[38] The exception is that, whereas in the 1867 Act the limitation on the right of a sole trustee to resign applied to " any trustee entitled to resign his office," in the 1921 Act it applies to a trustee " entitled to resign his office by virtue of this Act." [39] It appears therefore not to apply to a gratuitous trustee who has power to resign under the trust deed or at common law. But in view of the common law duty acted on in *Shand* v. *Macdonald* [40] and *McConnell's Trustees* [41] and emphasised in *Maxwell's Trustees* v. *Maxwell*,[42] this difference seems of no importance, and it may be said that if the effect of the resignation will be to leave the trust with no administrator the resigning trustees must first apply for the appointment of new trustees or a judicial factor.

When all the trustees propose to resign for reasons unconnected with the administration of the trust, new trustees will probably be appointed. On an application by a sole trustee for the appointment of a judicial factor the court appointed as trustees beneficiaries who appeared and stated that they were willing to act.[43] But if they resign because of disputes and difficulties, a judicial factor will probably be necessary, if only because third parties are unlikely to be willing to accept nomination and involve themselves in these disputes.[44]

Removal of trustees or sequestration

If it is desired to bring trustees' management to an end and they are unwilling to resign, either they may be removed from office or the estate may be taken out of their control by sequestration. These are alternative remedies with different legal effects. If trustees are removed, their office is at an end, but if the estate is sequestrated, they remain in office,[45] though with no power over the estate.[46] Where a trust estate had been sequestrated and a judicial factor appointed, the sole trustee granted a deed of assumption and conveyance in favour of himself and two other persons. In a petition for recall of the sequestration and factory the court expressed the opinion that the deed would be brought into effect by recall of the sequestration. Another view is that the deed took effect immediately as a deed of assumption, though its effect as a conveyance was postponed until the recall of the sequestration.[47] The court has emphasised the distinction between removal of trustees and sequestration

---

[36] ss. 3 (a) and proviso (1), and 19 (2).
[37] s. 1.
[38] s. 10.
[39] s. 3 (a) and proviso (1).
[40] (1864) 24 D. 829.
[41] (1897) 25 R. 330.
[42] (1874) 2 R. 71.
[43] *Walker* v. *Downie* (O.H.) 1933 S.L.T. 30, 1932 S.N. 88.
[44] *Maxwell's Trustees* v. *Maxwell* (1874) 2 R. 71 (interlocutor).
[45] *Foggo* (1893) 20 R. 273 at p. 275. See observations in *Morris* v. *Bain* (1858) **20 D. 716.**
[46] McLaren, *Wills and Succession* (3rd ed.) II, 1275.
[47] *Shedden* (1867) 5 M. 955.

of the estate by allowing petitioners for removal to amend by adding
an alternative crave for sequestration, which it granted.[48] Nevertheless,
if the reports are correct, they have been craved cumulatively,[49] and in
one case both granted.[50] Although the legal effects of these remedies are
different, the practical results are usually the same. The trustees' powers
are ended or, if suspended, are probably seldom restored. But removal
is the more extreme, granted only when the trustees have by their conduct
shown themselves to be unfit to hold the office.[51] Removal thus involves a
stigma, and unnecessary insistence on removal as opposed to sequestration
may affect expenses.[52]

Removal of the trustees or sequestration of the estate is a sign of disputes, and there appears to be only one reported case where the court,
after removing the sole trustee, appointed new trustees, and they were
already involved as trustees on a related trust.[53] With that exception the
court in all decisions mentioned below, where it made any appointment,
appointed a judicial factor.

Grounds for superseding trustees

It cannot be said that every case was decided on one isolated ground,
but an attempt has been made to group the decisions according to the
general principle most prominent as ground either of decision or of
unsuccessful argument. Strong reasons are required for the removal or
suspension of trustees in whom the truster has shown his confidence,[54]
and the wishes of the beneficiaries have some weight, partly because the
expense of a factory falls on them.[55] The court will not appoint a judicial
factor on the application of a claimant for the purpose of ascertaining
his rights when these could be ascertained by an action against the
trustees.[56]

(a) *Breach of trust.* A judicial factor was appointed where a person
described as a factor *loco absentis* on a trust estate embezzled the funds and
absconded[57]; where the sole trustee was liferenter and had paid most
of the funds to himself[58]; where the sole trustee sold feuduties belonging
to the trust to his own clerk, granted a title without payment and obtained

---

[48] *Carmont* v. *Mitchell's Trustees* (1883) 10 R. 829 at p. 834; *Morris* v. *Bain* (1858) 20 D.
716 at p. 717. See also *Carmont*, 1922 S.C. 686.

[49] e.g. *Harris* v. *Howie's Trustee* (1893) 21 R. 16; *Henderson* v. *Henderson* (1893) 20 R. 536;
Foggo (1893) 20 R. 273.

[50] *Thomson* v. *Dalrymple* (1865) 3 M. 336. In *Birnie* v. *Christie* (1891) 19 R. 334, the judges
said the executors must be removed from office, but in fact they sequestrated the estate.

[51] *Gilchrist's Trustees* v. *Dick* (1883) 11 R. 23 at p. 24; *Harris* v. *Howie's Trustee* (1893)
21 R. 16 at p. 19.   [52] *Stewart* v. *Morrison* (1892) 19 R. 1009 at p. 1112.

[53] *Lamont* v. *Lamont*, 1908 S.C. 1033.

[54] *Taylor* v. *Taylor's Trustees* (1857) 19 D. 1097 (removal); *McPherson* v. *A.B.* (1840) 3
D. 315 (sequestration).

[55] *Yuill* v. *Ross* (1900) 3 F. 96 at pp. 98, 99; *Stewart* v. *Morrison* (1892) 19 R. 1009 at p. 1112;
M'Whirter v. *Latta* (1889) 17 R. 68 at p. 70; *Scott* (O.H.) (1905) 13 S.L.T. 589; *Henderson*
(O.H.) (1901) 9 S.L.T. 16.

[56] *Simeone* (O.H.) 1950 S.L.T. 399; *Finlay* v. *Dymock* (1854) 16 D. 868; *Williamson* (O.H.)
(1900) 8 S.L.T. 195.

[57] *Miller* (1859) 12 D. 911. The sole trustee was abroad.

[58] *Fleming* v. *Craig* (1863) 1 M. 850 (removed).

a loan on the security of the feuduties [59]; where a sole trustee kept large balances in his hands and £2,000 was not accounted for [60]; where more than two years after the truster's death the beneficiaries obtained decree in absence against the sole trustee in an action of court, reckoning and payment and he failed to obtemper the decree [61]; on the application of one trustee where the other had acted fraudulently [62]; where the trustees after twelve years had taken no steps to ingather the estate [63]; where a sole trustee wilfully failed to carry out the directions of the truster [64]; where trustees had delivered funds to third parties for investment, and part of these were lent without security [65]; where a majority of executors-dative had bound themselves to further the claim of one claimant [66]; where the trustees were interfering with the rights of a liferentrix.[67]

On the other hand, the court refused to remove a sole trustee who had in good faith traded with the trust funds, successfully,[68] or trustees who were said to have paid claims unjustifiably and failed to oppose an application for sequestration of the estate,[69] or to sequestrate where a sole trustee had in good faith paid a debt not fully vouched,[70] or where trustees, who were empowered to leave funds in the hands of the truster's children (one of whom was bankrupt), had failed to insist on repayment.[71] An appointment was refused where it was averred (without any supporting facts), and denied, that the trustees intended to remove the estate to England and that the petitioner intended to raise an action to reduce the settlement,[72] and where one of three trustees made allegations against another, but not of *mala fides*.[73]

(b) *Deadlock*. Where the absence or recalcitrance of trustees renders a trust unworkable the absent [74] or recalcitrant [75] trustees may be removed and the trust administration continued by the remaining trustees, or the recalcitrant trustees may be ordained to act, at least where the difference

---

[59] *Jackson* v. *Welch* (1865) 4 M. 177 (removed). See also *Soutar's Creditor's* v. *Brown* (1852) 15 D. 89 (removed).

[60] *Goold* (1856) 18 D. 1318.

[61] *Morris* v. *Bain* (1858) 20 D. 716. See also *Henderson* (O.H.) (1901) 9 S.L.T. 16.

[62] *Macarthur* v. *Gemmill* (1839) 1 D. 1174. It does not appear why the defaulting trustee was not removed. See *Whittle* (1896) 23 R. 775.

[63] *Thomson* v. *Dalrymple* (1865) 3 M. 336 (removed).

[64] *Whyte* (1891) 28 S.L.R. 901 (removed).

[65] *Carmont* v. *Mitchell's Trustee* (1883) 10 R. 829. For subsequent history see *Mitchell Bequest Trustees*, 1959 S.C. 395.

[66] *Birnie* v. *Christie* (1891) 19 R. 334.

[67] *M'Whirter* v. *Latta* (1889) 17 R. 68; *Gibson-Smith* v. *Gibson-Smith* (O.H.) 1930 S.N. 35.

[68] *Gilchrist's Trustees* v. *Dick* (1883) 11 R. 22, distinguished in *MacGilchrist's Trustees* v. *MacGilchrist*, 1930 S.C. 635 at p. 638.

[69] *Taylor* v. *Taylor's Trustees* (1857) 19 D. 1097. See also *Hay* v. *Binny* (1861) 23 D. 594.

[70] *Harris* v. *Howie's Trustee* (1893) 21 R. 16.

[71] *Dryburgh* v. *Walker's Trustees* (1873) 1 R. 31.

[72] *Bowman* v. *Russell's Trustees* (1891) 19 R. 205.

[73] *Bannerman* (O.H.) (1895) 3 S.L.T. 208.

[74] Trusts (Scotland) Act 1921, s. 23. See *Smith* v. *Smith* (1862) 24 D. 834, Lord Deas (*diss.*).

[75] *Neilson* (1865) 3 M. 559, where the court refused to appoint a factor.

arises over a particular issue.[76] Further, where there is an equal division of opinion the court may appoint additional trustees to provide a majority.[77] But if none of these remedies is suitable, possibly because removal seems too drastic or no suitable person is willing to take office as trustee, the difficulty may be removed by sequestration and the appointment of a factor. Factors were appointed where trustees were evenly divided and the administration of the trust was at a standstill,[78] but refused where the division merely caused trouble,[79] and where one trustee refused to pay without investigation a claim on the estate by the other trustee and a doctor's account.[80]

(c) *Insolvency of trustee.* The insolvency of one trustee out of several is in itself no ground for the appointment of a factor,[81] though it may justify the removal of the insolvent trustee from office.[82] In two early cases the court appointed factors apparently because a sole trustee was insolvent,[83] but later dicta[84] raise a doubt, and in a subsequent case the court had to be satisfied that the sole trustee was mismanaging the estate.[85] Factors were appointed where two out of three trustees were insolvent and were trying to get the estate into their own hands,[86] and where one trustee was insolvent and the other in debt to the estate, and both were in England.[87]

(d) *Adverse interest.* A mere conflict of interest is enough. It is not necessary to shew that the estate will suffer. The court refused to recall the sequestration of a trust estate and the appointment of a factor when the result would have been to put the estate under the control of a sole trustee who had been cautioner for the former trustee, had acted as factor for him on the trust and was one of his heirs.[88] Where a sole trustee left the country under a cloud and before doing so assumed two trustees and also appointed them to be his mandataries and attorneys in connection with his own affairs, the court appointed a judicial factor, although there was no personal objection to the assumed trustees.[89] Factors were appointed where one trust had claims on another and the same trustees controlled both[90]; where the fiar had come to be the sole trustee[91]; where one execu-

---

[76] *Lord Lynedoch* v. *Ouchterlony* (1827) 5 S. 359, referred to in *Neilson (supra).*

[77] *Taylor,* 1932 S.C. 1; *Dick* (1899) 2 F. 316; *Aikman* (1881) 9 R. 213.

[78] *Stewart* v. *Morrison* (1892) 19 R. 1009; *Forbes* v. *Forbes* (1852) 14 D. 498; *Adie* v. *Mitchell* (1835) 14 S. 185; *Pott* v. *Stevenson* (O.H.) 1935 S.L.T. 106; 1934 S.N. 114.

[79] *Yuill* v. *Ross* (1900) 3 F. 96; *Hope* v. *Hope* (1884) 12 R. 27; *Laird* v. *Miln* (1833) 12 S. 187; *Purdie* (O.H.) (1897) 4 S.L.T. 258.

[80] *Scott* (O.H.) (1905) 13 S.L.T. 589.

[81] *Dryburgh* v. *Walker's Trustees* (1873) 1 R. 31. See *Philips* v. *Thomson* (1853) 2 Stu. 164.

[82] *Whittle* v. *Carruthers* (1896) 23 R. 775. See *Neilson* (1865) 3 M. 559.

[83] *Smith* (1832) 10 S. 531; *Towart* (1823) 2 S. 305.

[84] *McPherson* v. *A.B.* (1840) 3 D. 315.

[85] *Sawers* v. *Sawers' Trustee* (1881) 19 S.L.R. 258.

[86] *Barry* v. *Thorburn* (1847) 9 D. 917.   [87] *Stott* (1854) 16 D. 867.

[88] *Hunter* v. *Hume* (1834) 12 S. 406.

[89] *Foggo* (1893) 20 R. 273. See also *Fleming* v. *Craig* (1863) 1 M. 850 at p. 854.

[90] *Thomson* v. *Dalrymple* (1865) 3 M. 336; *Halcomb* v. *Thoms* (1853) 15 D. 861.

[91] *Henderson* v. *Henderson* (1893) 20 R. 536.

tor-nominate had claims against the estate and the other was abroad [92]; where the next-of-kin challenged the will and the title of the executrix-nominate *qua* universal legatee [93]; and where a sole trustee was serving his own ends.[94] But the trustees with the adverse interest must be in control. Where of three trustees one had been a partner of the testator and there were claims to be settled, the court refused to appoint a factor, pointing out that the case might have been different if the partner had been the sole trustee.[95] The same result followed where three out of five trustees applied for a factor on the ground that the other two trustees, sons of the testator, were carrying on his business and the question of selling it would arise.[96] The fact that one of two trustees was solicitor for creditors of the trust was no reason for appointing a factor, though one was appointed on other grounds.[97]

(*e*) *Miscellaneous*. The court appointed a factor where heritage was conveyed in liferent and fee and on the death of the liferentrix some of the fiars could not be traced [98]; where heritable bonds destined in liferent and fee could not be discharged because the fiars could not be ascertained [1]; where trustees were directed to pay to other trustees and raised a multiple-poinding, but the second trustees were unable to claim as such because their beneficiaries had conflicting claims [2]; where there was danger to the estate and an application for confirmation was refused [3]; where one of three trustees sued for recovery of a trust debt and was held to have no title [4]; to receive money which a trustee was ordained to pay to the estate, so that his co-trustees, who were equally at fault, should not benefit as beneficiaries [5]; where interference by the Court of Chancery obstructed the trustees in their administration [6]; where trustees had no power to act by a majority and one was a minor.[7] In contrast with the preceding case, an appointment was refused where an *ex officio* trustee died while a case to which the trustees were parties was at avizandum.[8] An application was also refused from a trustee who had taken no part in the administration and wanted a factor to investigate his co-trustee's actings.[9]

[92] *Thomson* v. *McNicol* (1871) 8 S.L.R. 623.
[93] *Tegner* v. *Henderson* (O.H.) 1930 S.L.T. 23; 1929 S.N. 130.
[94] *Soutar's Creditors* v. *Brown* (1852) 15 D. 89.
[95] *Young* (O.H.) (1901) 9 S.L.T. 20.
[96] *Young's Trustees* (O.H.) 1930 S.L.T. 731; 1930 S.N. 128.
[97] *Pott* v. *Stevenson* (O.H.) 1935 S.L.T. 106; 1934 S.N. 114.
[98] *Doig* (O.H.) (1882) 20 S.L.R. 10.
[1] *Montignani* (1866) 4 M. 461; *Gowans* (1849) 11 D. 1028. See Trusts (Scotland) Act 1921, s. 8 (2).
[2] *Govan* (O.H.) (1903) 11 S.L.T. 78. Factors were appointed on each legacy and share of residue.
[3] *Campbell* v. *Bamber* (1895) 23 R. 90.
[4] *Morison* v. *Gowans* (1873) 1 R. 116, commented on at p. 32.
[5] *Raes* v. *Meek* (1889) 16 R. (H.L.) 31.
[6] *Orr Ewing's Trustees* v. *Orr Ewing* (1885) 13 R. (H.L.) 1. See observations of Lord Blackburn, at pp. 21, 22, and of Lord Watson at p. 31, on *Ewing* v. *Orr Ewing* (1883) L.R. 9 App.Cas. 34.
[7] *Wylie* (1850) 12 D. 1110. The appointment was during the minority.
[8] *Boe* v. *Anderson* (1861) 23 D. 726.
[9] *Hill* v. *Hill* (1855) 17 D. 308.

Parties

There does not seem to be any reported decision except *Morison* [4] where the title of a petitioner has been questioned in the case of a private trust, and petitions have been entertained at the instance of beneficiaries, of one or more of the trustees, or of a combination of these, of the representatives of a deceased trustee [10] and of the trustees on a related trust.[11]

All interested must be made respondents and cited, including trustees whose declinature has made the application necessary,[12] and intimation must be made.[13] If there has been failure to cite, the court may recall an appointment.[14] Where a factor was appointed against the opposition of most of the beneficiaries, it was held that only a trustee, not the beneficiaries, had a title to reclaim.[15]

Specialties of the Office

Title to trust securities

A difficulty may arise in completing a factor's title to stock of English companies. No notice of any trust may be entered on the register of a company registered in England.[16] Accordingly, while a factor appointed on a trust has the certified copy interlocutor to establish his appointment, there may be nothing on the stock certificate or in the company's records to show that any particular stock is part of the trust property. Section 25 of the Trusts (Scotland) Act 1921 appears to meet this situation. It provides that application for authority to complete the title of a judicial factor to any trust property or estate may be contained in the petition for appointment. Effect appears to have been given to the corresponding section of the Trusts (Scotland) Act 1867,[17] but the only reported application under the 1921 Act was refused. A sole surviving trustee died leaving the trust stocks registered in his own name as an individual, and a crave for authority to complete title to these stocks was contained in a petition for the appointment of a factor. In refusing the crave for authority the court intimated that the factor ought to apply to the accountant for a certificate under seal that the stocks formed part of the trust estate, but except for a reference to section 66 of the Finance Act 1916,[18] which did not apply to the stocks in question, it was not explained why the appeal should be to the good offices of the accountant, who was under no statutory obligation to grant a certificate, rather than to section 25.[19]

---

10 *Burnett* v. *Boyd* (1829) 7 S. 314; *Shaw* v. *Steele* (1852) 24 Sc.Jur. 266.
11 *Seton* v. *Seton* (1855) 18 D. 117; *Halcomb* v. *Thoms* (1853) 15 D. 861.
12 *Russell* (1855) 17 D. 1005.
13 *Taylor* v. *Taylor's Trustees* (1857) 19 D. 1097.
14 *Wodrow* v. *Hodges* (1836) 15 S. 244; *Wood* v. *Mackintosh* (1862) 24 D. 563.
15 *Courage* v. *Ballantine*, 1946 S.C. 351, commented on at p. 137.
16 Companies Act 1948, s. 117. The distinction from Scots law is commented on in *Muir* v. *City of Glasgow Bank* (1878) 6 R. 392 at p. 400, (1879) 6 R.(H.L.) 21 at p. 26.
17 *Royal Bank of Scotland* v. *Greenlees* (1887) 15 R. 9 (narrative).
18 See p. 87.
19 *Brower's Executor*, 1938 S.C. 451.

Exercise of discretionary powers conferred by testator on trustees

Like other factors the factor on a trust estate is appointed " with the usual powers," and these include all powers normally necessary to enable him to carry out his duties. If, for example, the testator's directions can be carried out only by sale of heritage, a factor, apart from the power conferred by the Trusts (Scotland) Act 1921, s. 4, has power to sell.[20] But the usual powers do not include discretionary powers conferred by the testator on his trustees. If a factor desires such powers he must obtain them from the court as special powers.[21] Moreover, the court will not grant the power in the wide general terms in which the testator may have phrased it, but will adhere to its normal rule of granting only a power to do a specific act.[22] In that case the opinion was expressed in general terms and no reference seems to have been made to the observations of Lord President Cooper in *Angus's Executrix* v. *Batchan's Trustees*.[23] The question there was whether a factor on an executry estate had power to select amongst charities, but the Lord President in dealing with a particular argument referred to discretionary powers conferred on trustees and drew a distinction between discretionary powers of a purely administrative character and the fiduciary discretion reposed in a person designated as the selector of beneficiaries within a defined class. He appears to hold that, unless there was *delectus personae*, a discretionary power of the former character might be exercised by a factor, and to treat *Shorter*,[24] of which he expressed no disapproval, as an example. In that case a testator gave his trustees power to make advances to beneficiaries from their shares, and the Lord Ordinary dismissed as unnecessary a note by the factor craving power to make such advances. There may therefore be room for distinctions.

When a testator has made a bequest to a defined class with power to his trustees, nominated or assumed, to select the actual beneficiaries, a factor cannot exercise the power.[25]

Power to disregard truster's directions

Trustees are not bound to carry out the truster's directions, however specific, if they are convinced that to do so would imperil the safety of the estate.[26] A judicial factor would be wise to consult the Accountant of Court and to apply for special power before deciding to act on this principle, since the attitude of the court where it has been asked for such powers suggests that it will approve of their exercise only in extreme circumstances. A judicial factor applied for power to sell heritage which

---

[20] *McLeay* (O.H.), 1921, 1 S.L.T. 340; *Stirling's Judicial Factor* (O.H.), 1917, 1 S.L.T. 165.

[21] *Carmichael's Judicial Factor*, 1971, S.L.T. 336.

[22] *Carmichael's Judicial Factor*, 1971, S.L.T. 336. See p. 79.

[23] 1949 S.C. 335 at p. 368.

[24] 1930 S.L.T. 535.

[25] *Angus's Executrix* v. *Batchan's Trustees*, 1949 S.C. 335, overruling *Woodard's J.F.* v. *Woodard's Exrx.*, 1929 S.C. 534, and applying *Robbie's J.F.* v. *Macrae* (1893) 20 R. 358. *Macrae's J.F.* v. *Martin*, 1937 S.N. 69 is also overruled; *Vollar's Judicial Factor* v. *Boyd*, 1952 S.L.T.(Notes) 84; *Brown (Macfarlan's J.F.)*, 1910, 1 S.L.T. 29.

[26] *Thomson's Trustees* v. *Davidson*, 1947 S.C. 654.

the testator had forbidden his trustees to sell, stating that he could not even pay the interest on the bonds, and the Lord Ordinary remitted to a man of skill, but the Division recalled his interlocutor and, without delivering opinions, dismissed the petition.[27] The Lord President probably had this and similar trust cases in mind when in *Thomson's Trustees* v. *Davidson* [28] he reserved his opinion as to the holding of heritage, and it may be that a different view would now be taken of a case like *Whyte's Factor*.[27] Power to disregard the testator's directions was refused where sale of heritage would have been more convenient.[29] Where a testatrix directed division of her estate *in specie* and the beneficiaries agreed to sale and division of the proceeds, the court refused to authorise the judicial factor to carry out the agreement, observing that if he did he must take the responsibility himself.[30] Where a testator had directed accumulation of surplus income and the factor applied for power to make payments out of accumulated income to the testator's daughter and her children, who were in penury, but none of whom had a vested right, power was refused for the daughter, but granted for her children, who were said to be " in a different position " from their mother.[31]

If a factor is of opinion that it is impossible to carry out the provisions of the settlement he may apply to the court for directions,[32] and a factor may be authorised to give effect to the testator's purposes in a more convenient way than that provided by the trust deed. Where a testator directed that after the fulfilment of prior purposes his estate should be conveyed in terms of an entail, and the only prior purpose unfulfilled was the payment of a small annuity, the court authorised the factor to convey the estate in terms of the entail, the annuity being made a real burden on the lands, prestable by the factor, who remained in office and responsible for payment of the annuity.[33] On the other hand, the court refused to authorise a factor to convey the estate to the residuary legatee on her granting a personal bond in favour of an alimentary annuitant and, on this being done, to discharge him.[34] There are three distinctions between these cases. In one the annuity was alimentary and in the other it was not. In one it was to be secured on a personal bond and in the other made a real burden. But the third distinction is of general application. In *Munro* the factor remained responsible for payment of the annuity. In *Smith and Campbell* he proposed that the court should relieve him of his office while one of the trust purposes was still unfulfilled.

---

[27] *Whyte's Factor* v. *Whyte* (1891) 18 R. 376.
[28] 1947 S.C. at p. 658.
[29] *Watson* v. *Crawcour* (1856) 19 D. 70; *Conage's Judicial Factor* (O.H.), 1948 S.L.T.(Notes) 11.
[30] *Keegan* (1857) 19 D. 382.
[31] *Latta* (1880) 7 R. 881.
[32] *Hay's Judicial Factor* v. *Hay's Trustees*, 1952 S.C.(H.L.) 29; *Tait's Judicial Factor* v. *Lillie*, 1940 S.C. 534.
[33] *Munro* v. *Macarthur* (1878) 12 S.L.R. 126.
[34] *Smith and Campbell* (1873) 11 M. 639.

Variation of trust purposes

While there has so far been no application by a judicial factor on a trust estate under section 1 of the Trusts (Scotland) Act 1961 such an application would seem to be competent. " Trust " and " trustee " have the same meanings as in the Trusts (Scotland) Act 1961, as amended.

Public trusts

A public trust is one which is intended to benefit a section of the public and may be enforced by an *actio popularis*.[35] Here there is little room for the appointment of a judicial factor. If the trustees fail the court under the *nobile officium* will appoint new trustees, and it is incompetent to appoint a judicial factor to manage a public trust.[36] A judicial factor may, however, be appointed as an interim measure.[37]

---

[35] *Anderson's Trustees* v. *Scott*, 1914 S.C. 942 at p. 955, citing McLaren, *Wills and Succession* (3rd ed.), II, p. 917; *Andrews* v. *Ewart's Trustees* (1886) 13 R.(H.L.) 69 at p. 73.

[36] *Forbes* v. *Dalziel* (1877) 5 R. 328.

[37] *Carmont* v. *Mitchell's Trustees* (1883) 10 R. 829 (challenge of trustees' actings); *Wylie* (1850) 12 D. 1110 (temporary failure of trustees).

CHAPTER VII

FACTOR UNDER SECTION 163 OF THE BANKRUPTCY (SCOTLAND) ACT 1913

Competency

Section 163 enacts:

" It shall be competent to one or more creditors of parties deceased, or to persons having an interest in the succession of such parties, in the event of the deceased having left no settlement appointing trustees or other parties having power to manage his estate or part thereof, or in the event of such parties not accepting or acting, to apply . . . for the appointment of a judicial factor, and . . . the Lord Ordinary or sheriff may appoint such factor, who shall administer the estate . . . in accordance with the Judicial Factors (Scotland) Acts 1880 and 1889 and relative acts of sederunt, and in case of an insolvent estate shall divide the same among the creditors thereof in accordance with the rules obtaining in sequestrations in virtue of the provisions of this Act."

The section replaces section 164 of the Bankruptcy (Scotland) Act 1856. The only substantial differences between that section and section 163 are (1) that the former required to qualify a petitioning creditor a debt of £100, and the latter does not, (2) that, whereas under the 1856 Act the factor was bound to apply the common law rules as to ranking,[1] under the 1913 Act he applies in case of insolvency the rules of that Act, and (3) that the Rules of Court 1965 deal with the procedure for the distribution of any surplus after paying creditors [2] and that no such provision was made under the 1856 Act.[3] The other differences are that section 163 omits details as to the factor's duties, which have been rendered unnecessary since the general code applies to him, confers a limited jurisdiction on the sheriff, and contains a particular reference to insolvent estates. Otherwise decisions under section 164 of the 1856 Act apply to cases under section 163 of the 1913 Act.

The section applies whether the estate is testate or intestate,[4] solvent or insolvent.[5] Further, subject to the suggestion of Lord Deas mentioned below, it applies in all cases where the deceased's nominees have not accepted or at least are not acting. Two possible ambiguities in the section were resolved in " the first application under the new statute." [6] On a

---

[1] *Wight's Trs.* v. *Jamieson* (1863) 1 M. 815.
[2] r. 201 (*o*).
[3] *Alexander* (1862) 24 D. 1334.
[4] Goudy, *Bankruptcy* (4th ed.), p. 499.
[5] *Masterton* v. *Erskine's Trustees* (1887) 14 R. 712 at p. 716; *Alexander* (1862) 24 D. 1334 at pp. 1339, 1341.
[6] *Macfarlane* (1857) 19 D. 656.

petition by creditors under section 164 for the appointment of a factor on an intestate estate the court granted the prayer, and Lord Ivory said this [7]: " The petitioners are creditors on the estate, and there is no person to manage it under powers derived from the deceased. Therefore it appears to me that the statute applies." This makes it clear (1) that the words " in the event of the deceased . . . not accepting " apply to petitions both by creditors and by parties having an interest in the succession, not merely to the latter, and (2) that the section applies where no one has been appointed by the deceased to manage his estate, either expressly or impliedly [8] or by operation of statute.[9] The first point has never been questioned, but in *Macfarlane* [10] Lord Deas suggested that " having left " might have two meanings, *viz.* having left no settlement and having left (in the sense of being survived by) no parties having power to manage his estate, *e.g.* an heir who might serve or a person entitled to be appointed executor-dative. This construction, in itself difficult, involves placing an almost impossibly strained meaning on the words " in the event of such parties not accepting or acting," and it has not been further noticed. In five cases where there were executors-dative or potential executors-dative this question of competency was not raised, and factors were appointed in three [11] and refused in two [12] as matter of discretion. A person who has a possible claim of damages against the deceased is not a " creditor." [13]

It has not been decided whether an application competent when presented becomes incompetent if an executor-nominate is confirmed before the motion for appointment is made, but the opinions support the view that a competent application remains competent.[14] The question is not likely to arise, since confirmation of an executor *pendente processu* is a good ground for refusing an application as matter of discretion. A second appointment is competent, if after the discharge of the factor new assets emerge.[15]

Intimation

The Rules of Court 1965 specify the form of the petition and the necessary averments.[16] They require, besides intimation on the walls and in the minute book, intimation in the *Edinburgh Gazette* and service on such of the parties named in the petition as representatives of the deceased

---

[7] At p. 659.

[8] *Martin* v. *Ferguson's Trustees* (1892) 19 R. 474.

[9] Executors (Scotland) Act 1900, s. 3.

[10] (1857) 19 D. 656 at p. 659.

[11] *Macdonald, Fraser & Co.* v. *Cairns' Executrix*, 1932 S.C. 699; *Lamb* (O.H.) (1902) 9 S.L.T. 438; *Masterton* v. *Erskine's Trustees* (1887) 14 R. 712.

[12] *Bathgate* v. *Kelly* (O.H.) 1926 S.L.T. 155, 1926 S.N. 3; *Begg & Co.* (O.H.) (1893) 1 S.L.T. 274.

[13] *Dunn* v. *Britannic Ass. Co.* (O.H.) 1932 S.L.T. 244; 1932 S.N. 16.

[14] *London & Brazilian Bank* v. *Lumsden's Trustees* (O.H.) 1913, 1 S.L.T. 262 (where Lord Hunter thought the petition incompetent when presented); *Curle's Trustees* (O.H.) (1893) 1 S.L.T. 340; *Welsh* v. *Fife Coal Co.*, 1926 S.C. 807 at p. 811.

[15] *Wright* (O.H.) (1901) 9 S.L.T. 278.

[16] r. 201 (*a*).

as are not parties thereto.[17] No appointment may be made, except on cause shewn *ad interim*, until fourteen days after intimation and service.[18]

Appointment

The Lord Ordinary has a discretion. Appointments were refused where executors-nominate had obtained confirmation since the presentation of the petition,[19] where the deceased's widow [20] or children [21] had been decerned executors-dative, and where the estate was being administered by a person who had right to the liferent under a marriage contract.[22] But it was granted where the executor-dative had an adverse interest,[23] where, although the widow had been executrix-dative for three years, the petitioners under an arrangement were to a large extent controlling her administration,[24] and where an interim factor had been appointed in the sheriff court.[25] Where the next of kin had been decerned executor-dative after the appointment of a factor, but immediately went abroad, the court refused to recall the appointment.[26] The appointment is equivalent to a duly intimated assignation of the deceased's rights,[27] but it does not prevent the subsequent sequestration of the estate.[28]

While an application is competent if the deceased has nominated no one to manage the estate " or part thereof," the only power conferred on the court is to appoint a factor, " who shall administer the estate." Read literally, this requires the factor to administer the whole estate, including any part in the hands of executors-nominate. It seems unlikely that the court would adopt this construction, especially in the absence of express power to sequestrate, but a common law factory might be suitable in such a case.[29]

Factor's duties

Since the factor is to administer the estate in accordance with the Acts of 1880 and 1886, his general duties, *e.g.* to find caution and to ingather the estate, are the same as those of other factors, and the duties peculiar to his office are prescribed in paragraphs (*d*) to (*o*) of rule 201 of the Rules of Court 1965. The following is an outline of these paragraphs as applied in practice. If the estate is insolvent, the factor in ranking creditors applies the provisions of the Bankruptcy Act,[30] the date of his appointment

---

[17] r. 201 (*b*).
[18] r. 201 (*c*)
[19] *London & Brazilian Bank* v. *Lumsden's Trustees* (O.H.) 1913, 1 S.L.T. 262; *Curle's Trustees* (O.H.) (1893) 1 S.L.T. 340.
[20] *Begg & Co.* (O.H.) (1893) 1 S.L.T. 274.
[21] *Bathgate* v. *Kelly* (O.H.) 1926 S.L.T. 155, 1926 S.N. 3.
[22] *Marshall* v. *Graham* (1859) 21 D. 203.
[23] *Lamb* (O.H.) (1902) 9 S.L.T. 438.
[24] *Macdonald, Fraser & Co.* v. *Cairns' Executrix*, 1932 S.C. 699.
[25] *Youngson* (O.H.) 1911, 2 S.L.T. 448.
[26] *Masterton* v. *Erskine's Trustees* (1887) 14 R. 712.
[27] *Campbell's Judicial Factor* v. *National Bank of Scotland* (O.H.) 1944 S.C. 495.
[28] *Arthur* (O.H.) (1903) 10 S.L.T. 550.
[29] *McDougall* (1853) 15 D. 776.
[30] Bankruptcy (Scotland) Act 1913, s. 163. *Wight's Trs.* v. *Jamieson* (1863) 1 M. 815, is no longer law.

being equivalent to the date of sequestration.[31] Out of the first funds realised he reserves sufficient to defray the estimated cost of his administration and may pay privileged debts without waiting for the expiry of six months from the date of death.[32] Within fourteen days of receiving the first certified copy interlocutor of his appointment he inserts in the *Edinburgh Gazette* and any appropriate newspapers a notice calling for claims both by creditors [33] and by persons interested in the succession (hereinafter referred to as " persons interested ").[34] Within six months of receiving the first certified copy interlocutor of his appointment he lodges with the accountant an inventory of the estate and at the same time, or, with the accountant's sanction, later, a state of debts appearing to be due, including the claims both of creditors and of those interested.[35] Having adjudicated on the creditors' claims, he gives effect to his adjudication by laying before the accountant a state of funds and a scheme of division amongst the creditors.[36] On lodging the state of funds, scheme of division and the accountant's report in court he gives notice that he has done so to each person who has lodged a claim and, in the case of a creditor, stating the decision on his claim. He must also notify persons who have not lodged claims, but who he has reason to believe are creditors or persons interested.[37] Although only creditors' claims are being dealt with at this stage, those interested have the radical right and are entitled " to keep an eye on the claims of the creditors." [38] Any objections to the state of funds or scheme of division, whether by creditors or persons interested, are disposed of by the court,[39] and this settles the amount of the surplus, if any. Where there is no dispute as to the rights of those interested the factor proposes a scheme of distribution of any surplus, based in case of intestacy normally on a family tree showing that all the heirs have been accounted for, and in case of testate succession on the testamentary writings. He incorporates this in a report to the accountant, who in turn reports to the court, and both reports with any objections are considered by the court. The factor then pays to those found entitled by the court.[40] Where there is a serious dispute of law or fact among the claimants a factor would be well advised not to attempt to decide it himself but to propose that he should raise a multiplepoinding. But where the dispute seems to him, on advice, to be unreasonable or trivial he may make his decision, leaving it, if wrong, to be corrected.

Judicial factors have a title to sue for reduction of a transaction

---

[31] r. 201 (*e*).
[32] para. (*n*).
[33] In practice affidavits are not insisted on for trade debts if invoices and statements of account are available.
[34] para. (*d*), as amended by A.S., March 17, 1967.
[35] para. (*f*), as amended by A.S., March 17, 1967.
[36] paras. (*e*) and (*g*).
[37] para. (*h*).
[38] *Alexander* (1862) 24 D. 1334, Lord Neaves at pp. 1341, 1342.
[39] paras. (*j*), (*k*).
[40] para. (*o*).

harmful to the estate,[41] and, although a factor appointed under section 163
cannot found on the statutory right of challenge conferred on a trustee in
bankruptcy, a decision that such a factor had no title *qua* factor to challenge
seems to have proceeded on a misapprehension.[42] A factor appointed
under the section brought an action founded on the Bankruptcy Act 1621
for reduction of a declaration of trust granted by the deceased. In sustain-
ing a plea of no title to sue the Lord Ordinary held that the pursuer stood
in place of the trustees, whose rights were derived from the deceased,
and that the deceased had no right to challenge his own alienation, and
referred to *Fleming's Trustees* v. *McHardy*,[43] where it was held that
trustees under a trust deed for creditors had no title as such to challenge a
prior alienation. But in *Reid's Judicial Factor* the trustees were defenders,
not pursuers, and the pursuer derived his rights not from them, but from
the court, just as any judicial factor does. The actual decision might
have been supported on the terms of the Act of 1621, which confers the
title to sue on " the true and just creditor," but a person who represents
creditors for debts incurred before the alienation has a title to sue.[44]
Since the first duty of a factor under section 163 is to ingather the assets
and pay the creditors he represents them in the same way as a trustee in
bankruptcy does. But as the case did not develop on these lines, the
report does not disclose whether there were creditors at the date of the
declaration of trust still unpaid at the deceased's death.

Discharge

The factor must serve his petition for discharge on the representatives
of the deceased and on his cautioner and insert a notice in the *Edinburgh
Gazette*,[45] but as the state of funds has already been judicially approved,
or at least can no longer be objected to, while payments have been judicially
approved, the discharge seems to be a matter of course. The form of
discharge in the Styles [46] appears to overlook the fact that the scheme of
division referred to in rule 201 [47] is the scheme of division amongst the
creditors and that if the estate is solvent, a scheme of division amongst
the creditors is not the same as a scheme of division of the estate. If
there is a surplus, a second report by the accountant is necessary.[48]

---

[41] *Tait* v. *Muir* (1904) 6 F. 586 (judicial factor on the estate of a corporation); *Blaikie* v.
Milne (1838) 1 D. 18 (curator *bonis*).
[42] *Reid's Judicial Factor* v. *Reid* (O.H.) 1959 S.L.T. 120.
[43] (1892) 19 R. 542.
[44] *Obers* v. *Paton's Trustees* (1897) 24 R. 719 (trustee in foreign bankruptcy); *Edmund* v.
Grant (1853) 15 D. 703 (trustee in bankruptcy, who at that time had no statutory title).
[45] Rules of Court 1965, r. 201 (*p*).
[46] *Encyclopaedia of Scottish Legal Styles*, Vol. VI, form 94. See also Form 33 of the Rules.
[47] Rules of Court 1965, r. 201 (*g*).
[48] para. (*o*).

Chapter VIII

FACTOR ON PARTNERSHIP ESTATE

Introductory

While a factor may be appointed on a partnership estate either for the purpose of winding it up or of continuing the business in terms of the contract of copartnery,[1] there appear to be only three reported cases where a factor has been appointed simply to continue the business. In one,[2] dissolution of the partnership was imminent, and in two[3] the appointment was pending disputes. It is difficult to imagine any other circumstances in which the court would appoint a factor on the estate of a continuing partnership, and the remainder of this chapter deals with appointments made after dissolution for the purpose of winding up. Frequently dissolution and the appointment of a factor are craved in the same petition.[4] No appointment will be made unless it appears prima facie that there is or has been a partnership.[5]

Dissolution of partnership

" A distinction is to be marked between those events which *eo ipso* dissolve the partnership and those which only afford a ground of dissolution," [6] *i.e.* dissolution by the court. The Partnership Act 1890 preserves this distinction between events by which a partnership is dissolved[7] and cases in which the court may decree a dissolution.[8]

Subject to special agreement, a partnership for a fixed term is dissolved by the expiry of the fixed term, unless renewed by tacit relocation[9]; if entered into for a single adventure, by the termination of the adventure; if entered into for an undefined time, by notice; by the death or bankruptcy[10] of a partner; or by the business becoming illegal.[11] Should a dispute arise as to whether a partnership has been dissolved by any of these events it ought to be decided by an action of declarator with other appropriate conclusions.[12]

---

[1] *Haldane* v. *Girvan and Portpatrick Junction Railway Co.* (1881) 8 R. 669 at p. 673.

[2] *McCulloch* v. *McCulloch*, 1953 S.C. 189.

[3] *Booth* v. *MacKinnon* (O.H.) (1908) 15 S.L.T. 848; *Paterson* v. *Mackay* (O.H.) (1894) 1 S.L.T. 564. In *Drysdale* v. *Lawson* (1842) 4 D. 1061, the court refused to appoint, but gave no reason.

[4] See *Macnabs* v. *Macnab*, 1912 S.C. 421 at p. 423.

[5] *Gatherer* (O.H.) (1893) 1 S.L.T. 401; *Anderson* v. *Blair* (O.H.) 1935 S.L.T. 377. See also *Scott* (O.H.) 1910, 2 S.L.T. 234.

[6] Bell, Prin. (10th ed.), s. 373; Comm. (7th ed.) II, 524, 525.

[7] ss. 32, 33, 34.

[8] s. 35.

[9] s. 27; *Neilson* v. *Mossend Iron Co.* (1886) 13 R. (H.L.) 50.

[10] *i.e.* sequestration; s. 47.

[11] ss. 32, 33, 34.

[12] As in *Hannan* v. *Henderson* (1879) 7 R. 380; *Hill* v. *Wylie* (1865) 3 M 541. See *Encyclopaedia of the Laws of Scotland*, XI, s. 149. See also *Macnabs* v. *Macnab*, 1912 S.C. 421 (a case under s. 35).

On the other hand, the Act provides that " on application by a partner the court may decree a dissolution of the partnership " in any of six cases. The first four relate to the partners and are permanent insanity,[13] permanent incapacity in any other way to perform his part of the partnership contract,[14] conduct prejudicial to the business, and persistent breach of the partnership agreement or other conduct such that it is not reasonably practicable for the other partners to carry on the business.[15] The last two cases are that the business can be carried on only at a loss [16] and that it is just and equitable that the partnership should be dissolved.[17] The word " application " at the beginning of section 35 includes petition,[18] but obviously some of the statutory grounds may raise serious issues of interpretation or of fact more suitable for decision in an action. In such a case, if the only crave is for dissolution, the petition will be dismissed,[18] but if there is also a crave for appointment of a factor, supported by relevant averments,[19] a sist is the appropriate procedure, so that, after the action has been decided, the crave for appointment can be granted or refused according to circumstances.[20] But in some cases a remit to a reporter may be appropriate.[21] The phrase " decree a dissolution " appears to be of English origin,[22] but its meaning seems plain enough. In contrast with the phrase " a partnership is dissolved," used where the partnership is dissolved by an event,[23] it gives the court power to dissolve, which could be done by an interlocutor " dissolving " the partnership. It therefore seems inappropriate for petitioners who were founding on section 35 to crave the court " to find and declare that the partnership . . . is dissolved, and to decree a dissolution thereof "[24] or " to declare the copartnership . . . to be dissolved from and after " a date three months before the presentation of the petition.[25] Both petitions were dismissed, and the court did not require to consider whether the craves were consistent with section 35.

Grounds for appointment

On dissolution, in the absence of special terms, which must be established by the person founding on them,[26] any partner or the representatives

---

[13] In this case the partner's curator *bonis* may also apply. In *Cleghorn* (O.H.) (1901) 8 S.L.T. 409, the *incapax* was respondent.

[14] *Eadie* v. *MacBean's Curator Bonis* (1885) 12 R. 660, where under the partnership contract the duties of the incapacitated partner did not require his personal services and the application for winding up and appointment of a factor was refused.

[15] *Macpherson* v. *Richmond* (1869) 6 S.L.R. 348; *Thomson* (O.H.) (1893) 1 S.L.T. 59.

[16] *Miller* v. *Walker* (1875) 3 R. 242, a common law case.

[17] s. 35.

[18] *Macnabs* v. *Macnab*, 1912 S.C. 421.

[19] *Anderson* v. *Blair* (O.H.) 1935 S.L.T. 377.

[20] *Blake's Trustees* v. *Jolly* (1920), 1 S.L.T. 304, 57 S.L.R. 431.

[21] *Sons of Temperance Friendly Society*, 1926 S.C. 418, especially at p. 428.

[22] Bell, Comm. (7th ed.) II, 525, note 1.

[23] ss. 32, 33, 34.

[24] *Wallace* v. *Whitelaw* (1900) 2 F. 675, where there was a further crave for the appointment of a factor.

[25] *Macnabs* v. *Macnab*, 1912 S.C. 421.

[26] *Ferguson* v. *M'Bean* (O.H.) (1899) 7 S.L.T. 315.

of a deceased partner are entitled to have the assets realised, the debts paid and any surplus divided amongst the partners and the representatives of any deceased partner.[27] Prima facie, the surviving partners, if any, have the right to conduct the winding up, and at common law the court appointed a factor to do so only in case of necessity. The Partnership Act 1890 provides that any partner or his representatives may apply to the court to wind up the business and affairs of the firm.[27] This is taken to empower the court, if applied to by petition, to sequestrate the estate, if there are surviving partners, and to appoint a judicial factor,[28] but it will not do so unless such appointment is necessary.[29] " The reason why in the ordinary case the law gives to the surviving partner the whole control of the winding up is that he has an interest in the concern and the best qualifications for winding it up. So strong is his right that he cannot be superseded by a judicial factor, unless he is in some way disqualified for the office." [30] Surviving partners are, for example, more fitted than a factor to recover debts, for they know the customers,[31] and, from their familiarity with the business, to conclude pending contracts [32] and to realise the assets to the best advantage. As these considerations do not apply where there are no surviving partners and the representatives of the last surviving partner have no contractual right to wind up,[33] the court will in that case appoint a factor.[34] Nor do they apply where the surviving partners are unfitted for business by age or general incapacity.[35] But, where the winding up is in the hands of surviving partners their conduct may be such as to justify sequestration and the appointment of a factor.

Winding up is not just a matter of closing the door of the office or the gate of the factory and, with the aid of a small staff retained for the purpose, paying and collecting debts and selling any property. Not only do current contracts continue as a rule, but the most profitable method of realisation may be that the business be taken over on terms by the surviving partners or that it be sold as a going concern. There is almost bound to be some delay, and in the meantime the business must be carried on.[36] A partner's delay in winding up was found not unreasonable in the under-noted case,[37] but where a partner was in effect carrying on the business for his own benefit a factor was appointed.[38]

Disputes between partners or their representatives as to the past administration of the business or as to the proper distribution of the surplus

[27] Partnership Act 1890, s. 39.
[28] Encyclopaedia of Scottish Legal Styles, VII, Forms 156, 157.
[29] Carabine v. Carabine, 1949 S.C. 521 at p. 526.
[30] Nicoll v. Reid (1877) 5 R. 137 at p. 140; Collins v. Young (1853) 1 Macq. 385, 15 D. (H.L.) 35; Thomson (O.H.) (1893) 1 S.L.T. 59, where the last two lines of the report are obscure.
[31] Gow v. Schultze (1877) 4 R. 928; Elliott v. Cassils & Co. (O.H.) (1907) 15 S.L.T. 190.
[32] Bell, Comm. (7th ed.) II, 528; Partnership Act 1890, s. 38.
[33] Dixon v. Dixon (1822) 6 W. & S. 229.
[34] Dickie v. Mitchell (1874) 1 R. 1030 at p. 1033.
[35] Dickie v. Mitchell (1874) 1 R. 1030. In Robertson (O.H.) (1902) 10 S.L.T. 417, the averments of incapacity were held irrelevant.
[36] Robertson (O.H.) (1902) 10 S.L.T. 417; Dickie v. Mitchell (1874) 1 R. 1030 at p. 1035.
[37] Robertson (O.H.) (1902) 10 S.L.T. 417.
[38] Carabine v. Carabine, 1949 S.C. 521; Allan v. Gronmeyer (1891) 18 R. 784.

are not a ground for appointment. A judicial factor is not an arbiter and has no power to decide such disputes, which must be settled by an action of accounting, or a multiplepoinding.[39] An appointment was refused where the only question at issue was whether the business had a goodwill.[40]

Factor's duties

In so far as his duties are peculiar to his office they are the same as those of a partner who is winding up. It was apparently thought necessary to appoint with power " to manage and wind up " so that the factor should be able to continue the business with a view to profitable realisation.[41] But since the partnership is dissolved, mere sequestration, if necessary, and appointment are sufficient.[42] The court will not tolerate attempts to " bye-pass " the factor [43] or to interfere with him in the course of his duties, unless he is failing in them.[44] Since his duty is to realise the estate the factor is entitled to sell heritage.[45]

---

[39] *Gow* v. *Schultze* (1877) 4 R. 928; *Elliot* v. *Cassils & Co.* (O.H.) (1907) 15 S.L.T. 190; *Menzies* (O.H.) (1899) 7 S.L.T. 235.
[40] *Mackenzie* v. *MacFarlane* (O.H.) 1934 S.N. 16.
[41] *Dickie* v. *Mitchell* (1874) 1 R. 1030 at p. 1035.
[42] *Carabine* v. *Carabine* (1949) S.C. 521.
[43] *Fullarton* v. *Dixon* (1833) 11 S. 962. See *McCulloch* v. *McCulloch*, 1953 S.C. 189.
[44] *Dixon* v. *Fullarton* (1833) 12 S. 248; *Fullarton* v. *Dixon* (1834) 12 S. 750. See *McCulloch* v. *McCulloch*, 1953 S.C. 189.
[45] *Cooper & Sons' Judicial Factor* (O.H.) 1931 S.L.T. 26; 1930 S.N. 134.

CHAPTER IX

FACTOR PENDING DISPUTE[1]

General

The purpose of this appointment is to provide for the administration of property in dispute, or, if parties agree, for its sale and administration of the price, until parties' rights have been settled by agreement or litigation. Appointments have been made without application by any party where confirmation of an executor-nominate was suspended pending a reduction of the will.[2] They have also been made on the petition of an owner of property, still in possession, who maintained that he had sold it, without opposition from the alleged purchaser, whose position was that he had not bought the property and therefore was not concerned,[3] and of an apparent owner, whose title was challenged and her rights interfered with.[4] But the usual case, and that with which this chapter is almost entirely concerned, is an application by a claimant for the appointment of a factor on disputed property of which no one has control or which is under the control of another claimant. Such control may arise from the right of an apparent heir to continue his ancestor's possession,[5] but it usually rests on actual possession, with or without a title.

It has been stated that a factor will not be appointed if one of the parties has obtained peaceful possession before the competition arose,[6] and in the same case Lord President Inglis was of opinion that such possession would " exclude our jurisdiction." [7] If these *obiter dicta* mean that an appointment is incompetent in such circumstances, their soundness has not been tested in a case where the possession, however long and peaceful, was clearly without right or title. Nevertheless, there appears to be only one reported case where a person who had enjoyed peaceful possession on an *ex facie* good title was ousted, and that decision was reversed.[8]

Grounds for appointment

Since the court in making or refusing an appointment is exercising a discretion, it takes all the circumstances into account, and it would be

---

[1] The usual term is " Factor pending litigation " (*Leslie's Judicial Factor*, 1925 S.C. 464, Lord President Clyde at p. 469; *Faculty Digest*, Vol. 2, col. 1362), but a factor may be appointed before any litigation has begun.

[2] *Simpson's Exrx.* v. *Simpson's Trs.*, 1912 S.C. 418; *Campbell* v. *Barber* (1895) 23 R. 90.

[3] *Esson* (1851) 14 D. 10; *Buchanan* v. *Paterson* (1833) 12 S. 232.

[4] *Waddell* v. *Waddell* (1837) 16 S. 79. See also *Viscountess Hawarden* v. *Dunlop* (1861) 23 D. 923, narrative at p. 925, and sequel (1862) 24 D. 1267.

[5] Ersk., Inst. III, 8, 58; Bell, Prin. (10th ed.), s. 1682; *Padwick* v. *Steuart* (1871) 9 M. 793 at pp. 794, 797; *Borthwick* v. *Glassford* (1861) 23 D. 632 at pp. 633, 634.

[6] *Campbell* v. *Campbell* (1864) 2 M. (H.L.) 41 at p. 45.

[7] (1863) 1 M. at p. 998.

[8] *Viscountess Hawarden* v. *Dunlop* (1861) 23 D. 923 (*quoad* heritage).

unwise to assume that because it has founded particularly on one circumstance in one case the presence of that circumstance will necessarily
lead to the same result in another case.

The ostensible aim of all parties is to preserve the estate until their rights
are determined. Accordingly, one obvious reason for appointing a factor is
that there is no one with a title to intromit,[9] and probably this consideration influenced the court to appoint where confirmation of an executor-
nominate was suspended.[10] Another reason is to prevent dilapidation of
the estate. A factor was appointed where one *pro indiviso* owner, who held
the property in trust for himself and the other owners, had granted a bond
over the property and apparently used the proceeds for his own purposes.[11] The element of dilapidation was present in the undernoted cases,[12]
and in other cases the absence of averments of dilapidation has been
commented on.[13] Offer of caution may be an answer to such suggestions.[14]
But these considerations do not bulk largely in the reports, and it may be
inferred that the main reason for such applications is the desire to deprive
the possessor of the advantages arising from possession. He is a trustee
for the person ultimately found to be the true owner and bound to account
to him,[15] but in the meantime he enjoys the fruits and is " equipped by
possession of rents to fight the battle." [16] Probably the plea of *bona fide*
perception and consumption is open to him, at least until the first decision
against him in the main dispute.[17]

The question usually comes to depend on the strength of the respondent's right to possess and the strength of the petitioner's attack, as these
appear from " the admitted facts and the reasonable inferences to be
drawn from the state of the pleadings " [18] and the documents. An application will not be granted unless it is " in harmony with and derives support
from uncontested facts." [19] It is therefore useless for a petitioner to
found on an averment which is denied and requires proof. The court
disregarded an averment that the respondent's title had been impetrated [20]
and refused appointments where the only averment was that a deed had
been obtained by fraud [21] or granted on deathbed.[22] On the other hand,

---

[9] *Viscountess Hawarden* v. *Dunlop* (1861) 23 D. 923 at pp. 931, 932 (*quoad* moveable estate).
[10] *Tegner* v. *Henderson* (O.H.) 1930 S.L.T. 23, 1929 S.N. 130; *Simpson's Exrx.* v. *Simpson's Trs.*, 1912 S.C. 418; *Campbell* v. *Barber* (1895) 23 R. 90; *Blackwood* v. *Reith* (O.H.) (1905) 13 S.L.T. 629. See also *Russell* v. *Mollison* (1872) 9 S.L.R. 267.
[11] *Bailey* v. *Scott* (1860) 22 D. 1105.
[12] *Simpson's Exrx.* v. *Simpson's Trs.*, 1912 S.C. 418; *Campbell* v. *Barber* (1895) 23 R. 90.
[13] *Campbell* v. *Campbell* (1863) 1 M. 991 at pp. 1000, 1008, (1864) 2 M. (H.L.) 41; *Marshall* v. *Graham* (1859) 21 D. 203 at p. 205.
[14] *Macdowall* v. *Loudon* (1849) 12 D. 170; *Leith* v. *Bryce* (1830) 8 S. 1027.
[15] *Fleeming* v. *Howden* (1868) 6 M. (H.L.) 113 at pp. 118, 120, 122.
[16] *Padwick* v. *Steuart* (1871) 9 M. 793, Lord Deas at p. 797; *Boyle & Co.* v. *Cochrane* (1847) 9 D. 1053 (" the sinews of war ").
[17] *Houldsworth* v. *Brand's Trs.* (1876) 3 R. 304 at pp. 308, 312.
[18] *Campbell* v. *Barber* (1895) 23 R. 90 at p. 93.
[19] *Pattison's Curator Bonis* (O.H.) (1898) 5 S.L.T. 400.
[20] *Thoms* v. *Thoms* (1865) 3 M. 776.
[21] *Macdougall* v. *Maclaurin* (1839) 1 D. 1241; *Lady Elibank* v. *Royal Exchange Ass. Co.* (1833) 11 S. 680.
[22] *Gilmour* v. *Gilmour's Trs.* (1850) 12 D. 1266; *Tod* v. *Hunter* (1833) 11 S. 516; *Keiling* v. *Kirkwood* (1839) 1 D. 1024.

appointments were made where it was proposed to reduce a deed on grounds which required proof, but there were undisputed extrinsic facts supporting these grounds, *viz.* that a curator *bonis* had been appointed to the granter [23] or that the testator had revoked a will in favour of his relations and left everything to his valet.[24] Where the main dispute arises on the construction and effect of admitted facts and documents these are naturally brought to the notice of the judges dealing with the petition, the petitioner maintaining that on them the respondent has no right to possess and the respondent that he has. Although judges have frequently said that in disposing of the petition they are indicating no concluded opinion on the main dispute, the emphasis is on the word " concluded," since they can hardly help forming and being influenced by a prima facie one. In fact, in this type of petition, so far as the main disputes have been traced in the reports, a factor has never been appointed to supersede the person ultimately held to be the true owner, and an application by the true owner has never been refused.[25]

A factor was appointed on the petition of the heir of entail where the testamentary disponees of the deceased heir completed title three days after the funeral and were in possession, and the petitioner had raised a reduction of the disposition as a breach of the entail [26]; on the petition of testamentary trustees where the heir had completed title and entered into possession and maintained that the trusts had lapsed [27]; on the petition of beneficiaries under a will where the respondent maintained that the will did not carry heritage [28]; on the petition of a purchaser who had completed title and obtained decree of removing against the deceased seller's heir, the heir being in possession and having raised a reduction of the decree apparently on some legal ground and of the sale on the ground of forgery [29]; on the petition of an heir of entail where there was a dispute as to the right to be sole trustee in a trust over the entailed estates [30]; and on the petition of the curator *bonis* of a deceased lady whose marriage contract was challenged as not her deed.[31]

The court refused to appoint where the testamentary disponee of a deceased heir of entail was infeft and in possession and her right was challenged by the next heir of entail on three grounds.[32] The first, that the disposition had been impetrated, required parole proof and therefore could not be taken into account.[33] The second was that the disposition

---

[23] *Pattison's Curator Bonis* (O.H.) (1898) 5 S.L.T. 400.
[24] *Campbell* v. *Barber* (1895) 23 R. 90.
[25] The decisions on the merits, so far as traced, are noted where the petitions are cited.
[26] *Speirs* v. *Speirs* (1877) 5 R. 75. The disposition was reduced: (1878) 5 R. 923. See also *Elliot* v. *Scott* (1843) 5 D. 1075; and *Cathcart* v. *Cathcart* (1829) 7 S. 392, where the respondent's title was reduced: (1831) 5 W. & S. 315.
[27] *Brown* v. *Robertson* (1845) 7 D. 745. The heir's case failed: *Ogilvie's Trs.* v. *Kirk Session of Dundee* (1846) 8 D. 1229.
[28] *Fraser* v. *Thorburn* (1855) 18 D. 264. The will was held to carry heritage: *Thorburn* v. *Thorburn* (1858) 20 D. 829, where " 1835 " on p. 831 must be a mistake for 1855.
[29] *Russell* v. *McInturner* (1847) 9 D. 989.
[30] *Home* v. *Hunter* (1833) 11 S. 538. See further *Hunter* v. *Home* (1834) 12 S. 406.
[31] *Pattison's Curator Bonis* (O.H.) (1898) 5 S.L.T. 400.
[32] *Thoms* v. *Thoms* (1865) 3 M. 776. [33] *Ibid.*, Lord Ordinary at p. 777.

was a breach of the entail. The Lord Ordinary and the Lord President [34] were not impressed by this point, and it was ultimately abandoned.[35] The third, that the disposition did not carry the lands, was considered too doubtful as a ground for appointing.[36] The court also refused applications at the instance of the testamentary disponee of a deceased heir of entail, who maintained that the entail was defective, the next heir of entail having completed title and exercised some proprietory rights [37]; at the instance of creditors who had adjudged the estates, where the debtor's heir of entail had completed title, entered into possession and raised a reduction of the adjudication on the ground that it contravened the entail [38]; at the instance of a purchaser from a deceased heir of entail, who maintained that the entail was invalid [39]; at the instance of the trustee in bankruptcy of a deceased heir of entail, who maintained that the entail was invalid [40]; at the instance of a trustee in bankruptcy, who had raised a reduction of a conveyance in favour of the bankrupt's wife excluding the *jus mariti* [41]; at the instance of the owners of property, who had raised a reduction of a bond and disposition in security on grounds not stated, where the creditors were in possession under a decree of maills and duties [42]; at the instance of a claimant to teinds which had long been in the possession of another party [43]; and on the death of the trustee at the instance of a creditor who had acceded to a trust deed.[44]

Litigants who have obtained judgment in their favour, which is under appeal, have usually failed to obtain an appointment merely on the ground that the judgment shows that their opponents ought not to be in possession,[45] but in one somewhat special case the court founded on the fact that the petitioner had obtained decree, although an appeal had been taken.[46]

Before the Bankruptcy (Scotland) Act 1856, the court appointed factors on heritable estates, although the owner's estates had already been sequestrated, particularly where a creditor had obtained decree of maills and duties or of ranking and sale.[47] But now the effect of a decree of

---

[34] *Ibid.*, at pp. 777, 778.
[35] *Thoms* v. *Thoms* (1868) 6 M. 704 at p. 705 (narrative).
[36] It was negatived: 6 M. 704.
[37] *Catton* v. *Mackenzie* (1870) 8 M. 713. The disposition was held not to carry the lands: (1870) 8 M. 1049. The entail was held valid: (1872) 10 M. (H.L.) 12.
[38] *Bogle & Co.* v. *Cochrane* (1847) 9 D. 1503. The petitioners at that stage had the Lord Ordinary's judgment in their favour, but this was reversed: (1850) 7 Bell's App. 65.
[39] *Padwick* v. *Steuart* (1871) 9 M. 793. The entail was held valid: (1874) 1 R. 697.
[40] *Borthwick* v. *Glassford* (1861) 23 D. 632. The Lord Ordinary found the entail valid: *Glassford* v. *Borthwick* (1862) 24 D. 1136 at p. 1137.
[41] *Boaz* v. *Liddell* (1828) 6 S. The reduction failed: (1829) 7 S. 555.
[42] *Watson* v. *Shand* (1849) 12 D. 394. See also *Hutchinson* v. *Gordon* (1833) 11 S. 395; *Lady Elibank* v. *Royal Exchange Ass. Co.* (1833) 11 S. 680.
[43] *Wood* v. *Mackintosh* (1862) 24 D. 563.
[44] *Hamilton* v. *Littlejohn* (1834) 7 W. and S. 380.
[45] *Bogle & Co.* v. *Cochrane* (1847) 9 D. 1503; *Clouston* v. *Anderson* (1825) 3 S. 437; *McGregor* v. *McNeill* (1821) 1 S. 160; *Berry* v. *Anderson* (1822) 2 S. 97. See also *Boak* v. *Boak's Trs.* (1872) 10 M. 822.
[46] *Paterson* (O.H.) (1894) 1 S.L.T. 564.
[47] *Scott* v. *Scott* (1847) 9 D. 921; *Inglis* (1850) 12 D. 913; *Cadell* v. *Bell* (1831) 9 S. 873; *Thistle Bank* v. *Steven* (1834) 13 S. 219, *cf. Tweedie* v. *Beattie* (1836) 14 S. 1078; *Bank of Scotland* v. *Ogilvy's Trustees* (1829) 7 S. 412.

maills and duties can be decided in a sequestration [48] and sequestration practically supersedes the necessity for a ranking and sale.[49]

Apparent legitimacy

The great importance attached to apparent legitimacy is illustrated by the leading case.[50] The dispute was as to which of two claimants was heir to an entailed estate. The respondent claimed through his father, who all his life, over fifty years, had been regarded as legitimate. The petitioner's case was that the father was illegitimate, and he produced documentary evidence which practically established that when the father's parents went through a ceremony of marriage his mother's husband was alive. Nevertheless, the court refused to appoint a factor, holding that the father might yet be legitimate, and it was ultimately held that, although the parents' cohabitation began in adultery, their marriage was established by cohabitation with habit and repute after the death of the first husband of the father's mother and before the father's birth.[51] An appointment was also refused where the respondent's legitimacy had been recognised by his reputed parents since his birth, seven years before.[52]

Recall of factory

The factory is recalled when its purpose has been served, normally when the dispute is finally settled.[53] It was no objection to recall that a new claimant had appeared.[54] The purpose of the appointment, as in other cases, is ascertained from the averments in the petition and the terms of the interlocutor appointing. The question which arose as to whether an appointment had been made pending the proving of the tenor of a trust deed or for the purpose of executing the trust was due to some unfortunately expressed averments in the petition.[55]

Attempts to obtain recall by the party who has obtained judgment in his favour are complicated by the fact that the lower court has power to regulate interim possession. It has been laid down that a petitioner has a right to recall if, when the petition is presented, no appeal has been taken, but that if an appeal has been taken the matter is one of discretion.[56] In that case on the suggestion of the court a petition for interim possession was presented and the court recalled the factory and granted interim

---

[48] *Budge* v. *Brown's Trustees* (1872) 10 M. 958.

[49] Goudy, *Bankruptcy* (4th ed.) 497, note (*a*).

[50] *Campbell* v. *Campbell* (1863) 1 M. 991, (1865) 2 M. (H.L.) 41.

[51] *Campbell* v. *Campbell* (1867) 5 M. (H.L.) 115.

[52] *Munro* v. *Graham* (1849) 11 D. 1202.

[53] *Burden* v. *Burden* (1834) 12 S. 871; *Borthwick* (1862) 1 M. 104; *White* (1860) 22 D. 1473.

[54] *Noble* v. *Brackenbury* (1859) 21 D. 1053. Decree had been granted in the main dispute, and the new claimant had known of her possible claim years before.

[55] *Drummond* v. *Lindsay* (1857) 19 D. 859.

[56] *Aikman* v. *Aikman* (1859) 21 D. 1374. The appeal failed: (1860) 23 D. (H.L.) 3, 3 Macq. 854.

possession. In a subsequent case where the judges had differed, the court held both petitions competent, but, as matter of discretion, refused the petition for recall in *hoc statu* and the petition for interim execution except *quoad* expenses.[57]

---

[57] *Howden* v. *Fleeming* (1867) 5 M. 676. No opinions were delivered. The appeal succeeded: (1868) 6 M. (H.L.) 113.

CHAPTER X

OTHER APPOINTMENTS

Under Bankruptcy (Scotland) Act 1913, s. 14

THIS section empowers a court to which a petition for sequestration is presented to take immediate measures for the preservation of the estate by appointing a judicial factor. The court in an ordinary sequestration [1] is either the Court of Session, *i.e.* any Lord Ordinary,[2] or the appropriate sheriff,[3] and in a summary sequestration [4] is usually the sheriff, but in certain circumstances may be a Lord Ordinary. The appointment may be made on the application of a creditor producing an affidavit,[5] with or without citation of other parties interested, or without such application, if the court thinks proper.[6] The purpose is to preserve the estate until a trustee is confirmed and, in spite of the marginal note, an appointment is competent although sequestration has been awarded,[7] provided that a trustee has not been confirmed.[8] An application requires specific averments of danger to the estate.[9] Since the estates of a deceased debtor cannot be sequestrated until six months after his death, unless he was notour bankrupt or his successors concur or renounce the succession,[10] this is a favourable case for an appointment,[11] and an appointment is also suitable if, before the election of a trustee, proceedings have been sisted for consideration of a deed of arrangement.[12] If the same person applies both for sequestration and for the appointment of a factor he ought to combine the craves in one petition as he is unlikely to be awarded the expenses of two.[13]

It is the factor's right and duty to take possession of the estate,[14] and he is entitled to make an inventory of all property which prima facie belongs to the debtor.[15] But, since his duty is merely to preserve, he may incur some personal risk if by his actings he, at least deliberately,

---

[1] 1913 Act, s. 16.
[2] *Ibid.*, s. 20, as amended by the Administration of Justice (Scotland) Act 1933, s. 3.
[3] See Chapter XX.
[4] 1913 Act, s. 175 (1) and (2).
[5] *Partridge* v. *Baillie* (1873) 1 R. 253 at p. 254.
[6] This repeats s. 16 of the Bankruptcy (Scotland) Act 1856, under which most of the cases were decided.
[7] *Partridge* v. *Baillie* (1873) 1 R. 253.
[8] *Brown* v. *Bailey's Trs.*, 1910 S.C. 76 at p. 78.
[9] *Cuthbertson* v. *Gibson* (1887) 14 R. 736; *McCreadies* v. *Douglas* (1882) 10 R. 108.
[10] 1913 Act, s. 13.
[11] *J. & G. Stewart Ltd.* v. *Waldie* (O.H.) 1926 S.L.T. 526.
[12] 1913 Act, ss. 34, 36. *Goudy on Bankruptcy* (4th ed.) p. 419, note (*a*); *Brown* v. *Bailey's Trs.*, 1910 S.C. 76, at p. 78.
[13] Maclaren, *Bill Chamber Practice*, pp. 215, 216.
[14] *Neilson's Judicial Factor*, 1927 S.C. 595; *McCulloch* v. *McCulloch*, 1953 S.C. 189.
[15] *McLachlan* v. *Bell* (1895) 23 R. 126.

alters the rights of creditors *inter se*.[16] He is amenable to the Lord Ordinary and the sheriff (meaning presumably the sheriff who appointed him), although resident beyond the territory of the sheriff, at the instance of any party interested, to account for his intromissions and management.[17]

The office terminates on confirmation of the trustee.[18] On general principles only the trustee would appear to have a title to oppose the factor's discharge, but it has never been decided whether the effect of section 82 is to give a title to any creditor or indeed to the debtor himself. If the sequestration is recalled, or for some other reason the proceedings take end, the title to oppose the factor's discharge appears to be in the debtor.[18a]

On Revenue of Public Utility Companies

The companies which formerly carried on public utilities, such as railways, tramways, waterworks, gas works and harbours, were usually incorporated by special Acts. These Acts contained, or incorporated from the Companies Clauses Acts,[19] provisions for the appointment of a judicial factor on the revenues of the company to protect mortgagees and debenture holders.[20] The provisions of the special Acts and the Clauses Acts were similar.[21] They entitled the lender, if interest or repayment of principal was in arrear, to apply for the appointment of a factor and empowered the court to appoint a person to receive the whole or a competent part of the revenues and make payment to the petitioner of the arrears. The factor's sole duty was to recover revenue until the arrears were fully paid, and he had no right to interfere with the management of the company.[22] Some difficulty was caused by an appointment as judicial factor on the undertaking as well as to receive the tolls.[23] As soon as the arrears due to the petitioning creditor at the date of the appointment have been paid the appointment is at an end, and the factor must account to the company for any surplus in his hands after deduction of his remuneration and expenses.[24]

On Intestate Estate

When a person dies intestate, or at least without providing, expressly or impliedly,[25] for the administration of his estate, the normal remedy

[16] *Urquhart* v. *Macleod's Trustee* (1883) 10 R. 991.

[17] 1913 Act, s. 82. See *Bell* v. *Gow* (1862) 1 M. 85 at pp. 86, 87.

[18] *Esson* (1842) 4 D. 739; Goudy, *Bankruptcy* (4th ed.) p. 156.

[18a] See *Bell* v. *Carstairs* (1842) 5 D. 318.

[19] Companies Clauses (Scotland) Act 1845, ss. 56, 57; Companies Clauses Act 1863, s. 25.

[20] Judicial factors on railways had powers to manage; *Haldane* v. *Girvan and Port Patrick Junction Ry. Co.* (1881) 8 R. 669, 1003.

[21] *Greenock Harbour Trustees* v. *Judicial Factor of Greenock Harbour Trust*, 1908 S.C. 944 at pp. 956, 958, 1910 S.C. (H.L.) 32.

[22] *Greenock Harbour Trustees* v. *Judicial Factor of Greenock Harbour Trust*, 1910 S.C. (H.L.) 32.

[23] *Cotton* v. *Beattie* (1889) 17 R. 262. *Cf.* interlocutor in *Greenock Harbour Trustees* v. *Judicial Factor of Greenock Harbour Trust*, 1908 S.C. 944 at p. 946, 1910 S.C. (H.L.) 32.

[24] *Cotton* v. *Beattie* (1889) 17 R. 262, interlocutor at p. 272. But in that case the factor agreed, with the consent of the company, to pay arrears due to other mortgagees in the same position as the petitioner.   [25] Executors (Scotland) Act, 1900, s. 3.

is the appointment of an executor-dative, who now has a title to administer both heritage and moveables,[26] or of a judicial factor under section 163 of the Bankruptcy (Scotland) Act 1913.[27] A creditor may obtain confirmation as executor-creditor,[28] and where there are no known heirs the Queen's and Lord Treasurer's Remembrancer has the right to administer the estate,[29] including estate in England and Wales.[30] There is therefore little room for the appointment of a judicial factor at common law, but in special circumstances such factors have been appointed at the instance of a remote relative,[31] the curator *bonis* of the deceased,[32] her solicitors [33] and a creditor.[34] It is doubtful whether all these cases can stand since decisions appointing at the instance of solicitors [35] and of a remote relative,[36] where the next-of-kin were unknown, have been over-ruled.[37] Appointments have been made at the instance of the next-of-kin [38] or the widow,[39] though it does not appear why an executor-dative was not confirmed. An application was granted where executors-dative had left part of the estate unadministered,[40] but refused where the estate was being administered by the apparent heir, the heir offering caution for the petitioner's debt, which was not constituted and appeared to fall under the triennial prescription,[41] and when the deceased's heir could not be found, but he had appointed factors to act for him.[42] On the appearance of the next-of-kin prepared to be confirmed executors-dative the factory will be recalled.[43]

On Estate of Solicitor

The Council of the Law Society of Scotland, on being satisfied that a solicitor has failed to a material extent to comply with the Accounts Rules and that in connection with his practice either his liabilities exceed his assets or his books are in such a condition that it is not reasonably practicable to ascertain definitely whether his liabilities exceed his assets, may apply to the Inner House [44] for the appointment of a judicial factor

---

[26] Succession (Scotland) Act, 1964, s. 14.
[27] Re-enacting in substance s. 164 of the Bankruptcy (Scotland) Act, 1856.
[28] Bell's Prin. (10th ed.), para. 1895.
[29] *Rutherford* v. *Lord Advocate*, 1932 S.C. 674.
[30] Law Reform (Miscellaneous Provisions) (Scotland) Act 1940, s. 6 (1), as amended by Administration of Estates Act 1971, s. 7, Sched. 1, para. 4.
[31] *Young* (1851) 13 D. 950.
[32] *Macdonald* (1849) 11 D. 1028.
[33] *Hope, Oliphant & Mackay* (1851) 13 D. 951; *Wood* (1855) 17 D. 580 (narrative); *Turnbull* v. *Ross's Judicial Factor* (O.H.) 1916, 2 S.L.T. 249 (narrative).
[34] *Hope* (1850) 12 D. 912.
[35] *Handyside* v. *Lord Advocate* (O.H.) 1909, 1 S.L.T. 268.
[36] *Murray* v. *Lord Advocate* (O.H.) 1916, 1 S.L.T. 369.
[37] *Rutherford* v. *Lord Advocate*, 1932 S.C. 674.
[38] *McMurtrie* (O.H.) 1939 S.N. 48.
[39] *Rutherford's Judicial Factor* (O.H.) 1931 S.L.T. 587, 1931 S.N. 98.
[40] *McDougall* (1853) 15 D. 776. See Executors (Scotland) Act 1900, s. 7.
[41] *Macdowall* v. *Loudon* (1849) 12 D. 170.
[42] *Steel* (O.H.) (1874) 11 S.L.R. 160.
[43] *Turnbull* v. *Ross's Judicial Factor* (O.H.) 1916, 2 S.L.T. 249.
[44] Rules of Court 1965, Rule 8 (*a*).

on his estate, and the court, after giving him an opportunity of being heard, may appoint.[45] A factor is not a trustee in bankruptcy.[45a] His duty is to preserve, like that of a factor under section 14 of the Bankruptcy (Scotland) Act 1913.

On Estate of Limited Company

An interim factor was appointed on the estate of a limited company on averments of dishonest conduct by the directors.[46]

On Common Property

The normal remedy in case of disagreement between co-owners is an action of division and sale, but a factor may be appointed if liferent rights on the property render such an action impossible.[47] Otherwise an appointment will be made only in exceptional circumstances.[48] Such circumstances were held to exist where one co-owner was in possession as trustee for himself and two other co-owners and had borrowed on the security of the property and used the money for his own purposes. The other co-owners had in 1855 raised against him an action of division and sale, in which they obtained decree in 1857, and of accounting for the rents, which was still in dependence in 1860, when they applied for the appointment of a factor.[49] In *Allan* [50] both co-owners were willing to sell, and while an appointment was refused on the specific ground that they had agreed on the appointment of a neutral person to collect the rents pending the sale, it would be unsafe to conclude that the Division in the absence of such agreement would have reversed the Lord Ordinary and appointed a factor on the property with all the expense of a sale by him. The rents might have been sequestrated and a factor appointed to collect them.[51] Where trustees were directed to convey to children the proportions of the estate provided for them, a factor on the estate was refused authority to divide the heritage and convey a part to a child, but granted authority to convey to him his *pro indiviso* share.[52] It is not clear why this authority was necessary.

Miscellaneous

A factor was appointed on a trust estate where the Court of Chancery had ordered the trustees to administer under its directions [53]; on an estate

---

[45] Solicitors (Scotland) Act, 1958, s. 15.
[45a] *Ross* v. *Gordon's J.F.*, 1973 S.L.T. (Notes) 91.
[46] *Fraser*, 1971 S.L.T.(Notes) 18.
[47] *Mackintosh* (1849) 11 D. 1029; *Gordon* v. *Macquater* (1839) 1 D. 1135.
[48] *Allan* (1898) 6 S.L.T. 106, 152, 36 S.L.R. 3, particularly *per* the Lord Ordinary; *Morrison* (1857) 20 D. 276, Lord Deas. See also *Watson* (1856) 19 D. 98.
[49] *Bailey* v. *Scott* (1860) 22 D. 1105.
[50] (1898) 6 S.L.T. 152, 36 S.L.R. 3.
[51] *Neilson* (1865) 3 M. 559.
[52] *Watson* v. *Crawcour* (1856) 19 D. 70.
[53] *Orr Ewing's Trustees* v. *Orr Ewing* (1885) 13 R.(H.L.) 1; *Wilson* (O.H.) (1895) 2 S.L.T. 567.

sequestrated under the Bankruptcy Act 1856, where the trustee died and no creditor appeared at the meeting called to elect a new trustee [54]; on shares of a trust estate where there was difficulty in obtaining a discharge [55]; on each legacy where the legatees had conflicting interests, but could only claim in a multiplepoinding through the same trustees [56]; and where a sole trustee died during the dependence of a multiplepoinding he had raised and there was a long dispute as to who should be sisted in his place.[57] Where an aunt carried off a girl to England and concealed their address the court on the application of the girl's father sequestrated the property of the aunt, including her interest in her father's estate, and appointed a factor.[58] On the aunt submitting to the jurisdiction of the court the sequestration and appointment were recalled.[59]

Interim Appointments

All appointments are in their nature interim,[60] because they are made pending the occurrence of an event. The term is however used to mean appointments made without intimation and service to take immediate effect,[61] and the Rules of Court preserve the power of the court, which includes a Lord Ordinary,[62] to make appointments at any stage of the cause.[63] This power was used at the time when all appointments were made in the Inner House in cases where the *induciae* would expire during vacation, but this element does not seem to have influenced the decisions in the undernoted early cases,[64] which depended on the existence of an emergency. In *McCulloch* v. *McCulloch* [65] the Lord President described an interim appointment as an extreme remedy rarely granted and indicative of urgency. It does not appear from the report why it was craved and granted, and in fact it was made after hearing the respondent. An interim appointment may be made pending the disposal of a reclaiming motion.[66]

---

[54] *Moncrieff's Trustees* v. *Halley* (1899) 1 F. 696. See also *Cheyne's Trustees*, 1933 S.L.T. 184, 1933 S.N. 3.
[55] *Lauder* v. *Lauder* (1851) 14 D. 14.
[56] *Maitland's Trustees* (1903) 11 S.L.T. 78.
[57] *Christy* v. *Paul* (1834) 12 S. 916.
[58] *Edgar* v. *Fisher's Trustees* (1893) 21 R. 59.
[59] *Fisher* v. *Edgar* (1894) 21 R. 1076. For miscellaneous appointments on trust estates, see p. 37.
[60] *Dowie* v. *Hagart* (1894) 21 R. 1052, Lord McLaren (*obiter*) at p. 1057.
[61] Bankruptcy (Scotland) Act 1913, s. 14.
[62] Administration of Justice (Scotland) Act 1933, s. 40.
[63] Rules of Court 1965, r. 197 (*b*).
[64] *A B* (1829) 8 S. 89; *Kirk* (1827) 5 S. 564; *Mason* (1852) 14 D. 761 (narrative); *Brown* (1849) 11 D. 1027.
[65] 1953 S.C. 189; *Goold* (1856) 18 D. 1318.
[66] *Sharp* v. *McCall* (1860) 23 D. 38 at pp. 39, 40.

CHAPTER XI

THE FACTOR

General

Unless there is some objection to him, the court usually appoints as factor the person suggested by the petitioner. He may be a lay relative or friend, but there are advantages in the appointment of a solicitor or a chartered accountant. It is easier for them to communicate with the accountant,[1] and their commission covers professional work, except for outlays.[2] A merchant in an old case was appointed in preference to an accountant as factor on an industrial concern,[3] but it has been observed that an accountant may, if necessary, employ skilled technical assistance.[4] On the ground of expense an Edinburgh accountant was rejected as factor on an estate in favour of a person resident near the lands.[5] Where a farmer was proposed as factor *loco tutoris* the court declined to proceed till satisfied as to his prudence and business habits,[6] and where an *incapax* had been neglected the court remitted to the sheriff [7] or to a curator *ad litem* [8] to report as to the fitness of the curator *bonis* suggested by the relatives. The court will not appoint an undischarged bankrupt [9] or a person who has bargained for the office.[10] It refused to appoint as factor on a trust a person who had been nominated trustee and had declined to accept,[11] and a person who had promised to employ a particular solicitor, unless he undertook not to.[12] The rule that a woman should never be appointed [13] has been departed from.[14] The duties of a minister of the Church of Scotland were at one time thought to disqualify him,[15] but this view has been abandoned.[16] A peer may be appointed.[17] It is uncommon to appoint the petitioner on his own application alone,[18] but the sole next-of-kin was appointed on his own petition to be curator *bonis*.[19] The

---

[1] *Johnstone* v. *Barbé*, 1928 S.N. 86.

[2] *Mitchell* (1878) 5 R. 1124. See p. 99.

[3] *Dixon* v. *Watson* (1832) 10 S. 209.

[4] *Haldane* v. *Girvan and Portpatrick Junction Railway* (1881) 8 R. 669 at p. 674.

[5] *McCulloch* v. *Forman* (1851) 14 D. 311.

[6] *Anderson* (1854) 17 D. 97. Recently a wife was appointed curator *bonis* to her husband on her undertaking to consult her solicitor in preparing her accounts.

[7] *Thomson* (1846) 8 D. 1073.   [8] *Carter* (1857) 19 D. 286.

[9] *Millar* v. *Jervis* (1840) 2 D. 1181; *Dixon* v. *Watson* (1832) 10 S. 209.

[10] *Doud* v. *Simpson* (1847) 9 D. 511.

[11] *Pennycook* (1851) 14 D. 311.

[12] *Gilzean* (O.H.) (1902) 10 S.L.T. 159.

[13] *Thorburn* (1846) 8 D. 1000.

[14] *Chalmer's Trustees* v. *Sinclair* (1897) 24 R. 1047 at p. 1050; *Smith Sligo* (O.H.), 1914, 1 S.L.T. 287.

[15] *Bissett* (1836) 15 S. 4; *Brodie* (1867) 3 S.L.R. 223, *contra Campbell* (1849) 12 D. 913.

[16] *Pool* (O.H.) (1896) 4 S.L.T. 216.

[17] *Elgin* (1890) 28 S.L.R. 271.

[18] *Allan* (1852) 14 D. 486. *Cf. Graham* (1851) 13 D. 951.

[19] *Barclay*, 1962 S.C. 594.

rule that the petitioners' solicitor should not be appointed [20] has been abandoned in practice.

Residence in Scotland

As an almost universal rule the court will not appoint a person resident furth of Scotland and so not subject to its jurisdiction.[21] Where a minor and his father lived in New York and the father had been appointed guardian under the law of that state, the father was appointed curator *bonis* in respect of heritage in Scotland to which the minor had succeeded.[22] In the only exceptions reported no reasons were given.[23] Thoms suggested that in *Scott* [23] the appointment was made *per incuriam*,[24] and *Duff* was impliedly disapproved in *Forsyth*. Acting under the Guardianship of Infants Act 1886, the court appointed a relation in London to be guardian along with the mother.[25] The Lord President described the proposal as unusual and relied on the fact that the court was bound to have regard primarily to the benefit of the pupil, though this does not seem to distinguish the case from any application for the appointment of a factor *loco tutoris*. Lord McLaren founded on *Lord Macdonald* v. *His Next of Kin*,[26] where the court sustained a minor's choice of an English curator, but without mentioning a subsequent case [27] where it refused to do so. There is this distinction from a judicial factor that neither a guardian nor a curator receives remuneration, and in *Sim* one guardian, the mother, lived in Scotland.

Adverse interest

The court refused to appoint as curator *bonis* the executor of and cautioner for the deceased curator *bonis* on the ground that his first duty would be to call himself to account as such executor and cautioner.[28] The same principle was applied to trustees,[29] but in another case the court did not raise the point, at least at the outset.[30] The court refused to appoint as curator *bonis* to an *incapax* the person with whom he was boarded,[31] the treasurer of the asylum where he resided,[32] and a brother-in-law with

---

[20] *Lawson* (O.H.) (1894) 2 S.L.T. 308.
[21] *Napier* (O.H.) (1902) 9 S.L.T. 439; *Robertson* (1846) 9 D. 210; *Forsyth* (O.H.) 1932 S.L.T. 462 (where the *incapax* lived in England and the whole estate was moveable). Such a person, if appointed, must prorogate the jurisdiction of the Scottish courts.
[22] *Ogilvy*, February 10, 1927 (unreported), sequel to *Ogilvy* v. *Ogilvy's Trustees* (O.H.) 1927 S.L.T. 83, 1926 S.N. 166.
[23] *Scott* (1851) 13 D. 951; *Duff* (O.H.) 1910, 2 S.L.T. 202 (where the *incapax* lived in England).
[24] (2nd ed.) p. 43.
[25] *Sim* v. *Robertson* (1901) 3 F. 1027.
[26] (1864) 2 M. 1194.
[27] *Fergusson* v. *Dormer* (1870) 8 M. 426. The facts resemble those in *Lord Macdonald*, but the court may have distrusted the step-father.
[28] *Leslie* (O.H.) (1904) 12 S.L.T. 359. See *Rannie's Factory* (1866) 3 S.L.R. 140; *Speirs* (1851) 14 D. 11.
[29] *Foggo* (1893) 20 R. 273. See also *McCulloch* (1851) 14 D. 311, and *Hunter* v. *Home* (1834) 12 S. 406 at p. 407.
[30] *Scott* (1855) 17 D. 362.
[31] *Montgomery* (1855) 17 D. 623.
[32] *Gatherer* (1852) 14 D. 1047.

whom she lived.[33] A person who is already judicial factor on a related estate is objectionable unless there is no conflict between the estates,[34] and a solicitor whose firm held £40,000 in trust for an *incapax* was appointed curator *bonis* only because all the next of kin asked for him.[35] The objection extends to the nominee of a person with an adverse interest.[36] If a factor comes to have an adverse interest, it may be his duty to resign.[37]

A particular instance of adverse interest was the nearest agnate, whom the law regarded with suspicion. He was entitled to serve tutor-at-law to a pupil [38] or to an *incapax* who had been cognosced,[39] but if he was the heir, the custody of the pupil [40] or *incapax* [41] was committed to the mother or the nearest cognate. Although a factor does not have custody of a ward, the court when making an appointment was inclined to give weight to this conflict of interest. They refused to appoint a brother to be curator *bonis* to an *incapax*, the Lord Justice-Clerk remarking that the brother had a strong motive to spend as little as possible on the maintenance of the *incapax*.[42] In a fuller report of the case [43] the Lord Justice-Clerk had no doubt that the opinion that the court would regard favourably the nearest agnate or his nominee [44] had been wrongly attributed to his father, and in *Jackson* [44] Lord Mackenzie concurred only because the proposed curator *bonis* was excluded by a settlement from any interest in the ward's succession. But such suspicions now have less weight.[45] The court refused to appoint the nearest agnate on the ground that he could serve tutor-at-law.[46] Where the nearest agnate was appointed it was usually on condition that he agreed to act gratuitously, as he would have had to do if he had served tutor,[47] though if the appointment is unconditional he is entitled to commission,[48] and in special circumstances the factor was allowed to charge commission.[49] The nearest agnate was appointed curator *bonis ad interim* until he served as tutor.[50]

Selection by the court

In case of dispute the court has appointed the sheriff clerk permanently

[33] *Ferguson* (1850) 12 D. 912.
[34] *Clark* v. *Barstow* (1856) 18 D. 1041; *McWhirter* (1852) 14 D. 761.
[35] *Hagart* (O.H.) (1893) 1 S.L.T. 62.
[36] *Raeburn* (1851) 14 D. 310; *McIntosh* v. *McIntosh* (1839) 15 Fac.Dec. 155.
[37] *Dunn* v. *Chambers* (1897) 25 R. 247 at p. 251.
[38] Tutors Act 1474; Stair I, 6, 8; Erskine I, 7, 5.
[39] Curators Act 1585; Stair I, 6, 25; IV, 3, 7 and 9; Erskine I, 7, 49 and 50.
[40] Stair I, 6, 15; IV, 3, 9; Erskine I, 7, 7.
[41] Stair IV, 3, 9; *Bryce* v. *Graham* (1828) 6 S. 425 at p. 440.
[42] *Armit* (1844) 6 D. 1088.
[43] 16 S.J. 471. See *Hutcheon* v. *Alexander* (O.H.) 1909, 1 S.L.T. 71.
[44] *Jackson* v. *Wight* (1835) 13 S. 961.
[45] *Dick* v. *Douglas*, 1924 S.C. 787 at p. 793.
[46] *Cameron* (1849) 12 D. 912. See *Urquhart* (1860) 22 D. 932.
[47] *Accountant of Court* v. *Watt* (1866) 4 M. 772; *Robertson* (1830) 8 S. 307, 435; *Jackson* (1821) 1 S. 203.
[48] *Accountant of Court* v. *Watt* (1866) 4 M. 772; *Macdonald* v. *Macdonald* (1854) 16 D. 1023.
[49] *Accountant of Court* v. *Watt* (1866) 4 M. 772.
[50] *Simpson* v. *Simpson* (1891) 18 R. 1207.

or *ad interim*,[51] and has remitted to the sheriff or sheriff-substitute to suggest a suitable person.[52]

New nominee pendenti processu

It is competent to appoint a person not named in the petition upon whom the parties appearing have agreed, without further intimation.[53]

---

[51] *Fraser* v. *Thorburn* (1855) 18 D. 264; *Wilson* (1849) 12 D. 248; *Brown* (1848) 11 D. 1027.

[52] *Cochrane* v. *Macaslan* (1849) 12 D. 147; *Mackintosh* (1849) 11 D. 1029; *Brown* (1849) 11 D. 1027; *Speirs* (1851) 14 D. 11; *Robertson* v. *Robertson* (1840) 2 D. 1382; *Grierson* v. *Menteath* (1840) 2 D. 1234; *Millar* v. *Jervis* (1840) 2 D. 1181; *Dewar* v. *Dewar* (1834) 12 S. 315.

[53] *Davidson* v. *Bogle & Co.* (1837) 15 S. 421; *Hay* v. *Murray* (1837) 15 S. 850. *Contra Scoullar* (1834) 13 S. 101.

Chapter XII
CAUTION [1]

Introductory

It was taken for granted in the Act of Sederunt of February 13, 1730,[2] that a judicial factor must find caution before entering on the duties of his office, but the statutory obligation was imposed on factors *loco tutoris* and *loco absentis* and curators *bonis* by section 2 [3] of the Pupils Protection Act 1849 and extended to all judicial factors by the Judicial Factors Act 1889.[4] Section 2, as amended, provides that every judicial factor shall find caution, that no factor shall enter upon the duties of his office, nor shall a certified copy interlocutor of his appointment be issued, until after such caution has been found and received as sufficient, and that the factor shall obtain a certified copy interlocutor without delay. The Act did not specify whose duty it was to decide whether the caution was sufficient, but by Act of Sederunt it was laid on the clerk of court,[5] subject to the instructions of the court.[6] The duty now lies on the accountant. On a judicial factor being appointed subject to caution being found, the process must forthwith be transmitted to the accountant, who must, on the bond of caution being delivered to him [7] and on being satisfied as to its form and due execution and as to the sufficiency of the cautioner, make a marking on the margin of the interlocutor sheet to the effect that caution has been received, stating the amount and the name of the cautioner, and adding his signature and the date. Such marking is authority for the issue of a certified copy of the appointment [8] and the factor's title to intromit. The expense of the necessary procedure in obtaining approval of the bond of caution and the limitation, increase or reduction of the amount is a proper charge against the estate.[9] But although a factor has no title to intromit with the estate until he has found caution and obtained the certified copy interlocutor,[10] a factor was held to be entitled to raise an action on behalf of his ward before finding caution.[11]

---

[1] A form of bond of caution approved by the accountant is printed in the Appendix to illustrate points mentioned in this chapter. The statutory provisions governing caution in the sheriff court are dealt with in Chap. XX.

[2] s. 11. Cautioners for a curator are at least a century earlier. *Pollock* v. *Corsbies* (1627) Mor. 2074.

[3] As amended by Act of Sederunt, March 17, 1967.

[4] s. 6.

[5] Act of Sederunt, November 25, 1857, s. 5.

[6] See *Fraser's Judicial Factor* (1892) 19 R. 500.

[7] Rules of Court 1965, r. 200 (*d*).

[8] *Ibid.* r. 200 (*e*) (i), as amended by Act of Sederunt, March 17, 1967.

[9] *Ibid.* r. 200 (*f*). This repeats an earlier Act of Sederunt, which removed the ground of judgment in *Guillan's Judicial Factor* (O.H.) (1897) 4 S.L.T. 325, and supersedes such cases as *Frame* (1901) 9 S.L.T. 204, and *Cadell* (O.H.) 1916, 2 S.L.T. 146.

[10] *Donaldson* v. *Kennedy* (1833) 11 S. 740.

[11] *Calver* v. *Howard Baker & Co.* (1894) 22 R. 1.

The position of a cautioner for a judicial factor differs in some respects from that of a cautioner in, for example, a cash credit bond or a fidelity bond. In the two latter the creditor is known and it is he who must be satisfied with the cautioner and the terms of the bond. But a person may be entitled to enforce a bond of caution for a judicial factor although his right emerged after the bond was executed, and it is the accountant who must be satisfied with the cautioner and the terms of the bond.[12] Accordingly, decisions on cash credit or fidelity bonds may not apply to a cautioner for a judicial factor, in particular in questions of fraud inducing the bond and of discharge of the cautioner by the actings of the creditor. Further, the law was developed at a time when the cautioner was an individual, and the statutes proceed on that assumption. Now the cautioner is usually a guarantee company, and this raises questions as to the effect of failure to pay the premium.

Sufficiency of cautioner

It is the duty of the accountant to satisfy himself as to the proposed cautioner's sufficiency.[13] If an individual is proposed the accountant is entitled as matter of practice [14] to receive from the petitioner's solicitor a certificate that having made due inquiry he is satisfied that the cautioner is sufficient. A minor is clearly insufficient since lesion is presumed.[15] A single woman may act,[16] and a married woman's common law disability [17] has been removed.[18] If there are several cautioners and the signature of one is forged, the remainder remain liable.[19] That case concerned a bond of judicial caution, but the ground of decision applies to caution for judicial factors. In distinguishing a previous case, where it had been held that a forged signature liberated the other cautioners, Lord Wood, with whom the other judges concurred, pointed out that the bond there was in security of a loan and that it was for the lender to see that the bond was properly executed, whereas in judicial caution that was a matter for the clerk of court. In his report in *Burnett* [20] the accountant drew attention to the weakness of the system of individual cautioners, relying apparently on his experience. The individual might never have been able to fulfil his obligations, or he might become unable to do so, or he might (unknown to those concerned) be acting as cautioner for several factors and be unable to meet a number of losses. On these grounds the

---

[12] *Wallace's Factor* v. *McKissock* (1898) 25 R. 642 at p. 651. See opinion of Lord Wood in *Simpson* v. *Fleming* (1860) 22 D. 679 (judicial caution).

[13] Rules of Court 1965, r. 200 (*e*) (i).

[14] *Anderson's Factor* (1869) 6 S.L.R. 675, a case under the Act of Sederunt of November 25, 1857, which required caution " to the satisfaction of the clerk of court." See *Lang* (1850) 12 D. 943. In the sheriff court the certificate is obligatory by Act of Sederunt. See Chap. XX.

[15] Bell, Comm. (7th ed.) I, 131.

[16] *Fraser's Judicial Factor* (1892) 19 R. 500.

[17] *Biggart* v. *City of Glasgow Bank* (1879) 6 R. 470 at p. 481.

[18] Married Women's Property (Scotland) Act 1920, s. 3 (1).

[19] *Simpson* v. *Fleming* (1860) 22 D. 679.

[20] (1859) 21 D. 1197; 31 S.J. 637. The report is printed only in the S.J.

accountant advocated the use of guarantee companies as cautioners. He might have added that, although it is the duty of the factor to intimate to him the death or insolvency of the cautioner,[21] the factor may, perhaps quite innocently, fail to do so.

Section 27 of the Pupils Protection Act 1849 empowered the court to authorise policies of the British Guarantee Association " or other public company incorporated by Act of Parliament carrying on guarantee business within Scotland " to be accepted instead of bonds of caution by private individuals. After some judicial doubts [22] it is settled that the phrase quoted includes companies registered under the Companies Act,[23] and this is now the normal method of finding caution. It is the duty of the accountant each January to submit a list of approved guarantee companies for the approval of the Lord President. If a company not on the list is proposed as cautioner the accountant, if the Lord President approves, must include it in the list.[24] The premium, or such part of it as the accountant thinks proper, is a charge against the estate.[25] Since a company acts as cautioner in consideration of an annual premium, the contract would fall on failure to pay the premium.[26] This difficulty is met in the sheriff court by a provision [27] that the company must be taken bound to intimate non-payment of the premium to the accountant, and this term is inserted in the form of bond approved for the sheriff court. There is no such provision in the Rules of Court and no such term in the form of bond approved for the Court of Session. But in practice companies do intimate failure to the accountant, who issues a notice to the factor requiring him to find new caution within thirty days, and a company which failed to intimate could hardly expect to remain on the list of approved guarantee companies.

Amount of caution

Section 27 of the Pupils Protection Act 1849 empowered the court to restrict the amount for which caution must be found to a sum less than the value of the estate. There are contradictory decisions as to whether the court has the power at common law,[28] but the point is now of no importance since there is statutory power in all cases.[29] The power, however, is limited by the Rules of Court 1965, which provide [30] that the caution must be not less than two-thirds of the value of the moveable and other easily realisable estate.[31] If the accountant fixes the caution at a figure

---

[21] Pupils Protection Act 1849, s. 11.
[22] *Sim* (1863) 2 M. 205.
[23] *McKinnon* (1884) 11 R. 676; *McKinnon* (1884) 12 R. 184.
[24] Rules of Court 1965, r. 200 (*e*) (iv).
[25] *Ibid.* r. 200 (*f*); Accountant's Notes, n. 1.
[26] *Liquidators of Employers' Insurance Co.* v. *Benton* (1897) 24 R. 908.
[27] C.A.S., L, VIII, 7.
[28] *Keating* (1862) 24 D. 1266 (negative); *McKinnon* (1884) 12 R. 184, *McKinnon* (1884) 11 R. 676 (*obiter*) (both affirmative).
[29] Judicial Factors (Scotland) Act 1889, s. 6.
[30] Rules of Court 1965, r. 200 (*e*) (ii).
[31] See *C. and Others*, 1939 S.C. 736, where the Lord President hinted that in a case of particular hardship the court might exercise its dispensing power.

above the two-thirds he must report to the court, provided the factor requires him in writing to do so.[32] In the first *McKinnon* case,[33] to which the Act of 1849 applied, caution was fixed at £10,000, the value of the estate being over £73,000, chiefly invested in heritable securities, with an annual revenue of about £2,500.[34] The accountant may vary the amount of caution during the subsistence of a factory,[35] and this is effected by the cautionary company preparing a memorandum of agreement increasing or reducing the caution, which is signed by the factor and the company and lodged with the accountant to be filed with the original bond.[36]

Period for finding caution

When not otherwise expressed in the interlocutor appointing a factor he must find caution within one calendar month of the interlocutor, but on a motion enrolled before the expiry of that period the court may, on cause shown, prorogate the time.[37] Under this power the time was extended where the factor, not a professional man, had difficulty over the premium and intended to obtain an individual as cautioner.[38] After the month has expired there are two possible courses. First, the court may relieve any party from the consequences of failure to comply with the Rules due to mistake, oversight or other cause, not being wilful non-observance.[39] Where a bond was presented timeously, but did not have appended to it the necessary certificate (presumably the solicitor's certificate of the sufficiency of the cautioner) and the month under the relevant Act of Sederunt had expired, the court authorised the clerks to receive the bond.[40] Secondly, the factor may be appointed of new, so that a fresh month begins to run. This was done where the head office of the insurance company was in England and owing to English holidays there was delay in having the bond sealed.[41] The Lord Ordinary intimated that if such companies were to be accepted in future they must either grant interim cover or authorise their officials in Scotland to issue the bond. It is understood that this difficulty has been overcome. The expenses of obtaining such re-appointment are not allowed against the estate.

Liability of cautioner

It is unnecessary to consider the common law as to the constitution and proof of cautionary obligations or the application and effect of the

---

[32] Rules of Court 1965, r. 200 (*e*) (ii).
[33] (1884) 11 R. 676.
[34] See also *Hagart* (O.H.) (1893) 1 S.L.T. 62.
[35] Rules of Court 1965, r. 200 (*e*) (iii).
[36] See Accountant's Notes, note 1.
[37] *Ibid.* r. 200 (*c*), repeating previous Rules and Act of Sederunt.
[38] *Harris* (O.H.) (1901) 8 S.L.T. 415.
[39] Act of Sederunt of November 10, 1964, s. 4.
[40] *Campbell* (1855) 18 D. 292. On the dispensing power generally see *Dalgety's Trustees* v. *Drummond*, 1938 S.C. 709.
[41] *Cuthbertson* (O.H.) (1905) 13 S.L.T. 205. This course was followed in *Earl and Countess of Harrowby* (1856) 18 D. 733, and *Lang* (1850) 12 D. 943, but no reasons are reported.

Mercantile Law Amendment (Scotland) Act 1856.[42] The Act of Sederunt of February 13, 1730, provides that the factor and cautioner shall be bound conjunctly and severally, and so long as it is uncertain whether writing is required for constitution it may be taken for granted that the accountant will require a probative deed.

Under the usual terms of a bond the cautioner obliges himself that the factor shall make forthcoming the whole estate for which he is responsible, including penal interest.[43] He is therefore responsible for defalcations by the factor before the bond was signed.[44] But he is liable only for the factor's acts as such.[43] Where the curator *bonis* to a lunatic continued to administer the estate after the lunatic's death in terms of his trust disposition and settlement and received a payment in the latter capacity his cautioner was held to have no liability for the money so received.[45] It is the factor's duty to give the accountant notice of the death or insolvency of the cautioner,[46] but, if, as is usual, the cautioner's representatives, including vitious intromitters, are taken bound, they are liable for the factor's actings until they are discharged.[47]

Ascertainment and enforcement of liability

This may be by action[48] or in the course of a petition, *e.g.* for the removal of the factor,[49] and since the cautioner is called as defender or respondent, he has, subject to the possible effect of sections 15 and 16 of the Pupils Protection Act 1849, an opportunity to answer. Section 16 of the Pupils Protection Act 1849 entitles a cautioner to appear and be heard before the accountant during the course of an annual audit or to state objections to the audit. There appears to be no trace of a cautioner attempting to use this right, which is hardly surprising. The cautioner receives no intimation of the audit, the accountant's audit and report are conclusive against him unless the factor has lodged objections,[50] and section 16 provides no procedure for giving effect to the cautioner's objections, however well founded.

The bond provides two methods of enforcement against the cautioner. First, it empowers the court, after ascertaining by a certificate from the accountant the balance due by the factor, to decern against the cautioner for the whole sum mentioned in the bond, " or for any smaller sum." This procedure never seems to have been carried through to decree. It is understood that in practice the accountant, on being asked for a certificate, communicates with the cautioner, who thus has an opportunity of being satisfied as to the amount due, and as the cautioner is normally a guarantee

---

[42] See Walker, *Law of Evidence in Scotland*, pp. 108, 109.
[43] *Maxwell's Trustees* v. *Jeffs* (1862) 24 D. 1181.
[44] *Wallace's Factor* v. *McKissock* (1898) 25 R. 642.
[45] *Morland* v. *Sprot* (1829) 8 S. 181, (1831) 9 S. 478.
[46] Pupils Protection Act 1849, s. 11.
[47] *Bremner* v. *Campbell* (1842) 1 Bell's App. 280.
[48] *Ross* v. *Mackenzie* (1842) 5 D. 151.
[49] *Wallace's Factor* v. *McKissock* (1898) 25 R. 642; *Stewart* v. *Scott* (1850) 12 D. 744.
[50] s. 15.

company there is no difficulty about payment. The court is not bound by the certificate. The word is " may." Accordingly, if the cautioner did not accept the accountant's figure and the case had to be enrolled for decree, the court would probably order intimation to the cautioner.[51] Secondly, the bond contains consent to registration for execution, but as it does not state the amount due, summary diligence cannot proceed on an extract unless that amount has been ascertained by a method binding on the cautioner.[52] The charge may be suspended, but in the only case [53] the court proceeded on a ground, viz. lack of supervision by the creditors, which has been disapproved.[54]

Relief

On paying the amount due the cautioner is entitled to relief from the factor,[55] and this is expressly provided in the bond. If the factor is bankrupt and the cautioner has paid he ranks in the sequestration,[56] but if he has not paid and the creditors rank, he is liable to the creditors for the whole amount they fail to recover in the sequestration and does not rank for what he pays them.[57]

Release of cautioner

This may result from (1) the exoneration of the factor and delivery of the bond, (2) withdrawal by the cautioner, or (3) the conduct of the creditors or some of them. The septennial prescription does not apply.[58]

(1) On termination of the factor's appointment the usual procedure is to present a petition for his exoneration and for delivery of the bond. The petition is served on the cautioner.[59]

(2) A cautioner may withdraw on " reasonable notice," [60] but this affects only his liability for the future.[61] He cannot obtain relief from existing liability and delivery or cancellation of his bond unless any balance then due by the debtor is paid, and he is entitled to have the debtor, in this case the factor, ordained to make payment or to put him in funds to do so.[62] It follows that failing payment by the factor the cautioner himself must pay. The bond gives effect to these rules by providing that the cautioner may give thirty days' notice of termination, that on the elapse of the thirty days " without objection stated thereto " the cautioner shall not be liable to make good any loss occurring after the thirty days, and that liability for earlier losses may be satisfied by payment. The

---

[51] *Pringle* v. *Tate* (1832) 11 S. 47.
[52] *Fisher* v. *Syme* (1828) 7 S. 97; Bell, Comm. (7th ed.) II, 382, 384.
[53] *Pringle* v. *Tate* (1834) 12 S. 918.
[54] *Biggar* v. *Wright* (1849) 9 D. 78, discussed *infra*.
[55] Ersk., Inst. III, iii, 65.
[56] Bell, Comm. (7th ed.) I, 365.
[57] *Anderson* v. *Mackinnon* (1876) 3 R. 608; *Goudy on Bankruptcy* (4th ed.) p. 561.
[58] *Bremner* v. *Campbell* (1842) 1 Bell's App. 280.
[59] See Chap. XVII.
[60] Bell, Comm. (7th ed.) I, 387; *Doig* v. *Lawrie* (1903) 5 F. 295 at p. 299.
[61] Bell, Prin. (10th ed.) para. 266.
[62] *Doig* v. *Lawrie* (1903) 5 F. 295.

" objections " might be to proposed unusual conditions of withdrawal. A cautioner, unless he has expressly agreed, cannot be compelled to remain bound, and the effect of withdrawal on liability past and future is clear.

(3) A cautioner is released if positive actings by the person claiming against him contributed to the loss, but only in a question with that claimant. When the heir of an *absens* without the knowledge of the cautioner made a bargain with the factor *loco absentis* which was detrimental to the estate and then, having been decerned executor-dative on the presumed death of the *absens*, sued the cautioner for the loss to the estate, the cautioner was assoilzied.[63] The same principle was applied in *Biggar* v. *Wright*.[64] Biggar's estates were sequestrated and he was discharged on a composition. Having obtained decree against the trustee for a sum due by him to the estate, which the trustee failed to pay, he brought an action for payment against the representatives of one of the trustee's cautioners. The second defence, not mentioned in the rubric, was that the pursuer had connived at or encouraged the trustee's malversation. The court held this to be a relevant defence,[65] but as it was not stated with sufficient specification, granted leave to amend. In the latter of these cases the pursuer had the sole interest and was, or was alleged to be, a party to the malversation. Such a defence would not be open to a cautioner against an innocent creditor even if he had the same interest as the accomplice.[66] In an analogous situation the House of Lords distinguished the rights of the innocent from those of the guilty.[67]

Mere inaction by the creditor or other party does not liberate the cautioner. In a number of cases where the cautioner for a trustee in a sequestration was sued the Court of Session had sustained a defence that the loss would not have occurred if the commissioners had fulfilled their statutory duties, and that the cautioner was entitled to expect them to do so. This was the first defence in *Biggar* v. *Wright*,[68] supported by detailed averments of failure by the commissioners in their statutory duties over a period of twenty-three years. But the court found itself obliged by two decisions of the House of Lords [69] to hold this defence irrelevant. The principle applies *a fortiori* to cautioners for judicial factors, where no one, except the accountant,[70] has any statutory duty of supervision, and his inaction is no defence to the factor [71] or, it follows, his cautioner. In an action by a curator *bonis* against the representatives of the cautioner for the previous curator *bonis* the defenders maintained, *inter alia*, that the claim was barred by neglect on the part of the relations of the lunatic,

---

[63] *Lawson* v. *Coldstream* (1837) 15 S. 930.
[64] (1849) 9 D. 78.
[65] See *Wallace's Factor* v. *McKissock* (1898) 25 R. 642 at p. 653.
[66] *Lawson* v. *Coldstream* (1837) 15 S. 930, observations on p. 935 as to the position of the pursuer's sister.
[67] *Raes* v. *Meek* (1889) 16 R.(H.L.) 31 at pp. 33, 35, 36.
[68] (1849) 9 D. 78.
[69] *McTaggart* v. *Watson* (1835) 1 Sh. & Macl. 553 (cautioner for trustee in sequestration); *Creighton* v. *Rankin* (1840) 1 Rob.App. 99 (cautioner under fidelity bond).
[70] Pupils Protection Act 1849, s. 13.
[71] *Hutton* v. *Annan* (1898) 25 R. (H.L.) 23.

whose duty it was to attend to the manner in which the factor performed the duties of his office. The judges in response to a remit from the House of Lords unanimously rejected this defence, distinguishing the case of a cautioner for a trustee in a sequestration where they thought such a defence might be open.[72] The ambiguous note in the House of Lords report cannot mean that this point did not form the subject of adjudication,[73] since the House remitted to the Court of Session to ascertain the amount of the appellant's liability.

Reduction of the bond

As a general rule a cautioner cannot obtain reduction of his bond on the ground that he was induced to sign by the fraud or misrepresentation of the factor.[74] But he may be able to do so if his obligation was gratuitous. " A gratuitous benefit . . . gained through the fraud of another cannot be retained by the person benefited, even though innocent of the fraud." [75] The consideration for a bond of caution is that it is a condition precedent to the factor obtaining a title to intromit. In the absence of this consideration the bond is gratuitous.[76] In that case, which seems to be unique in this branch of the law, the tutor-at-law to a lunatic obtained extract without finding caution and intromitted with the estate. Two years later his sister granted a bond of caution. In a reduction brought by her, which was defended by the lunatic's curator *bonis*, she averred that she had been induced to sign by the tutor's fraudulent misrepresentations. The Division, by a majority, allowed a proof before answer. The Lord Justice-Clerk and Lord Wood seem to have had no doubt that the pursuer's case was relevant, the bond being gratuitous (in the sense explained above) and the averments of fraud sufficient, and the proof may have been allowed before answer either because that was what the pursuer asked for or because Lord Cowan, the third judge in the majority, thought that the pursuer's right to reduction would depend on whether the tutor was in default when the bond was granted, on which there was no averment. Under modern practice where the bond is granted by a guarantee company in return for a premium chargeable against the estate, it cannot be described as gratuitous.

Fraud by the creditor is a ground of reduction. The cautioner failed in *Wallace's Factor* v. *McKissock* [77] only because he had not made relevant averments of fraud against the beneficiaries under the trust. A more difficult question, not raised at least directly in any reported case, arises where there has been fraud by one of a number of creditors. On

---

[72] *Kerr* v. *Bremner* (1839) 1 D. 618 at p. 629, also printed in 1 Bell's App. at p. 298.

[73] *Bremner* v. *Campbell* (1842) 1 Bell's App. 280 at p. 304.

[74] *Wallace's Factor* v. *McKissock* (1898) 25 R. 642.

[75] *Gibbs* v. *British Linen Bank* (1875) 4 R. 630, Lord Shand at p. 634; *Clydesdale Bank* v. *Paul* (1877) 4 R. 626 at p. 626; *Traill* v. *Smith's Trustees* (1876) 3 R. 770 at p. 780.

[76] *Wardlaw* v. *Mackenzie* (1859) 21 D. 940 at pp. 946, 949. On this case, see *Gloag on Contract* (2nd ed.), pp. 333, 536.

[77] (1898) 25 R. 642.

the analogy of fraud by the factor it would appear that the rights of innocent creditors depend on whether the obligation was gratuitous or not.
In *Wardlaw* v. *Mackenzie* [78] the Lord Justice-Clerk, at p. 948, after referring
to English cases where it had been held that innocent beneficiaries could not
take under a will obtained by the fraud of another beneficiary, added,
" In all these authorities it is of course assumed that the innocent third
party has given no consideration for that which has been obtained by the
fraud, but is seeking gratuitous advantage." In the ordinary case therefore,
where the bond is not gratuitous, it would appear to be reducible *quoad*
the fraudulent creditor only. Partial reduction so as to settle the true
rights of parties is competent. [79]

---

[78] (1859) 21 D. 940.
[79] *Bain* v. *Lady Seafield* (1887) 14 R. 939; *McConechy* v. *McIndoe* (1853) 16 D. 315; *Glasgow
Feuing & Building Co.* v. *Watson's Trs.* (1887) 14 R. 610.

CHAPTER XIII

POWERS, DUTIES AND LIABILITIES: GENERAL

Introductory

The heading of this chapter is taken from the *Faculty Digest* and is justified by the fact that these three matters cannot be satisfactorily dealt with separately. The " usual powers " conferred on a factor on appointment depend upon the nature of his duties. A factor appointed to wind up a partnership estate has the duty and power to realise and distribute.[1] A factor *loco tutoris* has not. A special power is conferred on a factor only when he and the court are satisfied that he requires it for the proper exercise of his duties.[2] A factor's liability arises from exceeding his powers [3] or failing in his positive duties [4] or exercising a power imprudently.[5] Accordingly, it is proposed, after a general consideration of powers in the remainder of this chapter, to deal in the three following chapters with powers, duties and liabilities together under three heads— (1) recovery of estate and litigation; (2) the inventory and annual accounts, and (3) administration; any matters peculiar to a particular type of factory are considered in the chapter on that type.

Usual powers

Since the purpose of the appointment originally was to preserve the estate in an emergency, the powers granted on appointment, the " usual powers," were limited to those necessary to conserve the estate. Apart from cases where distribution was required, the factor's duty was to retain heritage and corporeal moveables as he received them [6] and to invest money and the proceeds of other assets in heritable or government securities.[7] Heritage in particular was regarded as sacrosanct,[8] and special power was required to sell [9] or feu [10] land, to grant a heritable bond [11] or to assign one,[12] to complete title to heritage, whether in name of the factor [13] or the ward,[14] or to a heritable bond,[15] to buy heritage,[16]

---

[1] *Cooper and Sons' Judicial Factor* (O.H.) 1931 S.L.T. 26; 1930 S.N. 134.
[2] *Russell* v. *Russell* (1874) 2 R. 93.
[3] *Hutton* v. *Annan* (1898) 25 R. (H.L.) 23.
[4] *Morrison* v. *Dryden* (1890) 17 R. 704.
[5] *Crabbe* v. *Whyte* (1891) 18 R. 1065.
[6] *McAdam's Judicial Factor* v. *Souter* (1904) 7 F. 179 at p. 181.
[7] *Grainger's Curator* (1876) 3 R. 479 at p. 481.
[8] *Marquess of Lothian's Curator Bonis*, 1927 S.C. 579 at p. 586.
[9] *Crighton* (1857) 19 D. 429; *Wood* (1856) 18 D. 732.
[10] *Alexander* (1857) 19 D. 888.
[11] *Wood* (1857) 19 D. 428.
[12] *Campbell* v. *Grant* (1869) 8 M. 227.
[13] *Meikle* (1856) 18 D. 988. [14] *Crighton* (1857) 19 D. 429.
[15] *Caird* (1848) 11 D. 232. [16] *Lambe* v. *Chapman* (1834) 12 S. 775.

or to grant a lease to endure beyond the expiry of the factory,[17] and was granted only if it was necessary to prevent serious loss or followed as a consequence of transactions by the owner or the previous owner.[18] But factors are now appointed with other duties besides conservation, and it is misleading to isolate Lord Justice-Clerk Inglis' description of the factor as " a conservator merely " [19] and treat it as applicable to all factors.[20] His Lordship was dealing with the particular apparently limited prayer before the court, which in the next sentence he contrasted with a prayer for an appointment " to execute the trust." Factors may have a duty and therefore a power to distribute the estate,[21] or in the case of a factor on a trust (before power to sell was conferred by the Trusts (Scotland) Act 1921) to sell heritage if the testator's directions can be carried out only by such sale,[22] or to pay debts incurred by the trustees during their administration.[23]

Powers under the Trusts (Scotland) Acts

It has never been doubted that " trustee " in sections 4 and 5 of the Act of 1921 includes judicial factor. Section 4, as adapted in terms of the amended definition section and amended by the Acts of 1961,[24] provides that a judicial factor shall have power to do certain acts, under seventeen heads, where such acts are not at variance with the terms or purposes of his appointment, and that such acts where done shall be as effectual as if such powers had been contained in the decree appointing him. The phrase " at variance with the terms or purposes " is more easily applied to a trust, the " terms " being the words used, as construed, and the " purposes " being the general intention of the granter as disclosed in the trust deed.[25] But it is awkward in relation to the appointment of a judicial factor. The " terms " of the interlocutor appointing him may indicate the nature of his functions, in fact the purposes of his appointment, e.g. a factor loco tutoris or a curator bonis, but in some cases they do not, and the " purposes " have to be discovered from the averments in the petition.[26]

In this connection judicial factors fall into three classes, the differences being illustrated mainly in relation to the alienation of heritage, absolutely

---

[17] Colt v. Colt (1800) Mor. 16387 (tutor-at-law): Stair II, 9, 2.

[18] Allan (1854) 16 D. 534.

[19] Neilson and Others (1865) 3 M. 559 at p. 560.

[20] Irons, Judicial Factors, p. 1, Thomson and Middleton, Manual of Court of Session Procedure, p. 264.

[21] Cooper & Sons' Judicial Factor (O.H.) 1931 S.L.T. 26, 1930 S.N. 134 (factor to wind up partnership); Wharrie's Judicial Factor (O.H.) 1916, 1 S.L.T. 345 (factor on trust estate when time for distribution had arrived).

[22] Stirling's Judicial Factor (O.H.) 1917, 1 S.L.T. 165; McLeay (O.H.) 1921, 1 S.L.T. 340. These and the earlier unreported Outer House decisions appear to conflict with Lord Curriehill's opinion in Morison (1855) 18 D. 132.

[23] Brown's Factor (O.H.) (1902) 9 S.L.T. 490.

[24] Trusts (Scotland) Act 1961, s. 4; Trustee Investments Act 1961, s. 10.

[25] See Weir's Trustees (1877) 4 R. 876.

[26] Leslie's Judicial Factor, 1925 S.C. 464 at p. 470. The difficulties which may be caused by ill-considered averments are illustrated in Drummond v. Lindsay (1857) 19 D. 859, where there was a dispute as to the purpose of the appointment.

or in security. The trust deed sets forth the terms and purposes of the appointment of a factor on a trust estate.[27] Where a factor is appointed to realise and distribute the estate the purpose is plain.[28] Examples are factors on executries, on intestate estates and on partnership estates where the partnership is to be wound up. The difficulties arise where the factor is appointed to administer an estate (other than a trust estate) until the occurrence of an event, for example a factor *loco tutoris* or a curator *bonis*. *Prima facie* alienation of any part of the estate is at variance with the purposes of the appointment.[29] But it is a factor's duty to sell unsuitable shares, and decisions and dicta provide broad guidance with regard to heritage.[30]

Section 5 of the 1921 Act, as adapted, empowers the court, on the petition of a judicial factor, to authorise him [31] to do any of the acts mentioned in section 4, notwithstanding that such act is at variance with the terms or purposes of his appointment, on being satisfied that such act is in all the circumstances expedient [32] for the execution of his appointment. In the only two reported cases under the Trusts (Scotland) Acts 1867 and 1884, the judicial factor was factor on a trust estate. Authority was refused in the first because of an express prohibition in the trust deed,[33] and in the second because of probable loss to some of the beneficiaries.[34] In the case of a factor *loco tutoris* the interests of his ward come first,[35] though this may be qualified in particular circumstances.[36] Where a judicial factor appeals to section 5 the court requires a report from the Accountant of Court before deciding on expediency.[37] If a judicial factor enters into a transaction with any person purporting to act under the powers contained in section 4 the transaction and any title acquired are not challengeable by that person " or any other person " on the ground that the act is at variance with the terms and purposes of the appointment.[38] The factor is, nevertheless, entitled to apply under section 5, because those interested in the estate, although they cannot reduce the title, may recover from him any loss.[39]

---

[27] *Marquess of Lothian's Curator Bonis*, 1927 S.C. 579 at p. 584. In *Tennent's Judicial Factor* v. *Tennent*, 1954 S.C. 215, the proposed act was at variance with the terms and purposes of the trust deed. For a trust case see *Naismith's Trustees* v. *Naismith*, 1907 S.C. 1380.

[28] *Leslie's Judicial Factor*, 1925 S.C. 464 at p. 473. See also *Cooper & Sons Judicial Factor* (O.H.) 1931 S.L.T. 26, 1930 S.N. 134.

[29] *Linton* v. *Inland Revenue*, 1928 S.C. 209 at p. 214.

[30] See p. 105.

[31] An unnecessary application will be dismissed as in *Cunningham's Tutrix* (O.H.) 1949 S.C. 275, and *Marquess of Lothian's Curator Bonis*, 1927 S.C. 579.

[32] As contrasted with the necessity required at common law for the grant of a special power to sell heritage: *Weir's Trustees* (1877) 4 R. 876 at p. 882.

[33] *Whyte's Factor* v. *Whyte* (1891) 18 R. 376.

[34] *Molleson* v. *Hope* (1888) 15 R. 665. A trust case is *Kerr's Trustees* v. *Kerr's Curator ad litem*, 1907 S.C. 678.

[35] See *Macqueen* v. *Tod* (1899) 1 F. 1069, application for special powers.

[36] *Marquess of Lothian's Curator Bonis*, 1927 S.C. 579 at p. 587.

[37] *Tennent's Judicial Factor* v. *Tennent*, 1954 S.C. 215. A trust case is *Darwin's Trustees* (O.H.) 1924 S.L.T. 778.

[38] Trusts (Scotland) Act 1961, s. 2.

[39] *Barclay* (O.H.) 1962 S.C. 594.

Under section 16 the court may authorise a factor to advance capital to minor beneficiaries.

Strictly speaking, authorisation by the court under sections 5 and 16 are not grants of special powers, since they could be granted by any Lord Ordinary,[40] whereas until 1933 a special power could be granted only by the Junior Lord Ordinary.[41] But the distinction is not always observed in practice. The report in *Marquess of Lothian's Curator Bonis* [42] is not specific, but the application seems to have been made under section 5. Yet it was made by note, not petition as required by the section, and came before the Junior Lord Ordinary, and the phrase " special powers " is used in the rubric and opinions. Authority to sell cannot be granted under a petition for appointment of trustees, and consequently of a factor, under section 8 (2) of the Act.[43]

An indirect effect of the Trusts Acts is to render obsolete a large number of decisions on special powers, since the court is most unlikely to apply decisions under the *nobile officium* to matters now regulated by statute.[44] But the fact that the court granted an application for special powers may yield an inference that the power was not within the " usual powers." This inference is, however, not inevitable. Special powers have been granted unnecessarily,[45] or where it was doubtful whether the factor had the power.[46]

Special powers

The " usual " powers are granted as matter of course when the factor is appointed. As a general rule, a special power is granted only if the factor satisfies the court that he requires it in order to carry out his duties, and therefore the general practice is not to grant a special power on appointment, but at a later stage on the application of the factor.[47] Special power to make up title was, however, granted on appointment when the estate was small,[48] and a common feature of other cases was that the main purpose of applying for the appointment was that the factor might use the special power asked.[49] When a factor had obtained special powers and died before exercising them they were granted to his successor on appointment.[50] The court has statutory power when making an appoint-

---

[40] s. 26.
[41] Distribution of Business Act 1857, s. 4.
[42] 1927 S.C. 579.
[43] *Gibson* (O.H.) 1967 S.L.T. 150.
[44] *Tennent's Judicial Factor* v. *Tennent*, 1954 S.C. 215 at p. 225; *Mitchell Bequest Trustees*, 1959 S.C. 395; *Tod* v. *Marshall* (1895) 23 R. 36.
[45] *Tosh's Judicial Factor*, 1913 S.C. 242; *Keegan* (1857) 19 D. 382 (reporter's report).
[46] *McBain* (O.H.) 1928 S.N. 103.
[47] *Russell* v. *Russell* (1874) 2 R. 93; *Beveridge* (1851) 13 D. 952; *Kerr* (1849) 12 D. 266; *Thomson* (1857) 19 D. 964; *Campbell* (1841) 4 D. 169.
[48] *Brodie* (1867) 3 S.L.R. 223. See also *Barclay*, 1962 S.C. 594.
[49] *Waring* (O.H.) 1933 S.L.T. 190, 1933 S.N. 14; *Muir* (O.H.) 1929 S.N. 113; *The Public Trustee of New Zealand* (O.H.) 1921, 2 S.L.T. 240; *Forbes* (1852) 14 D. 498. It is rather surprising that the application in *Drew* (O.H.) 1938 S.N. 73, to carry on a business, was even entertained.
[50] *Stodart* (1854) 16 D. 883; *Raeburn* (1851) 13 D. 951.

ment of a factor on a trust estate to grant him authority to complete title.[51] Occasionally the court has granted special powers at the instance of third parties. Most of these applications were designed to secure from the factor payments to the third party,[52] and in one case, where a curator *bonis* was unwilling to let his ward's house to the ward's wife, the court on the petition of the wife authorised him to do so.[53]

The circumstances in which special powers are required and granted in particular cases are mentioned in the chapter on Administration; but there are three general points. First the occasions for the grant of special powers are reduced by the Trusts Acts.[54] Secondly, in spite of the wide general statements by the whole court [55] they were at one time granted, in case of heritage at least, only on the ground of necessity,[56] but this doctrine was relaxed, at least where alienation of heritage was not involved, and expediency and desirability held sufficient.[57] Lastly, as a general rule, the court will grant only power to do a particular act,[58] although in very exceptional circumstances power to do acts of a particular kind may be granted,[59] and the factor must set forth how he proposes to exercise it so that the court, if it disapproves the proposal, may refuse the power or grant it in a modified form.[60]

In an *obiter dictum* Lord President Dunedin expressed the view that there is sometimes a little confusion as to what special powers are, and proceeded: " These applications for special powers might, I think, more accurately be called applications for special directions, because what the court is asked to do is to give a special direction to its own officer, namely, the factor." [61] " Direction " is an ambiguous word. It may mean command [62] or it may mean information,[63] in this connection, a finding as to the factor's powers. It was used in the former sense when it was said that it was " competent for the court to direct the curator *bonis* as to the way in which he ought to exercise his election " [64] and that a factor " is entitled to the direction of the court as to the course he should follow." [65] So read, these dicta conflict with the principle that responsibility for the exercise of his powers rests with the factor.[66] The other meaning was

---

[51] Trusts (Scotland) Act 1921, s. 25. See *Brower's Executor*, 1938 S.C. 451, discussed at pp. 38, 87.

[52] This anomaly is discussed at p. 111.

[53] *Graham* (1862) 24 D. 312. No opinions were delivered.

[54] *Tennent's Judicial Factor* v. *Tennent*, 1954 S.C. 215 at p. 225; *Mitchell Bequest Trustees*, 1959 S.C. 395.

[55] *Somerville's Factor* (1836) 14 S. 451.

[56] *Muller* v. *Dixon* (1854) 16 D. 536; *Maconochie* (1857) 19 D. 366.

[57] *Gordon's Curator Bonis* (1902) 4 F. 577; *Hamiltons Tutors*, 1924 S.C. 365.

[58] *Carmichael's Judicial Factor*, 1971 S.L.T. 336.

[59] *Grant's Curator* (1880) 7 R. 1014; *Lindsay* (1855) 18 D. 205.

[60] *Drummond's Judicial Factor* (1894) 21 R. 932; *Somerville's Factor* (1836) 14 S. 451, " the power necessary for accomplishing the object set forth in the petition."

[61] *Tosh's Judicial Factor*, 1913 S.C. 242 at p. 244.

[62] *e.g.* direction of labour.   [63] *e.g.* direction post.

[64] *Skinner's Curator Bonis* (1903) 5 F. 914 at p. 918. This case is commented on at p. 112.

[65] *Browning's Factor* (1905) 7 F. 1037 at p. 1044.

[66] *Tosh's Judicial Factor*, 1913 S.C. 242, Lord Johnston at p. 245; *Mathieson* (1857) 19 D. 917; *Drew* (1867) 5 M. 892; *Thoms on Judicial Factors* (2nd ed.) 107; *Irons on Judicial Factors*, 99.

placed upon the word when it was said that a factor was entitled to the direction of the court as to whether a lease was within the scope of the trust he was administering.[67] Such a direction is usually obtained by presenting an application for special powers and having it either considered on its merits or dismissed as unnecessary. None of these dicta influenced the interlocutors. In two of the cases [68] the court granted the power as craved in the ordinary way, while in the third [69] it both found that the factor was entitled to retain the shares and " allowed " him to do so. Nor do they appear to have influenced subsequent practice. Excluding cases relating to allowances to third parties,[70] there are three older cases where the court " directed " or " ordained " a judicial factor. Two arose out of proceedings in Chancery,[71] and the third related to the person of a pupil.[72]

The grant of a special power merely empowers the factor to do the act, or, as Thoms put it,[73] adds so much to his title. But no more than a " usual " power or authority granted under the Trusts (Scotland) Act 1921 does it relieve him from responsibility for imprudence in exercising it or protect the act from challenge on an extrinsic ground, possibly minority and lesion. Thoms, however, appears to hold that an act done under a special power is reducible on the ground that the court in granting the power misapplied the *nobile officium*.[74] Most of the dicta he cites refer to the factor's own responsibility or to challenge on an extrinsic ground, and the only cases which appear to lend any countenance to his view are *Vere* v. *Dale* [75] and *Muller* v. *Dixon*.[76] If the report in *Vere* v. *Dale* is correct the court reduced their own decree authorising the feu charter on the ground that as the tutors had no power to feu it was " therefore *ultra vires* of the court to authorise it." The reference to meliorations shews that the charter was treated as having fallen with the decree. Although the decision has been cited as authority for the proposition that the court would not grant authority to alienate heritage except in case of necessity, it has never been founded on in an attempt to induce the court to reduce its own exercise of the *nobile officium*. The clear distinction now drawn between actions and petitions (and notes) [78] makes the success of such an attempt less likely. *Muller* v. *Dixon* [79] was not a decision that in granting a power the court had misused the *nobile officium* and therefore that the

---

[67] *Tosh's Judicial Factor*, 1913 S.C. 242 at p. 245. The word is used in this sense in the Administration of Justice (Scotland) Act 1933, s. 17 (vi).
[68] *Tosh's Judicial Factor*, 1913 S.C. 242; *Skinner's Curator Bonis* (1903) 5 F. 914.
[69] *Browning's Factor* (1905) 7 F. 1037.
[70] See p. 111.
[71] *Allen* v. *Robertson* (1855) 18 D. 97; *Murray* v. *Baillie* (1849) 11 D. 710.
[72] *Moncreiff* (1891) 18 R. 1029.
[73] *Judicial Factors* (2nd ed.), p. 105.
[74] *Ibid.*, pp. 105–107. For possible results of the view see *Maconochie* (1857) 19 D. 366 at p. 369.
[75] (1804) M. 16389, " the well-known case," as Thoms called it.
[76] (1854) 16 D. 536.
[77] Gloag regarded the decision as founded on minority and lesion: *Contract* (2nd ed.) p. 78, note 7. But the only support for this view is that the pupil raised the action when he attained majority.
[78] *Tomkin's* v. *Cohen*, 1951 S.C. 22.
[79] (1854) 16 D. 536.

grant might be ignored. The most that can be said is that the procedure adopted yields an inference that the court considered such a decision open to them.[80] In 1852 the court granted a factor power to sell heritage. The Lord Ordinary's report pointedly drew attention to the legal position, so that it is improbable that the interlocutor was an " oversight." [81] The oversight may have been in 1854, when the opinions suggest that the judges were applying their minds, not to the question whether to find in effect that the interlocutor of 1852 should never have been pronounced, which they had no power to do,[82] but to the question whether they ought to grant the power. The case is thus an insecure basis for an inference.[83] There is also an *obiter dictum* by Lord Curriehill, with three concurring judges, in *Maconochie*.[84] The question was whether the court had power to authorise a curator *bonis* to sell or burden his ward's heritable estate, and Lord Curriehill observed that a negative answer would imply that all such powers previously granted were not lawfully granted and that persons who had trusted to their validity might be ruined.[85] This seems to mean that any previous grant might be set aside or ignored and the administration of the factory reconstructed as if the grant had never been. In *Bryce* v. *Graham* [86] no one suggested that if the court decided that it was incompetent to appoint a curator *bonis* without cognition (except as a temporary measure), every previous such appointment would fall.

Authorisation ex post facto

In very special circumstances the court has given subsequent sanction to an act beyond the powers of a factor.[87] This was done where an application for special powers would have disclosed the factor's reasons for wishing to buy heritage and raised the price against him,[88] where the factor had to act at once and did not have time to apply for special powers,[89] where the estate was small [90] and where the judges described the need as urgent.[91] But the court refused to sanction a sale of heritage by private bargain where power had been given to sell by public roup,[92] or expenditure on renewals far beyond the sums originally authorised.[93]

Effect of exercise of power

The exercise of his powers, usual or special, by a judicial factor does

---

[80] See *Maconochie* (1857) 19 D. 366 at p. 374.
[81] *Ibid.* at p. 375.
[82] *Beedie* v. *Beedie* (1889) 16 R. 648 at p. 651.
[83] *Skinner's Curator Bonis* (1903) 5 F. 914 at p. 917.
[84] (1857) 19 D. 366 at p. 369, a whole court case.
[85] Third parties would probably now be protected by s. 2 of the Trusts (Scotland) Act 1961.
[86] (1828) 6 S. 425, a whole court case.
[87] See *Horne's Trustees*, 1952 S.C. 70.
[88] *Gilray* (1876) 3 R. 619.
[89] *Blair's Curator Bonis* (O.H.) 1921 S.L.T. 248.
[90] *Hodge* (O.H.) (1904) 11 S.L.T. 709.
[91] *Hamilton's Tutors*, 1924 S.C. 364.
[92] *Drummond's Judicial Factor* (1894) 21 R. 932.
[93] *Maitland* (1863) 1 M. 1104.

not alter the succession to the estate unless the act was necessary in the interests of the ward [94] or was forced on the factor by operation of law.[95] All the cases arose from the distinction in the rules of intestate succession between heritage and moveables, and since this distinction has been abolished,[96] the question can arise as matter of succession only if there was a bequest of heritage.[97] It may, however, affect prior rights or legal rights.[98] The sale by a curator *bonis* of his ward's house and furniture might reduce considerably the rights of the ward's widow.

Relief under the Trusts (Scotland) Act 1921

Sections 29 to 33 provide a measure of protection to trustees,[1] but the question whether they apply to judicial factors does not seem to have been raised in any reported case, although some of their provisions have been in operation since 1891.[2] Sections 29 and 33 are peremptory, and there is nothing in the context to make them inapplicable to judicial factors. " The court " in sections 30,[3] 31 and 32 means any court in which a question relative to the actings, liability or removal of a trustee comes to be tried. This may well include proceedings for the discharge of a judicial factor or an audit of his accounts. " Beneficiary " has been given a wide meaning,[4] and section 31 may not be confined to factors on trust and executry estates.

---

[94] *McAdam's Executor* v. *Soutar* (1904) 7 F. 179; *Dick* v. *Dick* (O.H.) 1925 S.L.T. 337.
[95] *Macfarlane's Judicial Factor* v. *Greig* (1895) 22 R. 405 (division and sale); *Horn* v. *Espie* (1856) 18 D. 917 (compulsory purchase). See also *Kennedy* v. *Kennedy* (1843) 6 D. 40.
[96] Succession (Scotland) Act 1964, s. 1.
[97] *Chalmers* v. *Chalmers* (1851) 14 D. 57, with some alteration of the facts would illustrate this.
[98] Succession (Scotland) Act 1964, ss. 8, 9, 10.
[1] See volume on Trusts (in press).
[2] Trusts (Scotland) Amendment Act 1891, ss. 4, 5 and 6.
[3] See Trustee Investments Act 1961, s. 6 (7).
[4] *Bristow* (O.H.) 1965 S.L.T. 225.

CHAPTER XIV

RECOVERY OF ESTATE: LITIGATION

Introductory

General

It is the factor's duty to obtain control of the whole estate. This involves completing title, when necessary, to heritage and incorporeal moveables, and taking, or arranging for, possession of corporeal moveables. If there is a dispute about any property claimed as part of the estate, questions arise as to the factor's power and duty to enforce or resist such claims, his position *quoad* expenses of litigation, *res judicata*, compromise and arbitration.

Recovery of writs

A factor must ascertain the nature and amount of the estate, and he must, without delay, recover all writs and documents of importance belonging to the estate.[1] The normal method of enforcing this right would be an action for delivery, with a further conclusion or crave for warrant to search, but there does not appear to be any reported case where this course was followed. Factors, having obtained decree for delivery, have then by note applied for and obtained a warrant to search, apparently granted under the *nobile officium*.[2] In another case,[3] warrant to search followed a warrant authorising the factor to take possession of writs. The unusual procedure of authorising the factor to do what the statute required him to do may have been due to the complications caused by the interference of the English court.

Completion of Title

Heritage

There is a distinction between factories on the estate of a living ward, *e.g.* factories *loco tutoris* and curatories *bonis*, and factories where there is no owner, *e.g.* on trust estates or partnership estates. In the first case, title is as a rule completed in name of the ward and in the second in name of the factor. The reason is that a ward remains owner of his estate and the factor merely manages it for him. Where there is no *dominus*, the estate must be vested in the factor to enable him to grant conveyances and do any other necessary acts.[4] Accordingly, where the

---

[1] Pupils Protection Act 1849, s. 3. See *Hallpenny* v. *Howden* (1894) 21 R. 945.
[2] *McAlley's Judicial Factor* (1900) 2 F. 1198; *Ferguson's Curator Bonis* (1905) 7 F. 898; as to the right to search under s. 14 of the Bankruptcy (Scotland) Act 1913, see *McLachlan* v. *Bell* (1895) 23 R. 126.
[3] *Orr Ewing's Judicial Factor* (1884) 11 R. 682.
[4] *Scott* (1856) 18 D. 624 at p. 626; *Maconochie* (1857) 19 D. 366 at p. 372.

factory is on the estate of a living person and that person is already infeft, the factor need take no action.[5] Should it be necessary to complete the ward's title, and if the ward is a " person having right to land," this is done by notice of title,[6] or, if the ward has no title, by obtaining and recording a conveyance in favour of the ward, or by other method appropriate in the circumstances. No special power is required.[7] Any necessary conveyance is executed by the factor and, where the ward is a " person having right to land," but is not infeft, it may be enough to deduce his title in the conveyance.[8]

Where there is no existing *dominus* of the estate,[9] title is completed, where necessary, in name of the factor. Formerly all factors required special power to do so.[10] But since 1938 a factor " appointed by the court to administer a trust estate " is deemed to be a " person having right to land " [11] and, therefore, may complete title or grant a conveyance by deducing his title.[12] Prima facie the words " appointed . . . to administer a trust estate " appear to apply only where there is a pre-existing trust estate, but in *Lowe's Judicial Factor*,[13] there were opinions to the effect that a trust estate is created by the appointment of a factor, who is therefore a factor appointed on, or to administer, a trust estate. This view was treated with considerable reserve in *Leslie's Judicial Factor*,[14] and the then definition of judicial factor [15] goes a long way to shew that the opinions in *Lowe's Judicial Factor* were unsound. That definition is now amended,[16] possibly in order to meet the doubts of the Lord President as to whether it included more than factors on trust estates and factors on the estates of *incapaces*,[17] but section 1 of the 1938 Act itself demonstrates that the words " trust estate " mean a pre-existing trust estate. It refers to a trustee appointed by the court on " such a trust estate," and the court does not appoint a trustee unless there already exists a trust, express or implied. In *McMurtrie* [18] a crave for special power to a factor on an intestate estate to complete title to heritage was refused as unnecessary. The Lord Ordinary delivered no opinion, but section 1 of the 1938 Act figures prominently in the report, and the refusal bore to be " in respect that the judicial factor is a trustee on a trust estate within the meaning of the Trusts Acts." It would be unwise to count on this decision being followed. Professions of willingness by the only infeft trustee on a sequestrated estate to grant

---

[5] *Hodge* (O.H.) (1904) 11 S.L.T. 709 (factor *loco absentis*).
[6] Conveyancing (Scotland) Act 1924, s. 4.
[7] *Waring* (O.H.) 1933 S.L.T. 190, 1933 S.N. 14; *Melville's Curator Bonis* (O.H.) 1924 S.L.T. 119.
[8] Conveyancing (Scotland) Act 1924, s. 3.
[9] *Maconochie* (1857) 19 D. 366 at p. 372.
[10] *Leslie's J.F.*, 1925 S.C. 464, at pp. 471, 472.
[11] Conveyancing Amendment (Scotland) Act 1938, s. 1.
[12] Conveyancing (Scotland) Act 1924, ss. 3 and 4.
[13] 1925 S.C. 11.
[14] 1925 S.C. 464.
[15] Trusts (Scotland) Act 1921, s. 2.
[16] Trusts (Scotland) Act 1961, s. 3.
[17] *Leslie's Judicial Factor*, 1925 S.C. 464 at p. 469.
[18] (O.H.) 1939 S.N. 48.

any conveyances desired by the factor were held to be no ground for re-fusing the factor authority to complete title.[19] *A fortiori* such professions would be no ground for interfering with the statutory right of a factor on a trust estate to complete title.

The methods of completing title provided by earlier legislation, as amended, may still be used in cases where there is a ward or a trust estate, and, unless *McMurtrie* [20] was correctly decided, they must (leaving aside still earlier procedures [21]) be used in other cases, *e.g.* a factory on an in-testate estate. Where authority is asked for the completion of title to specified lands either in the petition for appointment or in a note by the factor the warrant is held to be a conveyance in favour of the factor or the ward, as the case may be, and on recording has the effect of a recorded conveyance. The title may be deduced from the person last infeft.[22] Section 44 of the Conveyancing (Scotland) Act 1874, as amended by the Conveyancing (Scotland) Act 1924, s. 3, provides that an interlocutor appointing a factor on a trust estate " shall specify " the trust deed and the lands, and that a recorded extract shall operate a title by infeftment in favour of the factor. " Notwithstanding the imperative words " of section 44, a factor on a trust estate may complete title under section 24 of the 1868 Act.[23] *A fortiori* he must be entitled to complete title under the later Acts of 1924 and 1938.

Questions as to title to real property situated abroad are governed by the *lex situs*.[24] Where a judicial factor on a trust estate wished to complete title to what was averred to be " real property " in England he applied for and was granted leave to apply to the Chancery Division for completion of title.[25]

Incorporeal moveables

Like heritage, stocks and shares are vested in the ward, if there is one, and otherwise in the factor.[26] Section 13 of the Judicial Factors (Scotland) Act 1889 does not alter this fundamental distinction. It means, not that a ward's property vests in his curator *bonis*, but that in a question with third parties the appointment is equivalent to a vesting of the estate in the curator *bonis*, so that they must account to him,[27] that is, treat him as if he were the owner.[28] As regards the recovery and transfer of stocks and shares there is, or at least may be, some difference according to whether

---

[19] *Paterson's Judicial Factor* v. *Lindsay* (O.H.) 1916, 2 S.L.T. 244.
[20] (O.H.) 1939 S.N. 48.
[21] Lord Ordinary in *Leslie's Judicial Factor*, 1925 S.C. 464 at p. 466.
[22] Titles to Land Consolidation (Scotland) Act 1868, s. 24, as amended by the Conveyancing (Scotland) Act 1924, s. 5 (3).
[23] *Hislop* (O.H.) (1901) 9 S.L.T. 176.
[24] *Bourne* v. *Gairdner* (1823) 2 S. 212. See also *Downie* v. *Downie's Trustees* (1866) 4 M. 1067.
[25] *Ayton's Judicial Factor* (O.H.) 1937 S.L.T. 86, 1937 S.N. 57.
[26] *Inland Revenue* v. *McMillan's Curator Bonis*, 1956 S.C. 142 at pp. 147, 149; *Yule* v. *Alexander* (1891) 19 R. 167.
[27] *Inland Revenue* v. *McMillan's Curator Bonis*, 1956 S.C. 142 at pp. 148, 149.
[28] It has been held competent to arrest in the hands of a factor *loco absentis* funds belonging to his ward's estate in respect of a debt due by the ward: *Mitchell* v. *Scott* (1881) 8 R. 875.

they are (a) securities of Scottish companies, (b) securities registered at the Bank of England, (c) securities of English companies or (d) securities in other countries.

(a) *Scottish companies.* Stock belonging to a ward at the date of the appointment remains registered in his name. The factor exhibits the stock certificate and a certified copy of the interlocutor appointing him, and some companies endorse the date of exhibition on the stock certificate, while others merely note the exhibition without marking the certificate. The company issues interest or dividend warrants in favour of the factor as factor and gives effect to transfers signed by him.[29] A curator *bonis* may have the right to vote on behalf of a member of unsound mind.[30] Should an insane ward recover, the company, on exhibition of an extract decree recalling the appointment of the curator *bonis*, cancels its note of the appointment, and the owner's right is complete. On principle stock acquired during the factory ought to be registered in the ward's name, but in practice it is frequently registered in name of the factor *qua* factor, who is then in the same position as a factor on an estate where there is no ward.

A judicial factor on an estate where there is no ward need not go on the register in respect of stock which on his appointment he decides to sell. The company gives effect to a transfer signed by him on delivery of the stock certificate and exhibition of a certified copy of the interlocutor appointing him.[31] If he retains or acquires stock he is registered *qua* judicial factor on the estate, unless the articles prohibit this. The only effect of the qualification is to identify the stock as part of the estate and not the personal property of the factor.[32] He incurs the same liabilities as other holders of that stock.[33] Special powers are not required to sell and transfer stock [34] or, except in special circumstances,[35] to acquire it. The factor may obtain a title through the executors of a sole trustee.[36]

Should the factor die or resign, his successor exhibits a certified copy of the interlocutor appointing him, and the company makes the appropriate changes.

(b) *The Bank of England.* The Government Stock Regulations 1965, which apply to certain stock [37] registered at the Bank, leave much to

---

[29] *Lindsay's Curator* v. *City of Glasgow Bank* (1879) 6 R. 671 at pp. 674, 678.

[30] Companies Act 1948, Table A, Reg. 64.

[31] *Buchan* v. *City of Glasgow Bank* (1879) 6 R. (H.L.) 44 at p. 46; *Wishart* v. *City of Glasgow Bank* (1879) 6 R. 1341 at pp. 1345, 1349 (both cases of executors); McLaren, *Wills and Succession* (3rd ed.), para. 2511.

[32] *Muir* v. *City of Glasgow Bank* (1878) 6 R. (H.L.) 21 at pp. 26, 30, 32, 34; *Royal Bank of Scotland* v. *Greenlees* (1887) 15 R. 9; *Elliot* v. *Mackie & Sons*, 1935 S.C. 81 at p. 90.

[33] *Lumsden* v. *Peddie* (1868) 5 M. 34 (registration " as curator *bonis* "), referred to in *Lindsay's Curator* v. *City of Glasgow Bank* (1879) 6 R. 671 at p. 677, and in *Muir* v. *City of Glasgow Bank* (1878) 6 R. (H.L.) 21.

[34] *Morison* (1901) 4 F. 144 at p. 147.

[35] In *Bontine's Curator* (1870) 8 M. 976, the curator *bonis* craved special powers because he proposed to acquire ordinary shares.

[36] Executors (Scotland) Act 1900, s. 6, as amended by Administration of Estates Act 1971, s. 7, Sched. 1, para. 2.

[37] See Schedule.

the discretion of the Bank,[38] and the practice is similar for all stock registered there and resembles that of Scottish companies. Where stock is already registered in name of a ward and is not detailed in the certified copy interlocutor of the appointment, the Bank, on a certificate by the accountant that the stock forms part of the estate under the factor's charge, notes the appointment, interest is sent to the factor, and he may transfer the stock. On exhibition of an extract decree recalling the appointment the note is cancelled, and the ward has all rights of ownership. Stock acquired for a ward may be registered in his name, the factor's appointment being noted. Alternatively, such stock may be registered in name of the factor described, *e.g.* " as curator *bonis* to. . . ." Where there is no ward registration can only be in name of the factor *qua* factor.

The requirement of the certificate from the accountant rests to some extent on section 66 of the Finance Act 1916, which applies to, *inter alia*, the Bank of England. That section, as amended,[39] provides that a certified copy interlocutor of an appointment as judicial factor, where any Government stock is specified in the certified copy interlocutor, or in a certificate under seal by the accountant, as forming part of the estate under the charge of the factor, is deemed to be a decree vesting the right to transfer such Government stock in the factor. " Government stock " was, and is,[40] defined, but the accountant is now expected to give, and does give, such certificates in respect of stocks which do not fall within the definition. This practice was certainly not discouraged in *Brower's Executor*.[41] Although none of the stocks involved was Government stock as then defined and only four out of the seven were inscribed at the Bank of England and none at any of the other institutions, the opinion of the Lord President, concurred in by the other judges, appears to imply that the accountant was obliged to, or at any rate would, give a certificate under seal in respect of them all.

On the death or resignation of the factor his successor acts as in the case of a Scottish company. Where one of several trustees became *incapax* the Lord Ordinary authorised her curator *bonis* to sign a transfer of War Stock registered in name of the trustees.[42]

(c) *English companies.* On exhibition of a stock certificate in name of a ward and of a certified copy of the interlocutor of appointment most English companies recognise the rights of a curator *bonis* or other factor, pay interest to him and give effect to transfers signed by him. Where an English company refused to recognise the authority of a factor to sell stock belonging to his ward without the express authority of the court, the Lord Ordinary granted authority.[43] They cancel their note of the appointment on exhibition of a certified copy of the interlocutor recalling

[38] See Regulation 15 (transfer).
[39] Act of Sederunt (Appointment of Judicial Factors etc.) 1967, s. 4.
[40] National Debt Act 1958, s. 15 (3).
[41] 1938 S.C. 451. See Chap. VI, p. 38.
[42] *Pennycuick* (O.H.) 1925 S.L.T. 362.
[43] *McCall's Curator Bonis* (1901) 8 S.L.T. 440.

it. But a difficulty arises where a factor elects or is compelled (because there is no ward) to have stock registered in his own name. No notice of any trust may be entered in the register of a company registered in England.[44] Consequently qualifying words such as " *qua* curator *bonis* for . . ." cannot be added to the factor's name and the stock appears to be his own property. An accepted solution is that the factor endorses on the stock certificate a note that he holds as curator *bonis* for a specified person or as judicial factor on a specified estate.[45] If there is real difficulty the accountant may grant a certificate that the stock forms part of the estate under the factor's charge. Where the factor dies or resigns and the stock is registered in name of the ward, the succeeding factor's rights are normally recognised on exhibition of a certified copy interlocutor of his appointment. If the stock is registered in name of the factor his executors will have to confirm and transfer the stock to his successor.

(d) *Other countries.* The only matter likely to arise is the recovery of such estate. A copy of the interlocutor of his appointment certified by the seal of the Court of Session is usually a sufficient title for the factor to take the steps required by the law of the country.

Corporeal moveables

While the distinction applies between estates of which the ward is owner and estates vested in the factor, discretion must play a large part. A minor or a pupil or an *incapax* living at home is entitled to the use of his own furniture. If an *incapax* is in a mental home, the curator *bonis* will probably allow the wife and family to continue to use the furniture rather than cause them inconvenience and the estate expense by storing it. The use of furniture belonging to a trust will be a matter of the terms of the trust deed and of arrangement between the factor and those interested. The factor may have possession, though a third party has custody.[46] Where a partnership is being wound up the factor may keep possession of the furniture by retaining the keys of the office. If the possessor of the estate refuses delivery the factor may obtain an order with warrant to search.[47]

Executor-dative under A.S. February 13 1730

Under section 7 of the Act of Sederunt [48] where a factor's ward, including an *absens*, has right to the estate of a deceased person, or part thereof, and no other person having a title offers to confirm to the estate, the factor may confirm in his own name as executor-dative on behalf of his ward and administer the estate for those entitled to it, including his

---

[44] Companies Act 1948, s. 117.
[45] *Brodie* v. *London & North Western Railway* (O.H.) 1912, 2 S.L.T. 477; *Accountant of Court* v. *Crumpton's Curator Bonis* (1886) 14 R. 55, a Bank of England case before the Bank adopted its present procedure.
[46] *Moore* v. *Gledden* (1869) 7 M. 1016 at p. 1022.
[47] *Neilson's Judicial Factor*, 1927 S.C. 595.
[48] Printed in Appendix.

ward.[49] In view of the way in which the section has sometimes been paraphrased [50] it should be emphasised that it does not apply unless there are two estates, that of a deceased person and that of a living person on which a factor has already been appointed,[51] and that the factor administers the first estate not as factor, but as executor. Consequently he cannot take credit against the factory estate for a debit balance on the executry estate.[52]

Since the factor is to confirm as executor-dative he must be decerned such [53] and find caution, whether the estate is testate or intestate. Where a sheriff in a testate case decerned a curator *bonis* executor-dative, the court reversed his decision, not on the ground that the section did not apply, but because in terms of the section others with a title offered to confirm.[54] On the reasoning in *Johnston's Executor* v. *Dobie* [55] the appointment as executor-dative is not brought to an end by the termination of the factory. The factor is already under the supervision of the accountant *qua* factor, and prima facie he would appear not to fall under that supervision *qua* executor-dative, except indirectly so far as his ward's interests are concerned. But the court may lay down a different rule.[56]

The factor *qua* executor-dative is entitled to convey heritage,[57] and has the powers, privileges and obligations of a gratuitous trustee.[58]

Commissary Factor

Where a minor or pupil would, if of age, be entitled to be decerned and confirmed executor-dative, the sheriff may appoint a commissary factor. He either decerns the minor executor-dative and appoints a factor or appoints a factor and decerns him executor-dative, and in either case the factor on finding caution is confirmed executor-dative *qua* factor for the minor,[59] or he may appoint the factor and then decern and confirm both minor and factor.[60] The factor is under the supervision of the accountant,[61] and his appointment does not fall on the minor attaining majority, but subsists until the administration has been completed.[62] The appointment has a drawback. Since a commissary factor's title extends

---

[49] *Martin* v. *Ferguson's Trs.* (1892) 19 R. 474 at p. 478; *Whiffen* v. *Lees* (1872) 10 M. 797 at p. 800; *Currie on the Confirmation of Executors* (6th ed.), pp. 108, 109.

[50] McLaren, *Wills and Succession* (3rd ed.), para. 1588; Ersk. III, 9, 32, note (*a*); Bell, Prin. (10th ed.) s. 1894, note (*i*), the first sentence.

[51] In *Keegan* (1857) 19 D. 382, there was only one estate and no ward, so that the reporter (p. 383) was mistaken in supposing that s. 7 applied.

[52] *Matheson's Curator Bonis* v. *Mathesons* (1889) 16 R. 701.

[53] *Matheson's Curator Bonis* v. *Mathesons* (1889) 16 R. 701, Lord President at p. 703.

[54] *Martin* v. *Ferguson's Trustees* (1892) 19 R. 474.

[55] 1907 S.C. 31.

[56] See *Accountant of Court*, 1907 S.C. 909.

[57] Succession (Scotland) Act 1964, ss. 14, 15. See volume on Trusts (in press).

[58] *Ibid.* s. 20.

[59] *Johnstone* v. *Lowden* (1838) 16 S. 541, referred to in *Whiffen* v. *Lees* (1872) 10 M. 797, at p. 800.

[60] *Currie on Confirmation* (6th ed.) p. 112.

[61] *Accountant of Court*, 1907 S.C. 909. See *Haston* (1930) 46 Sh.Ct.Rep. 141.

[62] *Johnston's Executor* v. *Dobie*, 1907 S.C. 31.

only to the executry estate, a curator *bonis* may have to be appointed to the minor if he acquires other property.[63]

Qua executor the factor is entitled to convey heritage,[64] and has the powers, privileges, immunities and obligations of a gratuitous trustee.[65]

Litigation

Title

A factor has power and a duty to enforce a claim on behalf of the estate by action and diligence [66] and to defend a claim against it,[67] but naturally he has no title to claim or retain property which does not fall within the terms of his appointment. A factor on heritable property, which had fallen into intestacy, had no title to sue third parties for rents uplifted by them before his appointment.[68] He has a title to sue before extract.[69] The Lord Justice-Clerk, who gave the leading opinion, dealt expressly only with a provision of the Act of Sederunt then in force, now repealed and not re-enacted, but the pursuer's real difficulty was section 2 of the Pupils Protection Act, and the Lord Justice-Clerk must have accepted the pursuer's argument that " the duties of his office " means those mentioned in the section, *viz.* intromissions. A factor has a right to appear at the audit of the accounts of his predecessor in office [70] and at his application for exoneration [71] and to sue an accounting against him.[72] He has a title to raise an action designed to relieve the estate of a possible liability [73] and to reduce a deed prejudicial to the estate.[74] He may bring a multiplepoinding,[75] and if he does not watch the competition, although he has no interest in its result, he may find that expenses have been awarded out of the estate.[76] He is entitled as nominal raiser to expenses as between agent and client.[77] There does not seem to be any direct authority as to reference to the oath of a judicial factor, but on the analogy of tutors [78] and trustees [79] it is competent to refer matters within his knowledge as factor. So far as the Scottish courts are concerned a factor is entitled to raise actions in foreign courts,[80] but it may be helpful to him there to have

---

[63] As in *Matheson's Curator Bonis* v. *Mathesons* (1889) 16 R. 701.

[64] Succession (Scotland) Act 1864, ss. 14, 15. See volume on Trusts (in press).

[65] *Ibid.* s. 20.

[66] *Fraser* (1850) 12 D. 914; *Henderson* v. *Watson*, 1939 S.C. 711. The defenders' first plea in *Kennedy* v. *McLean* (1851) 13 D. 705, that the factor had no title to sue without special powers, was not met by sisting the sisters as pursuers. It must have been repelled as unsound.

[67] *Mackintosh's Trustees* v. *Macqueen's Trustees* (1836) 15 S. 255.

[68] *Gordon* v. *Williams' Trustees* (1889) 16 R. 980.

[69] *Calver* v. *Howard, Baker & Co.* (1894) 22 R. 1.

[70] *Barlas* v. *Moncrieff* (1859) 21 D. 725.

[71] *Myles* v. *Ireland* (1855) 17 D. 590; *Port's Curator Bonis* (O.H.) (1901) 9 S.L.T. 271.

[72] *Simpson* v. *Doud and McCaul* (1855) 17 D. 314.

[73] *Watson* v. *Crawcour* (1843) 5 D. 1182.

[74] *Blaikie* v. *Milne* (1838) 1 D. 18; *Tait* v. *Muir* (1904) 6 F. 586.

[75] *Barstow* v. *Cook* (1862) 24 D. 790; *Tait's Factor* v. *Meikle* (1890) 17 R. 1182 at p. 1184.

[76] *Tait* v. *Grey* (O.H.) (1908) 15 S.L.T. 1068.

[77] *Wright* v. *Dalgarno* (*Miln's J.F.* v. *Spence's Trustees*) (O.H.) 1929 S.L.T. 279, 1929 S.N. 49.

[78] Ersk. IV, 2, 10; *Hepburn* v. *Hamilton* (1661) Mor. 8465, 12480.

[79] *Hotson* v. *Threshie* (1833) 12 S. 57.

[80] *Paul* v. *McIntosh* (1841) 3 D. 1145 (French decree).

his right to do so stated by a Scottish court.[81] Otherwise he may have to prove his right to sue.

In two reported cases decrees were granted for payment of money to judicial factors in actions at the instance of persons who had an interest to increase the estate.[82]

Failure to sue for debt

The accountant has power, with the approval of the Lord Ordinary where the sum involved exceeds £20, to dispense with the rules of exact diligence.[83] As some reported cases shew, it is not always wise to pursue a claim, and a factor who is in doubt would be well advised to report the circumstances to the accountant. If he does not obtain dispensation and fails to enforce a good claim, he will be debited with the amount unless he shews sound reason for his failure. On principle it appears to be for the objector to establish that the claim was good,[84] but the Trusts (Scotland) Act 1921 assumes the existence of a debt. It provides [85] that a factor may refrain from doing diligence for the recovery of any debt due to the estate which he reasonably deems irrecoverable. " Doing diligence " presumably includes the process of obtaining a decree, when necessary, and this was the view of Professor Mackenzie Stuart, who, by way of commentary on the provision, refers to decisions where at common law trustees were held entitled not to sue.[86] These and other decisions seem to establish that unless there has been great delay in raising the objection,[87] the onus lies on the factor to excuse his failure to recover [88] or, since 1921, to shew that he reasonably deemed the debt irrecoverable.[88] It is enough that he has good reason to think that an action will probably fail,[89] or that he establishes that nothing could have been recovered under a decree,[90] or, now, that he had reasonable grounds for such a belief. If the debtor is insolvent when the question of the factor's liability has to be determined, there is a presumption that he was solvent when the debt ought to have been recovered,[91] and even if the presumption is rebutted, the factor may be liable for any dividend he ought to have recovered. But, although a factor must not be influenced by sympathy or considerations of hardship,[92] he may exercise discretion. It may be bad estate manage-

---

[81] *Fullarton* v. *Dixon* (1833) 11 S. 962.

[82] *Rae* v. *Incorporation of Candlemakers of Edinburgh* (1858) 20 D. 461; *Thorburn* v. *Thorburn* (1858) 20 D. 829.

[83] Pupils Protection Act 1849, s. 14.

[84] See *Brown's Trustees* v. *Brown* (1888) 15 R. 581, interlocutor of Lord Ordinary (trustee); *Scrymgeour* v. *Wedderburn* (1673) Mor. 16289 (tutor).

[85] s. 4 (1) (*j*).

[86] *The Law of Trusts*, pp. 201, 242.

[87] *Condie* v. *McDonald* (1834) 13 S. 61 at p. 63.

[88] *Cranstoun* v. *Scott* (1826) 5 S. 62, interlocutor of Lord Ordinary.

[89] *Mores' Executors* v. *Malcolm* (1835) 13 S. 313 (executors).

[90] *Millar's Trustees* v. *Polson* (1897) 24 R. 1038 (trustees); *Watson* v. *Watson* (1623) Mor. 16242 (tutor).

[91] *Weir* v. *Hamiltons* (1751) Mor. 16355 (tutor).

[92] *Wardlaw* v. *Mackenzie* (1859) 21 D. 940 at p. 948.

ment to do diligence for rents,[93] and a curator *bonis*, who was suing his ward's daughter, was warned that he might be found personally liable in the expenses, if he persisted in the action, not because it was ill-founded in law, but because the family had arranged matters amongst themselves.[94]

Expenses

There are two questions, first, whether a factor is himself liable to meet expenses decerned for against him, and, second, whether he is entitled to recover from the estate expenses which he has incurred or which have been awarded against him.

(1) The answer to the first depends on the form of the decree, which must conform to that of the award.[95] If it is against him " as " or " *qua* factor," he is liable to the extent of the estate only; if it is unqualified, he may pay from estate funds, but if these are insufficient to meet the expenses, he must make up the deficiency himself.[96] The form of the award, and therefore of the decree, is matter for decision in the original action, and if the question of the factor's liability is raised in a suspension of a charge the court is concerned only with the meaning of the decree.[97]

The judges differed in *Craig* v. *Hogg* [98] as to whether as a general rule the award against a factor should be " *qua* factor " or unqualified, and the point has not been decided. The dicta in that and other cases in favour of an unqualified award rely largely on analogies from testamentary trustees, trustees in bankruptcy and liquidators. It is now settled that there is no general rule in the case of testamentary trustees.[99] A trustee in bankruptcy may consult the creditors and obtain an indemnity from them,[1] and the same consideration is used to support the practice of making unqualified awards against liquidators.[2] As was pointed out in *Barrie* v. *Barrie's Trustee*,[3] no such general test can be applied to testamentary trustees. It appears even less applicable to judicial factors, who

---

[93] *Condie* v. *McDonald* (1834) 13 S. 61 at p. 63; *Viscount of Oxford* v. *His Curators* (1684) M. 16305.

[94] *Ross* v. *Devine* (1878) 5 R. 1015.

[95] *Young* v. *Burgh of Darvel*, 1923 S.C. 745; Maclaren, *Expenses*, p. 40. In *Stewart* v. *Forbes* (1897) 24 R. 1112, all the judges, proceeding apparently on the award, assumed that the liability of the principal was " as trustee," and the decision depended on the interpretation of the bond of caution. No argument seems to have been founded on the fact that the decree for expenses against the principal was unqualified.

[96] *Craig* v. *Hogg* (1896) 24 R. 6 (seven judges). In view of this decision it is unnecessary to venture on an interpretation of the interlocutor in *Ferguson* v. *Murray* (1853) 16 D. 260. A factor may have no recourse against the estate: see next paragraph but one.

[97] *Craig* v. *Hogg* (*supra*) at pp. 19, 20, 24; *Anderson* v. *Anderson's Trustee* (1901) 4 F. 96 at pp. 102, 106.

[98] The rubric on this point is inaccurate. Lord McLaren adumbrated an intermediate position and Lord Moncreiff reserved his opinion. A somewhat different explanation of the opinions is given in *Kilmarnock Theatre Co.* v. *Buchanan*, 1911 S.C. 607 at p. 610.

[99] *Barrie* v. *Barrie's Trustee*, 1933 S.C. 132. The Lord Ordinary had found the pursuer entitled to expenses against the defender *qua* trustee only and found the defender entitled to expenses out of the estate, and the court was therefore dealing with both questions.

[1] *Cowie* v. *Muirden* (1893) 20 R. (H.L.) 81 at p. 88; *Drummond* (*Carse's Factor*) v. *Carse's Executors* (1881) 8 R. 449, Lord Justice-Clerk Moncreiff at p. 453.

[2] *Kilmarnock Theatre Co.* v. *Buchanan*, 1911 S.C. 607 at p. 610.

[3] 1933 S.C. 132 at pp. 139, 140, 146, 147.

are frequently appointed because the person beneficially interested in the estate is incapable of any legal act. The opposite view, *viz*. that as a rule the award against a judicial factor should be " *qua* factor," was supported on principle by Lord Fullerton. " If the party were not a lunatic he might have gone on with the action himself and the opposite party would have had no additional security for his expenses. . . . If we hold the curator who acts for him to be liable, we give the other party additional security: we just give him a cautioner for the expenses of the action." [4] The same point was made at greater length by Lord Young, with whom Lord Adam and Lord Kinnear concurred, in *Craig* v. *Hogg*,[5] and it is hardly met by Lord Trayner's observation [6] that the opponent would be prejudiced if he did not have recourse against the factor. The " prejudice " consists in the absence of a security which would have been the result of an accident. In *Barrie* v. *Barrie's Trustee* [7] Lord Hunter expressed the opinion that a person in the position of a paid trustee (which presumably includes a judicial factor) is as a general rule personally liable in expenses, and there are many dicta that a judicial factor is in this respect in a worse position than a testamentary trustee. This view, if correct, presents a dilemma to a factor bold enough or conscientious enough to accept office on a small estate with a claim for or against it, whose duty it is to consider only the interests of the estate.[8] Either he must litigate with the probability of an unqualified award of expenses against him in case of failure, or he must refuse to litigate to the possible injury of the estate, and face a possible debit in his accounts for the amount of the claim. An unqualified award was made against a factor whose conduct had been criticised by the Lord Ordinary.[9]

(2) The right of a factor to recover expenses from the estate cannot be determined in his favour in an action to which the beneficial owners are not parties,[10] but there seems to be no reason why the question should not be determined against him in their absence. The court may so determine by an award against a factor " personally " [11] or by a finding that he is not entitled to charge the expenses against the estate.[12] If the question has not been thus decided against the factor, it is open to those interested or to the accountant to raise it at an annual audit [13] or on the factor's petition for discharge.[14] A factor ought to obtain the accountant's appro-

---

[4] *Forbes* v. *Morrison* (1845) 7 D. 853 at p. 857.

[5] (1896) 24 R. 6, at pp. 14, 15, 17.

[6] *Ibid.*, at p. 23.

[7] 1933 S.C. 132, at p. 141.

[8] *Craig* v. *Hogg*, *supra*, at p. 17.

[9] *Paterson's Judicial Factor* v. *Paterson's Trustees* (1897) 24 R. 499.

[10] *Craig* v. *Hogg* (1896) 24 R. 6 at p. 20; *Paterson's Judicial Factor* v. *Paterson's Trustees* (1897) 24 R. 499 at p. 510.

[11] *Gorrie's Trustee* v. *Stiven's Executrix*, 1952 S.C. 1. See *Ross* v. *Devine* (1878) 5 R. 1015. Both were cases of unreasonable persistence in an action. See Maclaren, *Expenses*, pp. 171–181, on the ambiguity of the word " personally " in such an interlocutor.

[12] *Buckle* v. *Buckle's Curator Bonis* (1908) 15 S.L.T. 1002.

[13] *Accountant of Court* v. *Geddes* (1858) 20 D. 1174.

[14] *Rennie* v. *Morrison* (1849) 11 D. 457; *Drummond* v. *Carse's Executors* (1881) 8 R. 449 at p. 452.

val before entering into legal proceedings.[15] On the merits, a factor is entitled to take credit for all expenses, provided that he has acted reasonably and *bona fide* and has conducted the litigation properly,[16] even although they exhaust the estate before paying creditors.[17] A curator *bonis* was allowed credit for the expenses of recovering part of the lunatic's estate with which he had wrongly parted but only because the next-of-kin consented.[18] An award against a factor " *qua* factor " is a strong indication that he has acted properly.[19]

A factor requires special power to agree to pay his opponent's expenses from estate funds in any event.[20]

Res judicata

Although there appears to be no direct decision on either point it seems plain that, provided the subject matter and the *media concludendi* are the same, a decision for or against a judicial factor is *res judicata* in a question with any person representing the same position [21] and that a decision for or against such person is *res judicata* in question with the factor.[22] Any doubt on the matter [23] seems to be founded solely on an opinion attributed to Lord Mackenzie and to apply only to factors *loco absentis*. The Second Division were equally divided as to whether a factor *loco absentis* could competently continue an action raised by a factor who had been appointed by the *absens* and had died, and Lord Mackenzie was called in. He is reported to have said: " The great obstacle against admitting the powers of the factor to carry on actions at his own discretion is that he undoubtedly cannot bind the principal party as the mandatory would have done. The defender would not be safe by a decree of absolvitor, because the pursuer might disavow the proceedings of the factor." The court did not give effect to these views. It directed the Lord Ordinary to sist process so as to give the factor an opportunity (if so advised) of stating the reasons of necessity for insisting in the action.[24] Lord Mackenzie subsequently said that if he had been correctly reported he was wrong.[25] Where the court refused to appoint a factor *loco absentis* for the purpose of raising a reduction of a will their reason was that the *absens* might not want the will reduced.[26] It was never suggested that it was immaterial whether the factor obtained decree or

---

[15] Accountant's Notes, note 27 (*b*).
[16] Maclaren, *Expenses*, pp. 184, 228. See *Ross* v. *Devine* (1878) 5 R. 1015, where the factor was warned.
[17] *Drummond (Carse's Factor)* v. *Carse's Executors* (1881) 8 R. 449; *Stewart* v. *Forbes* (1897) 24 R. 1112 at p. 1120.
[18] *Accountant of Court* v. *Geddes* (1858) 20 D. 1174.
[19] *Barrie* v. *Barrie's Trustee*, 1933 S.C. 132 at p. 138.
[20] *Aikman* (1863) 1 M. 1140.
[21] *McCaig* v. *Maitland* (1887) 14 R. 295 at p. 297.
[22] See *Allen* v. *McCombie's Trs.*, 1909 S.C. 710 at pp. 715, 719; *Glasgow Shipowners' Association* v. *Clyde Navigation Trs.* (1885) 12 R. 695.
[23] *Irons on Judicial Factors*, p. 243; *Encyclopaedia of the Laws of Scotland*, VIII, p. 472.
[24] *Lumsdaine* v. *Balfour* (1827) 2 Fac.Dec. 472.
[25] *Kennedy* v. *M'Lean* (1851) 13 D. 705 at p. 710. The difficulty there arose from a doubt whether the *absens* was alive.
[26] *Watson* v. *Watson* (1864) 2 M. 1333.

not, and the opinions in *Kennedy* v. *M'Lean* [25] make it clear that a decree in an action properly raised and conducted by a factor *loco absentis*, provided the other conditions are fulfilled, is *res judicata* in a question with anyone claiming on behalf of the estate.

Compromise and Submission

A factor has power to compromise or submit all claims connected with the estate provided that the compromise or submission is not at variance with the terms or purposes of his appointment,[27] but this applies only to claims by a third party against the estate. A compromise between a factor on a trust estate and beneficiaries must be at variance with the trust since the beneficiaries or some of them receive either more or less than they are entitled to.[28] In that case the court stressed the importance of the opinion of the accountant, two of the judges using the word " approval." The claim must be connected with the estate. A decree arbitral was held not binding on the estate where the true issue was between the factor as an individual and the other party.[29]

[27] Trusts (Scotland) Act 1921, ss. 2, 4. For common law cases see *Anderson* (1855) 17 D. 596; *Anderson* (1857) 19 D. 329.

[28] *Tennent's Judicial Factor* v. *Tennent*, 1954 S.C. 215 at p. 226. On 29th June 1954 the Lord Ordinary, after considering on various assumptions of fact and law the probable result of a prolonged litigation, granted authority. A similar result was reached in *Telfer's Judicial Factor*, March 18, 1971 (unreported).

[29] *Aberdeen Town and County Bank* v. *Dean and Son* (1871) 9 M. 842.

CHAPTER XV

INVENTORY AND ANNUAL ACCOUNTS

(1) The Inventory

The factor, as soon as may be after obtaining a certified copy inter-locutor of his appointment and at latest within six months of reception of his bond of caution, must lodge with the accountant an inventory of the estate,[1] signed by him on every page.[2] Since this, when adjusted with the accountant and signed by him, forms " a clear rule of charge against the factor at the commencement of his office," [3] it must naturally show the estate as at the date of appointment, before the factor has intromitted.[4] The inventory is retained by the accountant.[5] Following the scheme of the Tutors and Curators Act 1672 and the Act of Sederunt of February 13, 1730, the inventory is divided into three parts, (1) list of funds, *i.e.* incor-poreal moveables, (2) moveable estate other than funds, *i.e.* corporeal moveables, and (3) rental, *i.e.* heritage, and in addition it requires a note of liferent and other interests and of the estimated amount of debts. The printed form and the Accountant's Notes [6] contain full instructions, and no question appears to have arisen in any reported case as to the form of the inventory. If any further property belonging to the estate is discovered the factor in his next annual account must report it to the accountant, who makes any necessary alteration in the inventory.[7] Failure in these duties renders the factor liable in penalties, but in all the reported cases where there was failure to lodge the inventory there was also failure to lodge accounts, and these are mentioned below under " Accounts." The penalties imposed on tutors and curators by the Tutors and Curators Act 1672 for failure to lodge inventories do not transmit against repre-sentatives,[8] but this does not apply to protect the representatives of judicial factors.[9]

The inventory is linked with the accounts by the requirement that the factor in his first annual account must charge himself with the items of the estate in the order in which they are given up in the inventory.[10]

---

[1] Pupils Protection Act 1849, s. 3, as amended by Act of Sederunt (Appointment of Judicial Factors, etc.) 1967, s. 2.

[2] Accountant's Notes, note 5.

[3] Pupils Protection Act 1849, s. 12.

[4] Note on Inventory Form.

[5] Pupils Protection Act 1849, s. 12.

[6] Note 5.

[7] Pupils Protection Act 1849, s. 3. See Accountant's Notes, note 9.

[8] *Mollison* v. *Murray* (1833) 12 S. 237; *Macturk* v. *Greig* (1830) 8 S. 995; *Graham* v. *Earl of Hopetoun* (1798) Mor. 5599. See *Rae* v. *Walker* (1877) 5 R. 34 at p. 36.

[9] *Kerr's Trustees* v. *Moody* (1850) 12 D. 1041.

[10] Note on printed form.

(2) The Accounts

Lodging and vouchers

On the bond of caution being received as sufficient the accountant assigns the day on which the factor is to close his first account, being not less than six months or more than eighteen months from the date of his intimation of receipt of the bond.[11] Thereafter the factor must close his account of charge and discharge once a year on a day fixed by the accountant and lodge it and the vouchers with the accountant within a month, but the accountant may on cause shown prorogate the time for lodging for three months.[12] Since the provisions as to the first account relate solely to the date of closing, the general provisions relative to annual accounts, *viz.* as to lodging, vouchers and possibly prorogation, are evidently intended to apply to it.[13] The Accountant's Notes [14] give full details as to the correct form of accounts and the information and vouchers required. Commission and expenses are dealt with below. It is the accountant's duty to see that accounts and vouchers are duly lodged.[15] At one time he made a practice of sending reminders or requisitions to dilatory factors,[16] but it would be unwise to rely on this now.[17] The statutory penalties for failure to lodge accounts timeously are fine, forfeiture of commission, suspension or removal from office, and payment of expenses.[18] The court now has a discretion in all cases. Until the Pupils Protection Act was applied to all factors,[19] factors not named in it were dealt with under the Act of Sederunt of February 13, 1730, and the minimum fine was half a year's commission.[20] Although these cases no longer apply, they may give a guide to the exercise of discretion, since some of them suggest that the court might have reduced the penalty if they had not been bound by the Act of Sederunt.[21]

The accountant's report

It is the accountant's duty to state the result of his audit in a short report and, if he has made any " corrections " in the account and is so required by the factor, to explain them and his reasons for making them.[22] But it has long [23] been the accountant's practice first to issue a draft report, which the factor is requested to revise and return within twenty-one

---

[11] Pupils Protection Act 1849, s. 11.
[12] *Ibid.* s. 4.
[13] This is assumed in the Accountant's Notes, notes 7 and 15.
[14] Notes 7–21 and Appendix, and note 22 (*b*) as to distinguishing between narrower range and wider-range investments.
[15] Pupils Protection Act 1849, s. 13. The accountant may report to the court immediately.
[16] See *Marshall* v. *Chisholm* (1901) 3 F. 642.
[17] 1947 S.L.T. (News) 55.
[18] Pupils Protection Act 1849, s. 6.
[19] Judicial Factors (Scotland) Act 1889.
[20] *Lowe* (1872) 11 M. 17.
[21] *Lowe* (1872) 11 M. 17 at p. 19; *Lambe* v. *Ritchie* (1837) 16 S. 219.
[22] Pupils Protection Act 1849, s. 13.
[23] *Accountant of Court* v. *Baird* (1858) 20 D. 1176.

days.[24] The accountant undertakes to deal with any objections " in accordance with the provisions of section 15 " of the Act of 1849, but this can only mean that he will give effect in his report to any objections to the draft report which he considers well founded.

The accountant's report is conclusive against the factor and his cautioner if written objections are not lodged by the factor within twenty days of its communication to the factor. But where a factor had charged no commission and the accountant had audited his annual accounts on that basis, the Lord Ordinary subsequently allowed commission for the whole period.[25] The court will on very special cause extend the time for lodging objections.[26] If objections are lodged and neither allowed nor departed from, the accountant must transmit the proceedings to the Lord Ordinary, who after hearing the factor or his agent and, if necessary, the accountant, may affirm, vary or reverse the audit and report, or may reserve any questions till the final audit. The Lord Ordinary's decision is not subject to review at the instance of the accountant, nor may a factor reclaim against a reservation. But if the decision is against the factor, he may bring the interlocutor under review, and the judgment of the court is not subject to appeal without leave. At the final audit any matter reserved may be opened up by the factor or his representatives or any succeeding factor or any person beneficially interested in the estate, and any matter decided may be opened up on cause shown.[27]

Section 17 appears to assume that any party beneficially interested in the estate may be heard at the audit. At least it entitles such party on cause shown to open up any account audited " in the absence of such party." The section applies to all audits, including annual audits. It provides that either at the termination of the factory or during its subsistence it shall be competent for any party beneficially interested in the estate or for any succeeding factor upon cause shown to open up the audit of all accounts audited in the absence of such party or succeeding factor and also all questions in the accounting which have either not been submitted for decision of the Lord Ordinary or have been reserved, and also all questions which have been decided merely as between the accountant and the factor or between the factor and some other beneficiary. Where a factor's appointment was recalled the Lord Ordinary at the instance of parties interested sustained objections to charges in his accounts which had apparently been allowed by the accountant at annual audits. His decision was reversed, but it was not suggested that he had acted incompetently.[28]

Commission and expenses of administration

It is the accountant's duty to " fix the amount of the factor's commission for the period embraced by the audit, according to what is just

[24] Accountant's Notes, note 23.
[25] *Graham's Curator Bonis* (O.H.) (1899) 6 S.L.T. 325.
[26] *Ross* (1856) 18 D. 795.
[27] Pupils Protection Act 1849, s. 15.
[28] *Sleigh* v. *Sleigh's Judicial Factor*, 1908 S.C. 1112.

in each particular case," [29] and the factor takes credit for it in the next annual account.[30] The amount of commission claimed may be indicated, with a note showing how it is arrived at, and when additional commission for distinctively special work is claimed a detailed note of the work should be supplied with an evaluation of each item.[31] The commission is in full of all work, professional or otherwise, done by the factor in connection with the estate. Accordingly, he is not entitled to fees for professional work done by himself or his firm, but only to outlays,[32] nor is he entitled to fees for meetings and trouble.[33] The usual amount mentioned *obiter* [34] or approved by the court in cases to which the Pupils Protection Act 1849 did not apply,[35] is 5 per cent. on revenue collected and 2 per cent. on capital realised, but it may in special circumstances be higher [36] or lower.[37]

The accountant has always held the view that the question of commission does not come under the " objections " mentioned in section 15 or, in other words, that his decision on commission cannot competently be brought under the review of the Lord Ordinary by the procedure laid down in section 15. The soundness of this view seems clear from the Act. Under section 13 the accountant is required to audit the factor's account and state the result of the audit in a short report. He is also required to fix the factor's commission for the period embraced by the audit. These are two separate duties, and it is only to the audit and the report stating its result that the factor has under section 15 a right to object. The accountant on one occasion, when the amount of the commission was the only question, did on the insistence of the factor transmit the proceedings to a Lord Ordinary for the purpose of obtaining judicial approval, or disapproval, of his view.[38] The result was inconclusive. According to the only note of the decision the Lord Ordinary " refused the appeal on the ground that the court could never go over all the accounts and weigh all the considerations known to the accountant. He held that the court could and would overturn the accountant's decision when it was evident that the accountant had failed to take into account all the relevant factors and as a consequence had offered flagrantly inadequate commission." The Lord Ordinary apparently did not consider the question of statutory construction at issue. But, even if the question of commission cannot be raised under section 15, the court would use its common law power to interfere, on a petition or note by the factor, if it were shown that the accountant had misused his powers.

---

[29] Pupils Protection Act 1849, s. 13.
[30] Accountant's Notes, note 18.
[31] Accountant's Notes, note 18.
[32] *Mitchell* v. *Burness* (1878) 5 R. 1124; *Sleigh* v. *Sleigh's Judicial Factor*, 1908 S.C. 1112 at p. 1118; *Lord Gray* (1856) 19 D. 1.
[33] *Kennedy* v. *Rutherglen* (1860) 22 D. 567.
[34] *Lord Gray* (1856) 19 D. 1 at p. 29.
[35] *Watt* (1866) 4 M. 772; *Hawkins* (1847) 9 D. 1484.
[36] *Wilson's Trustee* v. *Wilson's Creditors* (1863) 2 M. 9; *More* (1849) 11 D. 1495.
[37] *Lord Gray* (1856) 19 D. 1 at p. 29; *Sleigh* v. *Sleigh's Judicial Factor*, 1908 S.C. 1112 at p. 1113 (1 per cent.). [38] *Stewart's Judicial Factor* (1945) unreported.

The legal expenses in connection with the management of the estate are a proper charge, provided that the work has not been done by the factor or his firm,[39] but this rule does not apply to the proceedings leading up to the appointment.[40] The factor is not entitled to credit for fees paid to a solicitor for work which he himself could have done.[41] The law accounts must be submitted to the accountant, who transmits them to the auditor for taxation. The accountant can thus verify that the charges are for proper legal work. When the factor is a solicitor and he or his firm do legal work for the estate, the accountant may allow additional commission, in lieu of business charges, on due notice.[42] The ordinary expenses of administration fall on revenue, but the expenses of litigation,[43] of re-investment[44] and of obtaining special powers[45] are normally a charge against capital.

Income tax

A factor in whom the estate is vested is entitled to deduct the expenses of administration, but one who is administering for a ward is not.[46] A factor carrying on his ward's business was held not entitled to earned income relief on the profits on the ground that they were not derived by the ward from the carrying on by him of the business.[47] Any tax recoverable should be recovered each year.[48]

Personal profit from office

There is no doubt that if a factor trades with estate funds, the profits belong to the estate, and that he cannot charge professional fees against the estate. It is also settled that if he receives commission from a person dealing with the estate he must credit that to the estate.[49] On its facts the decision in *Sleigh* v. *Sleigh's Judicial Factor*[50] is not inconsistent with the rule as to professional fees. A factor, who was a member of a firm of solicitors, lent estate money on heritable security to clients of his firm, and in accordance with the usual practice the borrowers paid the fees to the firm. It was held, reversing the Lord Ordinary, that the factor was not bound to credit these to the estate. Gloag[51] appeared to doubt the decision, and Lord Moncrieff,[52] who regarded some of the dicta as unsound, pointed

---

[39] *Mitchell* v. *Burness* (1878) 5 R. 1124.
[40] *Watt* v. *Watt* (O.H.) 1909, 1 S.L.T. 103.
[41] *Wilson's Trustee* v. *Wilson's Creditors* (1863) 2 M. 9; *A.B.'s Curator Bonis*, 1927 S.C. 902 at p. 905; Accountant's Notes, note 27 (*a*).
[42] Accountant's Notes, note 13.
[43] *Baxter & Mitchell* v. *Wood* (1864) 2 M. 915; *Thomson* v. *Douglas* (1856) 18 D. 1240.
[44] *Smith* v. *Bennie* (1890) 18 R. 44; *Pearson* v. *Casamajor* (1840) 2 D. 1020.
[45] *Howden* v. *Simson* (1895) 23 R. 113.
[46] *Inland Revenue* v. *McMillan's Curator Bonis*, 1956 S.C. 142.
[47] *McDougall* v. *Inland Revenue*, 1919 S.C. 86.
[48] Accountant's Notes, note 32.
[49] *Sleigh* v. *Sleigh's Judicial Factor*, 1908 S.C. 1112 at p. 1118; *A.B.'s Curator Bonis* (O.H.) 1927 S.C. 902, affirming the Accountant. See Accountant's Notes, note 31.
[50] 1908 S.C. 1112.
[51] *Contract* (2nd ed.) 512.
[52] *A.B.'s Curator Bonis* (O.H.), 1927 S.C. 902.

out that it rested on the view that the factor and the borrowers were independent parties who happened to employ the same solicitors and that the borrowers in paying the fees were merely paying their own solicitors. On this explanation the decision leaves untouched the rule that a factor must communicate to the estate any profit (apart from his commission) which arises from his office.

Chapter XVI

ADMINISTRATION OF THE ESTATE

Cash balances

A factor is required to lodge money in his hands in one of the banks in Scotland established by Act of Parliament or Royal Charter in a separate account or on deposit in his own name as judicial factor.[1] The section provides two sanctions. First, if the factor keeps more than £50 in his hands for more than ten days,[2] he must be debited with interest at 20 per cent. on the excess for any time beyond the ten days. This provision was imperative,[3] but the accountant now has power to remit or modify the penalty.[4] At common law the court took the circumstances into account.[5] A factor might be treated like a trustee and held bound to credit the estate with the profits he had made by the use of the funds.[6] Secondly, unless the money has been kept in the factor's hands from innocent causes, he must be dismissed and has no right to commission. Where a curator *bonis* appointed in 1832 had acted in ignorance and had benefited his ward and lost himself, the court held innocent cause established,[7] but not where the factor had failed to lodge accounts and did not know what balance should be in his hands.[8] Every bank with which money has been deposited or lodged by any judicial factor, " whether on deposit-receipt or on account-current, or otherwise," must, once at least in every year, accumulate the interest with the principal sum so that both bear interest as principal. Any bank failing to do so is liable to account as if the money had been accumulated.[9] The Accountant of Court has power to require information from banks in connection with accounts opened by judicial factors.[10]

Estates for distribution

When a factor is appointed merely to ingather the estate and to distribute it to those entitled to it, and there is no " continuing administration," [11] *e.g.* a factor on an intestate estate, his duties are straightforward

---

[1] Pupils Protection Act 1849, s. 5.
[2] £25 in the sheriff court: C.A.S.L. VIII, 13.
[3] *Ballingall* (1853) 15 D. 711, where all interested, including the Accountant, wished to avoid the penalty; *Macdonald* v. *Macdonald* (1854) 16 D. 1023; *Maxwell's Trustees* v. *Jeffs* (1863) 24 D. 1181.
[4] Rules of Court 1965, r. 200 (*g*).
[5] *Blair* v. *Murray* (1843) 5 D. 1315; *Nairne* (1863) 1 M. 515; *Morrison* v. *Dryden* (1890) 17 R. 704, where the fault occurred and the petition was presented before the Judicial Factors Act 1889 applied the 1849 Act to all judicial factors.
[6] *Guthrie* v. *Fairweather* (1853) 16 D. 214, a case to which the Pupils Protection Act 1849 applied; *Cochrane* v. *Black* (1855) 17 D. 321; *Laird* v. *Laird* (1855) 17 D. 984.
[7] *Ballingall* (1853) 15 D. 711.
[8] *Macdonald* v. *Macdonald* (1854) 16 D. 1023.
[9] Pupils Protection Act 1849, s. 37.
[10] *Ibid.* s. 33.
[11] *Browning's Factor* (1905) 7 F. 1037 at p. 1042.

(subject to extrinsic questions of fact and law), and he has the powers necessary to carry them out. Accordingly, an application by a factor appointed to wind up a partnership estate for power to sell heritage was dismissed as unnecessary.[12] Such a factor probably fulfils his duty if, pending distribution, he places sums ingathered on deposit receipt.[13]

Continuing administration

The remainder of this chapter deals with factors whose duty is to hold the estate until the occurrence of some event, the attainment by a pupil of minority or by a minor of majority, the recovery or death of an *incapax*, or the arrival of the time for distribution of a trust estate. In some respects, particularly with regard to powers and to investment of the funds, the position of such a factor is identical with, or at least closely resembles, that of trustees, and decisions relating to trustees have been followed or distinguished by the court in cases involving judicial factors.[14] Some trustee cases are cited here, but for a full citation reference is made to the volume on Trusts, Trustees and Executors.

Duty to invest

A factor must, with due dispatch,[15] invest capital or surplus income in his hands. His duty to lodge money in bank has been mentioned, but he may not leave it on deposit receipt without some good reason, such as the difficulty of finding an investment suitable in the circumstances,[16] a possible need to pay out money,[16] or the small sum involved.[17] If he does leave funds on deposit receipt without good reason, he is liable for the difference between what they would have returned if properly invested and the interest actually received.[18]

Authorised investments

Until 1876 only three permissible forms of investment were recognised at common law, government stock, bank deposits and heritable securities.[19] In that year the court approved loans to local authorities secured on the rates, which it regarded as equally safe,[19] and later railway debentures, described by the accountant as " unexceptionable." [20]

The Trustee Investments Act 1961,[21] like the Trusts (Scotland) Amend-

---

12 *Cooper & Sons' Judicial Factor* (O.H.), 1931 S.L.T. 26, 1930 S.N. 134. See *Leslie's Judicial Factor*, 1925 S.C. 464 at p. 473.
13 *Clarke* v. *Clarke's Trustees*, 1925 S.C. 693 at pp. 701, 708, 713.
14 *Annan* v. *Annan's Curator Bonis* (1897) 24 R. 851 at p. 853, *sub nom. Hutton* v. *Annan* (1898) 25 R.(H.L.) 23 at p. 28; *Manners* v. *Strong's Judicial Factor* (1902) 4 F. 829, Lord Ordinary at p. 833.
15 Three months from the time the money becomes available was mentioned in *Nairne* (1863) 1 M. 515 at p. 516, but the range of suitable investments was then restricted. See interlocutor in *Sanders* v. *Sanders' Trustees* (1879) 7 R. 157 at p. 173.
16 *Manners* v. *Strong's Judicial Factor* (1902) 4 F. 829.
17 *Morrison* v. *Dryden* (1890) 17 R. 704.
18 *Melville* v. *Noble's Trustees* (1896) 24 R. 243.
19 *Grainger's Curator* (1876) 3 R. 479.
20 *Lloyd's Curator* (1877) 5 R. 289.
21 s. 1. See more fully volume on Trusts, and also Accountant's Notes, note 22 (*b*). In *Carmichael's Judicial Factor*, 1971 S.L.T. 336, it was taken for granted that the Act applies to judicial factors.

ment Act 1884 and the Trusts (Scotland) Act 1921, provides that a trustee
" may " invest in the securities described in the Act. In two cases to which
the 1884 Act applied the House of Lords and the Court of Session construed the word " may " as permissive and therefore, after deciding that
the investment in question was not permitted by the Act, went on to
hold that it was not justified at common law.[22] The detailed provisions
of the 1961 Act make it more difficult to read " may " as permissive, and
while the words " by virtue of the foregoing section " [23] shew that they
are not exhaustive, these words could be satisfied by the provisions as to
" special powers." [24] In any event, an investment which is not at least a
wider-range investment could hardly be justified at common law.

But the mere fact that an investment falls within a statutory class is
not enough. It must also be prudent.[25] A curator *bonis* in 1878 lent money
on heritable security, a form of investment which received statutory
sanction in 1884. In an action raised against him in 1890 he was held
liable for a loss on the ground that the loan was in the circumstances
imprudent.[26] It would, however, be difficult to say that a factor had acted
imprudently if he had acted under section 30 of the Trusts (Scotland) Act
1921 [27] with regard to a heritable security or under section 6 of the Trustee
Investments Act 1961 with regard to shares. Under the latter Act wider-
range investments appear to include shares with an uncalled liability. At
least they are not expressly excluded. Advice under section 6 that it is
proper to retain such shares may be a sufficient protection to a factor,
but it may be advisable to apply for special power. A factor was granted
leave to hold shares with an uncalled liability which he could get rid of only
by making a payment sufficient to exhaust most of the estate.[28]

It is the duty of the accountant to consider the investments and their
sufficiency [29] and, if he thinks proper, to require the factor to realise them.[30]
But the absence of such criticism is no defence to the factor.[31]

A factor on a trust estate has power, subject to the statutory condition,
to buy a suitable house for occupation by any of the beneficiaries.[32]
Otherwise special power is required to buy heritage.[33]

Usually a factor is not entitled to charge against the estate the expense
of changing from an unauthorised to an authorised investment. But

---

[22] *Hutton* v. *Annan* (1898) 25 R. (H.L.) 23 at pp. 24, 27, 28; *Cowan's Trustees* v. *Ferrie's
Curator Bonis* (1897) 24 R. 590 at p. 600.
[23] s. 2.
[24] s. 3.
[25] *Annan* v. *Annan's Curator Bonis* (1897) 24 R. 851 at p. 854, *sub nom. Hutton* v. *Annan*
(1898) 25 R.(H.L.) 23.
[26] *Crabbe* v. *Whyte* (1891) 18 R. 1065. In *Guild* v. *Glasgow Educational Endowments Board*
(1887) 14 R. 944, the Act of 1884 did not apply to the factor.
[27] See Trustee Investments Act 1961, s. 6 (7).
[28] *Browning's Factor* (1905) 7 F. 1037. The factor had no right by common law or statute
to hold ordinary shares. See also *Bontine's Curator* (1870) 8 M. 976.
[29] Pupils Protection Act 1849, s. 13.
[30] *Ibid.* s. 19. See *Grainger's Curator* (1876) 3 R. 479.
[31] *Hutton* v. *Annan* (1898) 25 R. (H.L.) 23.
[32] *Trusts (Scotland) Act* 1921, s. 4, as amended by Trusts (Scotland) Act 1961, s. 4. See
Bristow (O.H.) 1965 S.L.T. 225.
[33] *Gilray* (1876) 3 R. 619; *Watt* (1856) 18 D. 625.

where the factor on a trust estate had made the unauthorised investment with the approval of the liferenters for the purpose of increasing their income, the court indicated that the expense should be charged against income.[34]

Heritage: alienation

A judicial factor has power to sell, feu or dispone in security, provided that the act is not at variance with the purposes of his appointment,[35] and if the act is at variance he may apply for authority to do it,[36] possibly on terms approved by the accountant. A factor on a trust estate finds the purposes of his appointment in the trust deed.[37] The powers of other factors to sell or feu depend on the nature of the heritage and the purpose for which it is held. A factor does not require special authority to sell tenement property held as an investment,[38] or to feu land on a part of an estate dedicated to feuing.[39] On the other hand, a curator *bonis* would require authority to sell his ward's home or family estate.[38] In a doubtful case or to satisfy a purchaser it is proper to apply for authority, when the court may dismiss the application as unnecessary or, in a suitable case, grant it.[40] Whether a factor has power to dispone in security must depend on the purpose for which he proposes to use the borrowed money, and it is difficult to think of circumstances in which he would not be wise to apply for authority. But borrowing to pay off other debt might be an example.[41] A transaction at variance with the terms and conditions of the appointment cannot be reduced on that ground.[42]

Although heritage in Scotland forms part of an estate under administration abroad, *e.g.* by a receiver in England, a judicial factor must be appointed to administer it.[43] The factor is not entitled without leave of the court to send abroad the price received for heritage, and therefore if the receiver obtains authority to sell it, the factor will apply for authority to sell and to remit the proceeds of the sale to the receiver. At one time the court refused to allow the money to be sent abroad [43] unless it was required for the maintenance of the ward.[44] The practice now with

[34] *Morison* (1856) 19 D. 132.
[35] Trusts (Scotland) Act 1921, s. 4.
[36] *Ibid.*, s. 5. On these sections see also p. 77. The price is converted only if the sale is necessary: *Laurie's Trs.* v. *Stewart* (O.H.) 1952 S.L.T. (Notes) 20; *Dick* v. *Dick* (O.H.) 1925 S.L.T. 337.
[37] *Marquess of Lothian's Curator Bonis*, 1927 S.C. 579 at p. 584.
[38] *Cunningham's Tutrix* (O.H.) 1949 S.C. 275; *Leslie's Judicial Factor*, 1925 S.C. 464 at p. 473; *Public Trustee of New Zealand* (O.H.) 1921, 2 S.L.T. 240.
[39] *Marquess of Lothian's Curator Bonis*, 1927 S.C. 579.
[40] *Cunningham's Tutrix* (O.H.) 1949 S.C. 275; *Marquess of Lothian's Curator Bonis*, 1927 S.C. 579 at p. 585. In *Barclay*, 1962 S.C. 594, authority was thought necessary, although the house had been empty for a considerable time. See also *Brunton* (O.H.) 1928 S.N. 112, and *Forbes* (O.H.) 1922 S.L.T. 294, overruled in *Shearer's Tutor*, 1924 S.C. 445, but restored on the merits by Guardianship of Infants Act 1925, s. 10.
[41] See *Grant* (1889) 16 R. 365.
[42] Trusts (Scotland) Act 1961, s. 2. See *Barclay* (O.H.) 1962 S.C. 594, and p. 77.
[43] *Murray* v. *Baillie* (1849) 11 D. 710; *Allen* v. *Robertson* (1855) 18 D. 97. See, however, *Lamb* v. *Montgomerie* (1857) 19 D. 699, (1858) 20 D. 1323. See *Ogilvy* v. *Ogilvy's Trustees* (O.H.) 1927 S.L.T. 83, 1926 S.N. 166, where the authorities are reviewed.
[44] *The Public Trustee of New Zealand* (O.H.) 1921, 2 S.L.T. 240; *Robertson's Curator Bonis* (O.H.) 1921, 2 S.L.T. 242.

regard to England is to authorise the factor to remit the price to the receiver, provided that it is invested in name of the Accountant-General of the Supreme Court.[45] In the converse case, where the estate under the administration of a curator *bonis* includes real property in England, which he proposes to sell, the accountant, if the sale is necessary, *e.g.* to provide funds for the ward's maintenance, issues a certificate under seal certifying that special power would not be required in Scotland and authorising the factor to sell and to apply to the appropriate English court for any authority required. In other cases the factor must obtain authority to apply to the English court for power to sell.

Heritage: management

The general duties of a factor are to preserve the estate, to keep things going rather than to change, and to do nothing irretrievable unless in case of necessity.[46] The difficulty is to draw the line between preservation and change. Special power is required to rebuild [47] or add to [48] the mansion house. On the other hand, where a curator *bonis* applied for special power to repair farm buildings (to be let) and to instal a new drainage system into the mansion house the Lord Ordinary refused the application as unnecessary, contrary to the opinion of the Accountant of Court.[49] The grant of authority in some cases was accompanied by doubts as to whether the special power was necessary.[50] In one case authority to repair farm buildings was not even craved, except possibly by implication.[51] A factor requires special power to cut timber.[52]

A factor has power, subject to the statutory condition, to grant leases of any duration (including mineral leases).[53] This resolves the previous doubts as to whether a factor had power to grant urban leases,[54] but it still leaves unsettled the question as to whether he is entitled to grant a mineral lease of an unopened mine.[55] He also has power to accept a renunciation of a lease and to grant abatement or reduction of rent.[56] In the undernoted cases the court, at a time when special power was required, authorised a factor to accept a renunciation of a lease [57] or to grant an abatement of rent.[58] A factor is liable for interest on rents which

---

[45] *Forster's Curatory* (1968) unreported. The interlocutor in *Muir*, 1929 S.N. 113, was subsequently modified to meet this practice.
[46] *Macqueen* v. *Tod* (1899) 1 F. 1069 at p. 1075.
[47] *Semple* v. *Tennent* (1888) 15 R. 810.
[48] *Maitland* (1863) 1 M. 1104.
[49] *Pattison's Curator Bonis* (O.H.) (1895) 3 S.L.T. 110. See also *Aikman* (1863) 1 M. 639 (fifth head).
[50] *Bell* (1838) 1 D. 109; *Esson* (1856) 18 D. 676. The remark of the Lord Ordinary in *Moncreiff* (1864) 2 M. 1094, that a piece of ordinary and even necessary management would be authorised was *obiter*.
[51] *Robertson* (1855) 17 D. 1116.
[52] *Horsburgh's Curator Bonis* (O.H.) (1901) 9 S.L.T. 216; *Macqueen* v. *Tod* (1899) 1 F. 1069; *Thriepland* (1848) 10 D. 1234.   [53] Trusts (Scotland) Act 1921, ss. 4 and 5.
[54] *Tosh's Judicial Factor*, 1913 S.C. 242.   [55] *Campbell* v. *Wardlaw* (1883) 10 R. (H.L.) 65.
[56] Trusts (Scotland) Act 1921, ss. 4 and 5. See *Molleson* (1890) 17 R. 303.
[57] *Wink* (1851) 13 D. 952; *Milne* (1836) 14 S. 451.
[58] *Macgregor* (1837) 15 S. 1092; *White* (1849) 11 D. 1031 (a mineral lease). See also *Grant's Curator* (1880) 7 R. 1014.

he ought to have recovered after a year from the time when they ought to have been recovered.[59]

Where the heritage is part of an estate which is being administered abroad, the factor formerly required the leave of the court to remit the rents to the administrator. At one time he was authorised to send only as much as was necessary for maintenance of a ward,[60] but later the court did not adhere to this limitation.[61] More recently an application for authority to send rents to a receiver in England was dismissed as unnecessary,[62] and the matter is left to the factor's discretion, possibly with the accountant's concurrence.

Factor as tenant

Where the ward is,[63] or in the case of a trust estate the truster was,[64] tenant under a lease, the factor requires special power to renounce it. Should he adopt it, he is liable " as factor " [65] for the whole outstanding prestations, including arrears of rent.[66] But he does not adopt the lease merely by carrying it on for a short time until he has made up his mind.[67]

Carrying on business

A judicial factor has no power to carry on a business, and it has been doubted whether in view of the opinion in *Gilray* [68] the court can competently authorise him to do so.[69] But in *Gilray* [68] special powers were not craved, and in an earlier case the court indicated that it would have entertained an application by a factor *loco tutoris* for special power to continue trading with a sloop.[70] Authority was granted to carry on a farm until the next break in the lease where great loss would otherwise have occurred.[71] In both cases where power was refused the application was made not by the judicial factor, but in the petition for his appointment, though the reports do not suggest that this influenced the result.[72] This is a matter on which a factor would be wise to consult the accountant.

Maintenance of a ward

Since a judicial factor does not have custody of the ward, his duty

[59] *A.S.*, February 13, 1730, s. 1.
[60] *Murray* v. *Baillie* (1849) 11 D. 710.
[61] *Allen* v. *Robertson* (1855) 18 D. 97; *Laing* v. *Robertson* (1859) 21 D. 1011; *Public Trustee of New Zealand* (O.H.) 1921, 2 S.L.T. 240.
[62] *Gilchrist* (O.H.) 1950 S.L.T. (Notes) 42.
[63] *Warden* (1829) 7 S. 848.
[64] *Grahame* (1851) 14 D. 312.
[65] *i.e.* to the extent of the estate only: *Craig* v. *Hogg* (1896) 24 R. 6 at pp. 13, 19, 20, 25.
[66] *Dundas* v. *Morison* (1857) 20 D. 225; *Gibson* v. *Kirkland* (1833) 6 W. & S. 340 (where the interlocutor did not limit the liability).
[67] *Dundas* v. *Hood* (1853) 15 D. 752.
[68] (1872) 10 M. 715.
[69] *Drew* (O.H.), 1938 S.L.T. 435, 1938 S.N. 73. But see *McDougall* v. *Inland Revenue*, 1919 S.C. 86.
[70] *Macleod* (1856) 19 D. 133. In *Hamiltons* v. *Hamilton* (1834) 12 S. 924, a factor *loco tutoris*, who had in effect allowed the pupils' mother to trade with the estate, was not found liable for the ensuing loss.
[71] *Rutherford's Judicial Factor* (O.H.), 1931 S.L.T. 587, 1931 S.N. 98.
[72] *Drew* (O.H.), 1938 S.L.T. 435, 1938 S.N. 73; *Philip* (1827) 6 S. 103.

in regard to maintenance consists in making suitable payments from income to those in charge of the ward. It is therefore within his usual powers.[73] Many factors consult the accountant as to a suitable amount. Where the factor is unwilling to pay the whole sum claimed, the court has decided the proper amount.[74] An application by a father for a larger allowance for his pupil son was refused,[75] but the court *ex proprio motu* directed a curator *bonis* to increase the board paid for an *incapax* so as to add to his comfort.[76]

Although there is no definite decision, it seems clear that a factor is not entitled, without special power, to encroach on capital where the income of the estate is insufficient. A factor *loco tutoris* was granted power to borrow £250 and expend it on the pupil's maintenance.[77] This is a suitable method where the probable duration of the factory is known, but where it is uncertain, as in the case of an *incapax*, a frequent solution is an annuity. While this course is competent with special power at common law, it is specially provided for by statute. If a factor deems it proper for the comfort or welfare of his ward that the whole or part of the estate should be " sunk on annuity," he may submit the matter to the court with the opinion of the accountant, and the court may sanction the proposal.[78] Such a proceeding may disappoint the expectations of the ward's heirs, but the capital is still his and may be expended as his curator *bonis*, with the sanction of the court, thinks best for him.[79] The court accordingly gave its sanction where the interest on the capital was insufficient to maintain the lunatic.[80] But no special reason was given in *Towers*.[81] Factors *loco tutoris* have been authorised to buy annuities for the maintenance of pupils, the price to be paid on the pupils succeeding to entailed estates.[82] It has been judicially observed that if relatives undertook with sufficient security to pay an annuity higher than that obtainable from an insurance company, the court would not object.[83] There is however a practice, which has been judicially noted,[84] for factors to make advances from capital without special authority if they have the accountant's approval, which is given only for necessary or highly expedient specific purposes.

---

[73] In *Currie* (1904) 12 S.L.T. 30, the Lord Ordinary granted special power to a curator *bonis* to make payments for behoof of his ward, although the accountant reported that this was unnecessary, but it may have been because of the very large sums proposed. See also *Hamilton* (1842) 4 D. 627.

[74] *Grant* v. *Cameron* (1838) 16 S. 652 (1840) 2 D. 722; *Jackson* v. *Gourlay* (1836) 15 S. 313; *Hamilton* v. *Hamilton* (1835) 13 S. 452, an action by a mother against her pupil son and presumably his tutor, in which it is not clear whether the money was required for the pursuer and her daughter or for the son.

[75] *Scott* (1870) 8 S.L.R. 260. The son's estate was under the management of a judicial factor.

[76] *Myers* (1845) 7 D. 886.

[77] *McGruther* (1835) 13 S. 569.

[78] Pupils Protection Act 1849, s. 7.

[79] *Finlayson* v. *Kidd* (1836) 14 S. 219 at p. 220.

[80] *Paisley* (1857) 19 D. 653, where the court insisted on a Scottish insurance company; *McGilchrist* (1855) 17 D. 917; *Innes* (1846) 8 D. 1211 (a case at common law).

[81] (1848) 10 D. 720.

[82] *Earl of Buchan* (1837) 16 S. 238; *Miller* (1836) 15 S. 147.

[83] *Finlayson* v. *Kidd* (1836) 14 S. 219 at p. 220.

[84] *Rutherford's Judicial Factor* (O.H.), 1931 S.L.T. 587.

Allowances to third parties [85]

A judicial factor is justified in making such payments if either the third party has a right to support from the estate or the factor has obtained special power to make voluntary payments. These situations are thus entirely different in principle. In the first the factor is paying a debt; in the second he is making a gift with the approval of the court.

First, the right of support is an incident of the relationship of parent and child. Putting it broadly, a parent who can do so is bound to maintain a destitute child and set him up in life.[86] The obligation also exists between other ascendants and descendants, and an indigent person has a right to support from his ancestor's representatives, if *lucrati* by the succession, provided that he has not received a provision from the ancestor.[87] If such a claim is made against a factor, his proper course appears to be to concede it if he thinks it well founded,[88] and in one reported case the factor took this course.[89] If the factor rejects the claim, the proper method of enforcing it is by action, since it is an attempt to enforce a right.[90] This principle was followed for a time,[91] but abandoned, possibly for reasons to be suggested. The claim is an equitable one and may be met by an equitable answer.[92] A claim by a factor *loco tutoris* against the curator *bonis* of the pupil's paternal uncle was rejected on the ground that the pupil's father had succeeded to half the grandfather's estate.[93] Authority to make a payment to a ward's sister was refused, although his funds came from their father, possibly partly on the ground that she had received a provision.[94]

Since a wife has a right to support from her husband, the accountant was of opinion that special power to a curator *bonis* to make payments to his ward's wife was unnecessary, but the Lord Ordinary granted it, possibly because of the large sums involved.[95]

Secondly, factors have been authorised to make payments to persons with no legal right. At first curators *bonis* were empowered to continue voluntary payments which their wards had been making while *capaces*,[96]

---

[85] The right of a factor on a trust estate to exercise a power conferred on the trustees to make advances to beneficiaries is mentioned in Chap. VI.

[86] Bell, Prin. (10th ed.) paras. 1629–1634; *Graham* (1865) 3 M. 695. In *Hamilton* (1842) 4 D. 627, special power was granted probably unnecessarily.

[87] *Hutchison* v. *Hutchison's Trustees*, 1951 S.C. 108; *Aitkenhead* v. *Aitkenhead* (1852) 14 D. 584.

[88] The accountant's opinion to this effect was ignored in *Howe* (1859) 21 D. 486. See also the accountant's opinion in *Rutherford's Judicial Factor* (O.H.) 1931 S.L.T. 567, 1931 S.N. 98.

[89] *Blackwood* (O.H.) (1890) 17 R. 1093 (narrative).

[90] *Court* (1848) 10 D. 822; *Aitkenhead* v. *Aitkenhead* (1852) 14 D. 584 (narrative); *Hamilton's Tutors*, 1924 S.C. 364, Lord Anderson at p. 370.

[91] *Stuart* v. *Court* (1848) 10 D. 1275; *A* v. *B* (1858) 20 D. 778.

[92] *Beaton* v. *Beaton's Trustees*, 1935 S.C. 187 at pp. 195, 198.

[93] *Stuart* v. *Court* (1848) 10 D. 1275.

[94] *Robertson* (1853) 25 Sc.Jur. 554, commented on in *Hamilton's Tutors*, 1924 S.C. 364 at p. 369. *Balfour* (1889) 26 S.L.R. 268, may rest on that ground.

[95] *Currie* (1904) 12 S.L.T. 30.

[96] *Gardner* (1882) 20 S.L.R. 165; *Bowers* v. *Pringle Pattison's Curator Bonis* (1892) 19 R. 941 (narrative); *A.B.* (O.H.) (1894) 2 S.L.T. 311.

and this practice has continued.[97] It appears to rest on the principle that the court is empowering the factor to do what it is satisfied the ward would have done if he had remained *capax*, and this principle was expressly applied where the occasion for the payment arose after the ward became *incapax*.[98] It was probably on this ground that a curator *bonis* was authorised to pay an allowance for his ward's daughter after her marriage,[1] and its extension to tutors, and presumably factors *loco tutoris*, may be justified on the ground that the pupil, particularly in view of her pre-decessors' practice, would have made the payment if she had been old enough to understand, though this was not specifically stated in the opinions.[2] The decisions in *Gordon's Curator Bonis*[3] and *Hamilton's Trustees*[4] shake the authority of *Dunbar*,[5] where it was known that the *incapax* wished the payment to be made. The court refused to increase the amount which a curator *bonis* had been authorised, three years previously, to pay to indigent relatives of the ward, who averred that with advancing years their necessities had increased.[6] Whether such an increase might be authorised in view of the fall in the value of money [7] has not been considered in any reported case. There must, in any event, be ample funds in excess of what is required for the ward, and the proposed recipient must be in need.[8]

Although these justifications for making allowances are distinct, the first depending on a legal obligation and the second at best on a moral, they may both apply to the same situation. A father, as a general rule, has both a legal and a moral duty to support his destitute son. Further, it is certainly easier for the factor to put the facts before the court in a petition for special powers and leave the decision to it than either to take the responsibility of admitting a right to support or to refuse a claim and possibly find himself defender in an action or respondent in a petition. In these circumstances the distinction of principle has tended to be obs-cured, particularly since the court has entertained petitions for the enforce-ment of rights. A curator *bonis* was granted power to make payments to his ward's children, who had a right to support, partly because of the

---

[97] *Currie* (O.H.) (1904) 12 S.L.T. 30, where a curator *bonis* was authorised to continue payments to charities which the ward had supported; *Robertson's Curator Bonis* (1920) where payments were authorised to two nieces whom the ward had brought up: *Encyclopaedia of the Laws of Scotland*, VIII, p. 483.

[98] *Gordon's Curator Bonis* (1902) 4 F. 577.

[1] *Blackwood* (O.H.) (1890) 17 R. 1093. No opinion was delivered.

[2] *Hamilton's Tutors*, 1924 S.C. 364, where the authorities were reviewed; *Boyle* (1855) 17 D. 790, where this consideration may be implied; *Gardiner* v. *Montgomery* (1833) 11 S. 325, where the Lord Ordinary was favourable, but the remedy sought was incom-petent.

[3] (1902) 4 F. 577.

[4] 1924 S.C. 364.

[5] (1876) 3 R. 554. The curator *bonis* could not lawfully pay without special power, the brother having had a provision from their father and therefore having no right to main-tenance.

[6] *Bowers* v. *Pringle Pattison's Curator Bonis* (1892) 19 R. 941.

[7] *Kelly* v. *Glasgow Corporation*, 1951 S.C. (H.L.) 15.

[8] *Hamilton's Tutors*, 1924 S.C. 364 at p. 371.

presumed intention of the ward.[9] In a similar case the ward's intention was founded on,[10] but that decision was later regarded as based on the right of support.[11]

The court has granted petitions by third parties craving it to " ordain " or " direct " a factor to make payments to them,[12] and it has refused one on the merits.[13] This practice was criticised by Lord President Inglis. A testator left an annuity of £50 to his daughter with power to his trustees to increase it. A judicial factor was appointed on the estate, and the daughter presented a petition praying the court " to grant and award " to her " a free yearly annuity of £350." This was opposed by the petitioner's daughter and by the judicial factor, and in July 1867 it was dismissed as incompetent. The Lord President drew a distinction between an incidental proceeding in a factory and an independent proceeding, though he did not elaborate the distinction, and held that the petition was incompetent on either view. On the second alternative it was unprecedented, being a petition for a decree for an annuity. On the first the petitioner ought to have gone to the factor, and " if he should improperly refuse to apply to the court for authority, there is nothing to prevent a party . . . asking the interposition of the court." [14] In March 1869 the daughter did ask " the interposition of the court " by presenting a petition " asking an increased annuity," [15] and the Lord Ordinary " authorised " the factor [16] to pay an additional £150. In a reclaiming note by another party the court superseded further consideration in the meantime in order that the factor might make an application if so advised. On a petition by the factor he was authorised in November 1869 to pay an increased annuity. This prevented clarification. The fact that the court did not dismiss the March petition must mean that it differed from the 1867 petition, presumably because it craved authority only, and that, if the factor had not petitioned, consideration of it would have been resumed. If the factor's refusal had been found " improper," the court would presumably have granted the authority craved, and the prospect of removal for contumacy would have compelled the factor to exercise it, or it might, as the Lord President hinted,[17] have made some order on him. When, however, two ladies, to whom a curator *bonis* was paying an annuity under special power, presented a petition praying that the annuity " should be increased," [18]

---

[9] *Howe* (1859) 21 D. 486. See also *Russell* (1850) 12 D. 913.
[10] *Maconochie* (1857) 19 D. 366.
[11] *Graham* (1865) 3 M. 695, especially at p. 698.
[12] *Grant* v. *Cameron* (1838) 16 S. 652 (where the word " ordain " evidently required justification) (1840) 2 D. 722; *Marshall* v. *Gourlay* (1836) 15 S. 313; *Hope* (1858) 20 D. 390. *Hamilton* v. *Hamilton* (1835) 13 S. 452 was an action. In all these cases the proposed beneficiaries, or most of them, had a right to maintenance.
[13] *Graham* (1865) 3 M. 695.
[14] *Mackay* v. *Ewing* (1867) 5 M. 1004.
[15] The reporter's words: *Allan* v. *Mackay* (1869) 8 M. 139 at p. 140.
[16] " Petitioner " in the report must be a mistake.
[17] (1867) 5 M. at p. 1007.
[18] The reporter's words: *Bowers* v. *Pringle Pattison's Curator Bonis* (1892) 19 R. 941.

the court said nothing about approaching the curator *bonis*.[19] He left the matter in the hands of the court, who dismissed the petition on the ground that to grant it would create a bad precedent. This apparently entitles a judicial factor to stand aside and leave it to the third party to initiate the matter and to the court to decide it. In any event he would be wise to consult the accountant in any doubtful case.

Election

Until the decision in *Skinner's Curator Bonis* [20] the rule, illustrated entirely in cases of curators *bonis* to *incapaces*, was that, except in cases of necessity, the curator *bonis* was not entitled to elect, but must leave the right to the *incapax*, if he recovered, or to his representatives, if he did not, and that this right was not lost because the curator *bonis* in the meantime received payment of the testamentary provisions. But the curator *bonis* was bound to elect to take legal rights if this was necessary for the maintenance of the ward, and, like an individual,[21] he might be compelled to elect if delay was prejudicial to other persons interested in the estate, *e.g.* by delaying distribution. All this was settled by a tract of decision.[22] In none of these cases was there any suggestion that the curator *bonis* required special power. If he did require it, the first question of law in *McCall's Trustees* ought to have been answered in the negative and the eight pages of opinions in *Morison's Curator Bonis* could have been reduced to as many lines, since in the former it was not stated and in the latter it was not averred that the curator *bonis* had obtained special power.[23] Whether the question was raised by action, special case, multiplepoinding or, as in *Hope*, incidentally, the court required to decide parties' rights when the case began,[24] and references in opinions to " authorising," " allowing " and " the discretion of the court " cannot be taken literally.

In *Skinner's Curator Bonis*,[25] where third parties were entitled to compel election, a curator *bonis* applied for authority to accept the testamentary provisions. The Lord Ordinary expressed the view that the application was unnecessary, because the curator *bonis* had power to elect, and incompetent, because it craved power to elect in a particular way, and reported the case. The Division remitted to him to grant the prayer. There was no contradictor, a point apparently overlooked by Lord McLaren when he founded on agreement. Lords Adam and Kinnear seem to have

---

[19] *Mackay* v. *Ewing* (1867) 5 M. 1004, and *Allan* v. *Mackay* (1869) 8 M. 139, were not cited.
[20] (1903) 5 F. 914.
[21] *Watson's Trustees* v. *Watson*, 1910 S.C. 975.
[22] *Turnbull* v. *Cowan* (1848) 6 Bell's App. 222 (interlocutor); *Morison's Curator Bonis* v. *Morison's Trustees* (1880) 8 R. 205; *McCall's Trustee* v. *McCall's Curator Bonis* (1901) 3 F. 1065; *Nisbet's Trustees* v. *Nisbet* (1868) 6 M. 567; *Hope* (1858) 20 D. 390. See also *Paterson* v. *Moncrieff* (1866) 4 M. 706 at p. 709, and *Macadam's Executor* v. *Souters* (1904) 7 F. 179, where a curator *bonis* had, in 1896, claimed legal rights without special power, and no adverse comment was made.
[23] Session Papers.
[24] *Welsh* v. *Fife Coal Co.*, 1926 S.C. 807, Lord Sands at p. 811.
[25] (1903) 5 F. 914.

been misled by the inaccurate rubric in *Turnbull* v. *Cowan*,[26] which, while stating correctly the decision that it is for the court to say whether election must be made, contains the words " and [the election] will be exercised for him [the curator *bonis*] by the court." Since the decision was that the curator *bonis* was not bound to elect, these words represent an *obiter* opinion, which was not argued for by any party, and was based on English law,[27] extracted from a somewhat obscure passage in the Lord Chancellor's speech and certainly not concurred in by Lord Campbell.

The practice of the court, as stated by the accountant, accepted by the Lord Ordinary and based on *Skinner's Curator Bonis*, now is to grant authority to a curator *bonis* to elect, but only when there is urgent necessity for it, *i.e.* where the interests of the ward or of third parties demand that such election be made.[28] This implies that special authority is required and that what was previously decided by action or special case is now decided in a petition or note. In the latest reported case, where election was necessary, the Lord Ordinary was asked to decide how the election should be made, and did so.[29] This decision is now followed in practice, except where the factor proposes to make the obvious choice, *e.g.* to claim *jus relictae* for a wife who has been excluded, or practically excluded, from her husband's will. But if the factor proposes to make the less obvious choice, *e.g.* to accept an illusory or token provision, special power is applied for. This was the position in *Burns' Curator Bonis* v. *Burns' Trustees*,[30] where the Lord Ordinary gave effect to what would probably have been the wishes of the *incapax*, thus applying a test formerly applied by the curator *bonis*.[31]

It is very doubtful whether in view of the now established practice the court would reconsider *Skinner's Curator Bonis*.[32] Indeed it is not likely to have an opportunity to do so. The new practice is advantageous to factors, since it relieves them of a former responsibility. Apart from that personal consideration, a factor would not be justified in incurring in addition to the expense of a note for special powers that of a reclaiming motion and a hearing before Seven Judges, even if it were competent for him to reclaim against an interlocutor granting him the powers for which he had asked, nor is a factor likely to elect without special powers in a doubtful case, hoping that after three hearings a court of Seven Judges would overrule *Skinner's Curator Bonis* and hold that he had power.

The new practice would seem to be applicable to any judicial factor, but some doubt is cast on this by a case where the factor on an intestate

---

[26] (1848) 6 Bell's App. 222.
[27] See *Lamb* (1868) 20 D. 1323, where the Court of Chancery elected for an infant, and *Glasgow Corporation* v. *Central Land Board*, 1956 S.C. (H.L.) 1 at pp. 10, 13 and 20, for comments on the authority of House of Lords decisions based on English law.
[28] *Mitchell*, 1939 S.L.T. 91, 1939 S.N. 23, where the crave was refused on the ground that there was no necessity to elect.
[29] *Burns' Curator Bonis* v. *Burns' Trustees* (O.H.) 1961 S.L.T. 166.
[30] (O.H.) 1961 S.L.T. 166.
[31] *Morison's Curator Bonis* v. *Morison's Trustees* (1880) 8 R. 205 at p. 213.
[32] (1903) 5 F. 914.

estate sued for the deceased's legal rights, apparently without obtaining special power.[33]

Collation

The right of the heir at law to share in the moveable estate with the other next of kin on condition of collating the heritage is now of less importance. If the whole estate is intestate, it devolves according to the statutory rules without distinction between heritable and moveable property.[34] Under the previous law an heir at law who claimed a share in the moveable succession was bound to collate not only heritage to which he succeeded as heir, but also heritage he had received from the predecessor as a gift, whether by way of testamentary settlement or by deed *inter vivos*.[35] As the Act [34] affects only intestate estate, collation of heritage acquired as a gift would be a gratuitous alienation clearly beyond the powers of a judicial factor. It is doubtful whether under the old law special power to collate was necessary.[36]

---

[33] *Lawson (Neave's Judicial Factor)* v. *Cook (Neave's Trustees)* (O.H.) 1928 S.L.T. 411, 1928 S.N. 60.

[34] Succession (Scotland) Act 1961, s. 1.

[35] McLaren, *Wills and Succession* (3rd ed.) I, 152; *Anstruther* v. *Anstruther* (1836) 14 S. 272 at pp. 282, 302.

[36] *Robertson* (1841) 3 D. 345; *Mitchell* (1847) 10 D. 148, commented on in *Skinner's Curator Bonis* (1903) 5 F. 914 at p. 917.

CHAPTER XVII

EXONERATION AND DISCHARGE[1]

Introductory

The only statutory provision [2] empowers a factor at the termination of his office to present a petition for discharge, but this is not exhaustive. The petition may be at the instance of the factor's representatives,[3] a ward,[4] a beneficiary,[5] the owner of the estate,[6] or a trustee on the sequestrated estate of a deceased debtor.[7] Where the factor is not the petitioner and is alive, he must be called as a respondent, and in any event intimation must be made to all interested parties.

Should the estate be small and the factor willing to dispense with judicial discharge the accountant, on being satisfied that the estate has been fully accounted for, will report the facts to the court with a view to writing the case off, but delivery of the bond of caution will not be made.[8] This procedure is followed in practice in larger estates. For example, a curator *bonis* who on the ward's death becomes executor may be willing to dispense with a judicial discharge. The practice of granting warrant for delivery of the bond of caution following a private discharge is obsolete.[9]

Termination of Appointment

Crave for termination

The crave for exoneration must be preceded by a crave for recall of the appointment, or removal of the factor, unless the office has been terminated in earlier proceedings [10] or by the occurrence of an indisputable event.[11] The *Styles* recommend no crave for recall on the death of the ward,[12] where a minor has attained majority [13] and where a trust estate has been wound up.[14] On the other hand, the crave is necessary

---

[1] Special provisions govern the discharge of a judicial factor under s. 163 of the Bankruptcy (Scotland) Act 1913.
[2] Pupils Protection Act 1849, s. 34. The Lord Ordinary now has jurisdiction, and the provision as to finality does not apply to his interlocutors.
[3] *Rollo* (1852) 14 D. 990.
[4] *Semple* v. *Tennent* (1888) 15 R. 810.
[5] *Manners* v. *Strong's Judical Factor* (1902) 4 F. 829.
[6] *Livingstone* (1857) 19 D. 280, explaining *Williamson* (1857) 19 D. 99.
[7] *Borthwick* (1862) 1 M. 104.
[8] Accountant's Notes, note 33.
[9] *Aitken* (1893) 21 R. 62.
[10] *Doud* v. *Simpson* (1847) 9 D. 511.
[11] See *Kyle* (1862) 24 D. 1083 at p. 1085.
[12] *Encyclopaedia of Scottish Legal Styles*, Vol. V, Form 350.
[13] *Ibid.* Vol. VI, Form 89.
[14] *Ibid.* Vol. VI, Form 93.

where the fact may be disputable, *e.g.* whether an *incapax* has recovered,[15] or whether the factor's conduct has been such that he ought no longer to retain his office,[16] and where he wishes to resign.[17] While there is no reported application for exoneration where the absence of the preliminary crave has created difficulty, it is wiser to insert it in case of doubt. The danger of not applying for recall at the earliest possible date is illustrated by the undernoted case.[18]

Irregular appointment

Where there has been irregularity in the proceedings for appointment the practice has not been uniform. Failure to intimate to a pupil's agnates was held sufficient of itself to require the recall of the appointment of a factor *loco tutoris*.[19] On the other hand, where there had not been intimation to the proper parties, the court entered upon the merits and recalled a sequestration of teinds and the appointment of a factor thereon [20] and the appointment of a curator *bonis* [21] on the ground that if the objections now stated had been before them originally they would have refused to appoint. In the latest case the Lord Ordinary proceeded on both grounds.[22]

Factory at an end

A factory comes to an end when its purpose has been fulfilled, a matter dealt with, where necessary, in connection with particular types of factor. It also comes to an end on sequestration of the estate and confirmation of a trustee under the Bankruptcy Act.[23] It has never been considered whether in any of these circumstances it is necessary to crave recall of the factory as well as recall of the appointment, and the practice has not been uniform. The court has recalled the appointment [24] and both curatory and appointment.[25] The interlocutor in *Fisher* v. *Tod*,[26] if correctly reported, was wrong, since the factory was not at an end. The *Styles* are inconsistent, suggesting in one place [27] recall of the curatory only and in another recall of curatory and appointment.[28] It would appear in this state of uncertainty to do no harm to crave recall of both factory and appointment. Where the estate has been sequestrated it is necessary also

---

[15] *Ibid.* Vol. V, Form 352; *Tweedie* (1886) 14 R. 212.
[16] *Nairne* (1862) 24 D. 1086.
[17] *Kyle* (1862) 24 D. 1083 at p. 1085; *Halliday's Curator Bonis*, 1912 S.C. 509.
[18] *Gorman's Factor* (O.H.) (1907) 15 S.L.T. 645.
[19] *Fowlds* v. *Hodges* (1836) 15 S. 244.
[20] *Wood* v. *Mackintosh* (1862) 24 D. 563.
[21] *Gordon* v. *Gunn* (1832) 11 S. 235.
[22] *Lawson* (O.H.) (1894) 2 S.L.T. 308. See also *Turnbull* v. *Ross's Judicial Factor* (O.H.) 1916 2 S.L.T. 249.
[23] *Newall's Trustees* v. *Aitchison* (1840) 2 D. 1108; *Arthur* (O.H.) (1903) 10 S.L.T. 550; *Borthwick* (1862) 1 M. 104; *Mitchell* v. *Scott* (1881) 8 R. 875 at pp. 876, 878.
[24] *Tweedie* (1886) 14 R. 212; *Sawyer* v. *Sloan* (1875) 3 R. 371; *A. B.* v. *C. B.* (O.H.) 1929 S.L.T. 517, 1929 S.N. 85.
[25] *Lawson* (1863) 2 M. 355; *Drummond* (1858) 20 D. 1101.
[26] (1865) 3 M. 889.
[27] Vol. VI, Form 95.
[28] Vol. V, Form 352.

to crave recall of the sequestration.[29] Otherwise no one would have a title to administer.

Factory continuing

At one time it was doubted whether a factor was entitled to resign except for some cause outwith his control, such as ill health,[30] but it is now settled that he may. Since resignation, at least if it is voluntary, is for the benefit of the factor, not of the estate, it might have been expected that the expenses of discharge and the new appointment would as matter of principle fall on the factor, but where the court did impose such expenses on a factor it treated the question as one not of principle, but of degree, dependent largely on the size of the estate and the length of the factor's service.[31] In a subsequent case where the estate was larger and the factor's term of service somewhat longer the expenses were allowed out of the estate.[32] On the death of a factor his representatives may apply for exoneration and discharge,[33] but it is probably not necessary to crave recall of the appointment. Any person interested in the estate [34] or in the well-being of a ward,[35] who is dissatisfied with the factor's conduct, may apply for his removal from office or the recall of his appointment. The old procedural distinction between removal and recall no longer exists.[36] In all these cases the petition ought to contain a crave for the appointment of a successor, since the expenses of two petitions are not likely to be allowed out of the estate.[37] A factor may be removed on a report by the accountant.[38] It seems contrary to principle to appoint a new factor, even *ad interim*, without first removing the factor in office, but no comment was made on this procedure in the Inner House.[36]

Effect of termination of office

A factor's powers, except *quoad* acts necessary for denuding, cease on termination of his office. A curator *bonis* cannot sell heritage after his ward's death,[39] and his title to sue ceases on service of a curator-at-law.[40] But even if his appointment has been expressly terminated, his liability to account continues until he has divested himself of the estate by trans-

---

[29] *Fisher* v. *Edgar* (1894) 21 R. 1076; *Shedden* (1867) 5 M. 955; *Hunter* v. *Home* (1834) 12 S. 406. It has been held that a factor has no title to crave recall of sequestration: *Robertson* v. *Grahame* (1852) 14 D. 971, a case to which the Pupils Protection Act 1849 did not apply.

[30] *McEwan* (1857) 19 D. 936.

[31] *Halliday's Curator Bonis*, 1912 S.C. 509.

[32] *Kinloch's Curator Bonis* (1956) unreported.

[33] *Rollo* (1852) 14 D. 990.

[34] *Walker* v. *Buchanan* (1888) 15 R. 1102.

[35] *Marshall* v. *Chisholm* (1901) 3 F. 642, when the factor was removed and found liable in the petitioner's expenses.

[36] *Souter* v. *Finlay* (1890) 18 R. 86.

[37] *Dalziel* (O.H.) (1898) 5 S.L.T. 255.

[38] Pupils Protection Act 1849, ss. 6, 20. *Jaffray* (1851) 14 D. 292.

[39] *Duff* v. *Gorrie* (1849) 11 D. 1054. See *Ross* v. *Lockhart's Trustees* (1829) 3 W. & Sh. 481 (tutors after pupils attained minority).

[40] *Young* v. *Rose* (1839) 1 D. 1242.

ferring it to those entitled to it or by consignation.[41] A factor as an individual has a title to sue a person whose illegal acts have caused him expense in carrying out the duties of his office.[42]

Exoneration

The crave

Since exoneration cannot be granted until the estate has been conveyed to those entitled to it, or consigned, the crave varies according to circumstances. If the petition is at the instance of the factor and he has already conveyed the estate, he narrates the conveyance, produces the receipt and discharge and craves exoneration,[43] or he may have made over the bulk of the estate, retaining a balance to meet expenses and undertaking to pay over any surplus and produce a receipt.[44] On the other hand, if he has not yet divested himself of the estate he craves exoneration on payment of any balance due by him.[45] In all these cases he craves the court to find him entitled to the expenses of the petition out of the estate, which involves that he must retain sufficient to meet these.

Objections

The Act requires the petitioner to call all persons interested in the estate, so far as known to him, and they and any other persons showing right and interest may appear as parties.[46] Although the Act mentions only petitions by a factor, the provision is equally applicable where the petition is presented by another person. The cautioners should be called.[47] Where exoneration is required because the factor has died or resigned or been removed, his successor as factor is interested in the estate, and it has been held that in these circumstances the successor has the sole title to object to exoneration. A curator *bonis* was removed on a petition by the heir of the *incapax* and a new appointment made, and the heir was held to have no title to oppose the exoneration of the removed curator *bonis*, his title having shifted to the successor.[48] But while this decision appears justified in principle, its *ratio* cannot stand with an earlier case, where the person on whose application a factor had been appointed in succession to the former factor was held entitled to object to the former factor's accounts.[49] It is true that in *Ewing* [49] the reasoning is not very convincing and that the petitioner had a vested interest in the estate, whereas in *Port* [50] he apparently had not. But this is irrelevant if the sole title was in the new

---

[41] *Jaffray* (1851) 14 D. 292; *Duncan* (1851) 14 D. 313.
[42] *Paul* v. *McIntosh* (1841) 3 D. 1145.
[43] *Encyclopaedia of Scottish Legal Styles*, VI, Form 89.
[44] *Ibid.* Form 93.
[45] *Ibid.* Form 88.
[46] Pupils Protection Act 1849, s. 34.
[47] *Pringle* v. *Tate* (1832) 11 S. 47; *Adamson* (1848) 10 D. 684. The *Styles* provide for this.
[48] *Port's Curator Bonis* (O.H.) (1901) 9 S.L.T. 271, sequel to *Marshall* v. *Chisholm* (1901) 3 F. 642.
[49] *Ewing* v. *Barclay* (1864) 3 M. 127.
[50] (O.H.) (1901) 9 S.L.T. 271.

factor. It would appear to be in the interests of the new factor that any person interested should be allowed to state objections to the exoneration of the old. Otherwise he may find that his own exoneration is opposed on the ground that he had failed properly to call his predecessor to account,[51] in other words failed in his duty to recover the estate.

The purpose of objections is not to prevent the discharge of the factor, but to obtain an alteration of the terms on which discharge is craved on one or both of two grounds. The first is that the factor has not accounted for, or is not prepared to account for, the proper amount of the estate, and objections on this ground will fall naturally into the form of objections to accounts lodged in an action of accounting, *viz.* averments to show why a particular credit ought to be deleted or reduced, or a particular debit inserted or, if it already appears, increased.[52] Such objections raise questions as to the recovery and administration of the estate and may require investigation by proof or by remit to the Accountant, or both.[53] It is competent in such an investigation on cause shown to open up the annual audit of the factor's accounts.[54] Where one only of several beneficiaries is to raise such an objection a convenient practice is for the factor before applying for his discharge to present a note craving authority to consign with the Accountant the share of that beneficiary as ascertained by the factor. The beneficiary may lodge answers and the question is decided without bringing in all the satisfied beneficiaries. Secondly, there may be a dispute between claimants as to their proper shares of an estate admittedly correct in amount. This may be decided in a multiplepoinding, with the factor as real [55] or nominal [56] raiser. In condescending on the fund *in medio* the factor is entitled to deduct the expenses of management and his own remuneration.[57] An award of expenses from the estate taxed as between agent and client does not mean " third party paying." [58] A simpler method may be for the factor to present a petition for approval of his scheme of division and for discharge after payment in terms thereof. The scheme is remitted to the accountant for report, the claimants are heard on it, and it is approved or amended by the Lord Ordinary.[59]

The accountant's report

No discharge can be granted until the accountant has reported on the factor's accounts.[60] The remit to him is usually made in the interlocutor

[51] *Adamson* (1848) 10 D. 684.

[52] As in *Manners* v. *Strong's Judicial Factor* (1902) 4 F. 829; *Semple* v. *Tennant* (1888) 15 R. 810; *Newland's Curator Bonis* v. *Jaffray* (1863) 2 M. 146. See also *Matheson's Curator Bonis* v. *Mathesons* (1889) 16 R. 701.

[53] As in *Manners* v. *Strong's Judicial Factor* (1902) 4 F. 829; *Semple* v. *Tennant* (1888) 15 R. 810; *Newland's Curator Bonis* v. *Jaffray* (1863) 2 M. 146.

[54] Pupils Protection Act 1849, s. 34.

[55] *Barstow* v. *Cook* (1862) 24 D. 790; *Ross's Judicial Factor* v. *Martin*, 1955 S.C.(H.L.) 56.

[56] *Tait's Factor* v. *Meikle* (1890) 17 R. 1182.

[57] *Wright (Miln's Judicial Factor)* v. *Dalgarno* (O.H.), 1929 S.L.T. 279, 1929 S.N. 49; *Miln's Judicial Factor* v. *Spence's Trustees* (O.H.), 1927 S.L.T. 425.

[58] *Wright (Miln's Judicial Factor)* v. *Dalgarno* (O.H.), 1929 S.L.T. 279, 1929 S.N. 49.

[59] *Divers*, 1966 S.L.T. 181.   [60] *Aitken* (1893) 21 R. 62.

recalling the factor's appointment, if there is one, and the practice is set
forth in the Accountant's Notes for the Guidance of Judicial Factors,
which appear to proceed on the assumption that there are no objections, or
that these have been disposed of. It is the duty of the factor or his solicitor
to transmit the process to the accountant,[61] along with detailed vouchers
for all transactions since the last annual account,[62] and, where payment
has been made, receipts by the person or persons to whom the estate has
been conveyed, with evidence of their title to receive it.[63] The accountant
issues a draft report for the factor's observations, and, after considering
any observations, the report itself. The factor is entitled to be heard on
the accountant's report,[64] though there is no statutory provision to that
effect.

Discharge

When the Lord Ordinary is satisfied that the factor has accounted
properly for the estate and has conveyed it to the proper persons, the
factor is exonered and discharged and an order made for delivery of the
bond of caution.[65] Where payment has not been made, the interlocutor will
find the factor entitled to his discharge on payment as set forth in his
scheme approved by the accountant, but this is little known in practice.
No decree for exoneration and discharge may issue in favour of a factor
appointed to distribute a trust estate, an intestate, partnership or other
estate until there has been lodged a certificate by the Inland Revenue
that all income tax and death duties have been paid.[66]

Approval of a report shewing a balance due by the factor is normally
sufficient, but it is competent to decern against him and his cautioners
for payment or consignation.[67] It is incompetent in a petition for discharge
of a curator *bonis* on the death of the ward to decern against the ward's
executors for payment of a balance due to the curator *bonis*.[68]

Partial discharge

A factory may be recalled *quoad* a part of the estate for which it has
become unnecessary, for example where one part of property in dispute
has been found to belong to a particular claimant,[69] or where part of a
trust estate has fallen into intestacy and the factor was authorised to
convey it to the next of kin.[70] The reports in these cases do not indicate
whether the factor was to any extent discharged, but in a subsequent case

---

[61] Note 33.
[62] Note 12.
[63] Notes 35, 36.
[64] *Clark* v. *Barr's Trustees* (1903) 5 F. 856.
[65] Practice Note, May 14, 1970.
[66] Rules of Court 1965, r. 36.
[67] *Lowe* (1872) 11 M. 17; *Wallace's Factor* v. *McKissock* (1898) 25 R. 642; *Stewart* v. *Scott* (1850) 12 D. 744.
[68] *Wallace's Curator Bonis* (O.H.), 1910, 1 S.L.T. 167.
[69] *Noble* v. *Brackenbury* (1859) 21 D. 1053; *McGillivray's Executors* v. *Mason* (1857) 19 D. 1099 (narrative, first paragraph).
[70] *Nisbet* v. *Tod* (1848) 10 D. 361.

a factor was authorised to pay over capital set free by the death of life-renters and on a report that payment had been made to the proper persons and production of discharges by them the factor was discharged *ad interim*.[71] When the value of the estate is reduced in this way the accountant may authorise a decrease in the amount of caution.[72]

Exoneration by multiplepoinding

A judicial factor like any other holder of a fund may competently raise a multiplepoinding for the settlement of conflicting claims,[73] but he cannot in such a process obtain exoneration and discharge from office. Although *Campbell* v. *Grant* [74] was dismissed on the ground that there was no double distress, Lord Deas [75] and Lord Ardmillan expressly, and the Lord President and Lord Kinloch by implication, stated a conclusive reason for holding a conclusion for exoneration and discharge from office to be incompetent in any circumstances. The curator *bonis* had been appointed in exercise of the *nobile officium* and could not be discharged in an action. The same point had been made by Lord Ivory in an earlier case,[76] which was dismissed on the ground that it was incompetent in a multiplepoinding to review the conduct of a judicial factor as such. These were cases of factors on trust estates, to whom the Pupils Protection Act 1849 did not then apply, and the subsequent extension of that Act, with its provisions for exoneration and discharge, to all judicial factors, reinforces the opinions of these judges. Although factors are now appointed in the Outer House, it is generally understood that the Lord Ordinary is exercising the *nobile officium* by statutory delegation.[77] Further, a " process of judicial factory " [78] is initiated by petition, and only in the most exceptional circumstances could such a process be interfered with by an action.[79]

Action of count, reckoning and payment

This is incompetent against a factor in office.[80] One of the reasons for holding a multiplepoinding an incompetent method of obtaining discharge from office applies here, *viz.* that there is a recognised method, now statutory, of challenging the factor's administration. Accordingly, the Lord Ordinary founded on the opinions in *Carmichael* v. *Todd*,[81] where an attempt to challenge a factor's administration in a multiplepoinding was held incompetent. The Lord Ordinary's surmise that the action may be competent after the factor has been removed from office is borne out

---

[71] *Smith* (O.H.) (1883) 19 S.L.R. 435.
[72] Rules of Court 1965, r. 200 (*e*) (iii).
[73] See *Ross's Judicial Factor* v. *Martin*, 1955 S.C.(H.L.) 56 at p. 59.
[74] (1869) 8 M. 227, (1870) 8 M. 988.
[75] At both hearings.
[76] *Carmichael* v. *Todd* (1853) 15 D. 473 at pp. 476, 477.
[77] See p. 125.
[78] Rules of Court 1965, r. 200 (*b*).
[79] See *Sharp* v. *McCall* (1860) 23 D. 38, Lord Justice-Clerk Inglis at p. 38.
[80] *Cormack* v. *Simpson's Judicial Factor* (O.H.) 1960 S.L.T. 197.
[81] (1853) 15 D. 473.

by reports to which he was not referred. *Scott*,[82] which he mentions, is further reported,[83] and from the second of these reports it appears that the factor was removed on a petition and complaint before the action of count, reckoning and payment was advised. In *Simpson* v. *Doud*[84] a factor was removed from office and presented an application for his exoneration and discharge, to which the new factor lodged answers. Thereafter the new factor raised an action of count, reckoning and payment against his predecessor, to which only his cautioner lodged defences. The action was conjoined with the application for discharge, and the report does not disclose which interlocutors were pronounced in the petition and which in the action. In three earlier actions of count, reckoning and payment the factor was removed or his office had come to an end before the action was raised.[85] Such an action would require intimation to all claimants on the estate.[86]

---

[82] (1821) 1 S. 28.
[83] *Cranstoun* v. *Scott* (1824) 2 S. 783, (1826) 5 S. 62.
[84] (1855) 17 D. 314.
[85] *Lambe* v. *Ritchie* (1837) 16 S. 219; *Morland* v. *Sprot* (1829) 8 S. 181, (1831) 9 S. 478; *Fergusson* v. *Menzies* (1830) 8 S. 782.
[86] *Allen* v. *McCombie's Trustees*, 1909 S.C. 710.

CHAPTER XVIII

JURISDICTION[1]

General

The principle of effectiveness, on which jurisdiction mainly depends, is most frequently and clearly illustrated in actions, where a particular remedy is sought against a particular defender and the question is whether the court can enforce the remedy, if granted, against the defender.[2] The application of the principle to the appointment of a factor on property has not been expressly considered, but the decisions[3] are broadly in conformity with the proposition that the Court of Session has jurisdiction to appoint a factor if it could pronounce a decree effective against the person or property concerned. Accordingly, the court has jurisdiction to appoint a factor on a Scottish trust,[4] executry, intestate estate or partnership, on the estate of a minor or *incapax* resident in Scotland,[5] and on heritage in Scotland. Further, in view of the equitable nature of the remedy there is jurisdiction where either the person whose estate is affected or part of the moveable estate is in Scotland and in either case an emergency has arisen. The observation that a Lord Ordinary ought to have allowed proof as to the domicile of an alleged *incapax* resident in England[6] overlooks the fact that, unless status is in issue, domicile in questions of jurisdiction means residence,[7] or in other words that domicile of succession is irrelevant, except in questions of status.

Heritage in Scotland

On this ground curators *bonis* were appointed to minors[8] and to an *incapax*[9] living abroad. A probable claim to heritage may be enough.[10] It makes no difference that the ward's estate is already being administered abroad, *e.g.* in England by a receiver[11] or by guardians.[12] Nor does the subsequent appointment of administrators abroad affect the factor's posi-

---

[1] As to the jurisdiction of the sheriff see Chap. XX.
[2] *Fraser* v. *Fraser and Hibbert* (1870) 8 M. 400 at p. 405.
[3] Some of the reports, being directed to other points, do not disclose all the facts relevant to jurisdiction.
[4] *Orr Ewing's Trustees* v. *Orr Ewing* (1885) 13 R. (H.L.) 1.
[5] *Watson* (O.H.) 1933 S.L.T. 434, 1932 S.N. 66; *Harper* (O.H.) 1932 S.L.T. 496. Both were foreigners in asylums in Scotland. " Residence " is discussed in Chap. XX.
[6] *Alston* v. *Alston* (1895) 23 R. 16.
[7] *Joel* v. *Gill* (1859) 21 D. 929 at p. 938; *Carter* v. *Allison*, 1966 S.C. 257 at pp. 274, 278.
[8] *Waring* (O.H.) 1933 S.L.T. 190, 1933 S.N. 14; *Hay* (1861) 23 D. 1291; *Hay* v. *Boreland* (1837) 15 S. 850; *Collins* (O.H.) 1921, 2 S.L.T. 36; *Ogilvy*, February 10, 1927 (unreported), sequel apparently to *Ogilvy* v. *Ogilvy's Trustees*, 1927 S.L.T. 83, 1926 S.N. 166.
[9] *Dalrymple* v. *Ranken* (1836) 14 S. 1011.
[10] *Watson* (1864) 2 M. 1333.
[11] *Muir*, 1929 S.N. 113; *Laing* (1859) 21 D. 1011. See *Wilson* (O.H.) (1895) 2 S.L.T. 567.
[12] *Melbourne* (1857) 19 D. 699; *Lamb* (1857) 19 D. 699, (1858) 20 D. 1323; *Allen* v. *Robertson* (1855) 18 D. 97; *Viscountess Alford* (1851) 13 D. 950; *Wight* (1837) 15 S. 1197.

tion *quoad* the heritage.[13] A foreign administrator cannot complete title to heritage in Scotland,[14] or grant a discharge of an heritable bond.[15] At one time the court refused to restrict the appointment to the heritage in Scotland, but where a ward lives abroad and his estate is being administered in his own country the modern practice is to do so.[16] The factor requires special power to remit abroad the price of the heritage if it is sold, but not the rents.[17]

Emergencies

A curator *bonis* was appointed to a minor resident abroad whose claim in a multiplepoinding had been sustained, but who could not give a valid discharge,[18] and a similar appointment would have been made to minors abroad who had rights in a Scottish trust but for their own opposition.[19] The court appointed a curator *bonis* to an *incapax* living in England who had a liferent from a Scottish trust and to whom no receiver had been appointed, but recalled the appointment when a receiver was appointed.[20] On petitions presented before the appointment of the Custodian of Enemy Property factors were appointed in the assets of enemy aliens, in one case on the assets in Scotland [21] and in the other on the assets in any country except Germany and Austria.[22] Curators *bonis* have been appointed to foreigners becoming insane while temporarily in Scotland, as an *interim* measure until their own courts appointed administrators.[23]

---

[13] *Murray* v. *Baillie* (1849) 11 D. 710.
[14] *Gordon* v. *Earl of Stair* (1835) 135, 1073.
[15] *Young & Co.* v. *Thomsons* (1831) 9 S. 920; *Ogilvy* v. *Ogilvy's Trustees* (O.H.) 1927 S.L.T. 83, 1926 S.N. 166.
[16] *Ogilvy*, February 10, 1927, unreported.
[17] See pp. 105, 107.
[18] *Burns* (1851) 14 D. 311.
[19] *Macdonald* (O.H.) (1896) 4 S.L.T. 4.
[20] *Sawyer* v. *Sloan* (1875) 3 R. 271. See also *Duff* (O.H.) 1910, 2 S.L.T. 202, which discloses no connection wth Scotland (commented on in *Forsyth* (O.H.) 1932 S.L.T. 462), and *Buyers* (O.H.) 1910, 2 S.L.T. 201.
[21] *Hardie* v. *Smith* (O.H.) 1914, 2 S.L.T. 400.
[22] *Smith Laing & Co.* (O.H.) 1914, 2 S.L.T. 462.
[23] *Reid* v. *Reid* (O.H.) (1887) 24 S.L.R. 281; *Bonar* (1851) 14 D. 10.

CHAPTER XIX

PROCEDURE AND EXPENSES

Appointment of the Factor

Historical and general

Since the office originated in an exercise of the *nobile officium* [1] the power to appoint was at first confined to the court and, after its reconstruction in 1808, to the Inner House. The Court of Session Act 1857, usually known as the Distribution of Business Act, provided, by section 4, that petitions for the appointment of judicial factors, factors *loco tutoris* or *loco absentis*, or curators *bonis* should be enrolled before, and disposed of by, the Junior Lord Ordinary. After 1889 these were presented and disposed of in the Bill Chamber,[2] and that explains the phrase " petitions which, according to former practice, were presented in the Bill Chamber." [3] While it never seems to have been necessary to decide the nature of the jurisdiction conferred on the Junior Lord Ordinary by section 4, in incidental references it was taken for granted that the section empowered him to exercise the *nobile officium*,[4] and when section 4 was repealed [5] and replaced by the Rules of Court, the Rules in their earlier forms were assumed to have the same effect.[6] This view has never been disapproved, and if it is correct, the Rules of Court 1948 and those of 1965 in their original form were self-contradictory since they assigned petitions, *e.g.* for the appointment of factors to the Outer House, but excluded petitions invoking the *nobile officium* [7] and assigned all petitions invoking the *nobile officium* to the Inner House without exception.[8] These changes while they lasted do not seem to have affected practice or caused any difficulty, and the 1965 Rules have been amended so as to restore the pre-1948 position.[9]

A factor may be appointed *de plano* in place of a factor removed from office,[10] or to administer sums of damages awarded or agreed to be paid

---

[1] See Chap. I.

[2] Clerks of Session (Scotland) Regulation Act 1889, s. 3, repealed by Administration of Justice (Scotland) Act 1933; *Innes, Chambers & Co.* v. *T. D. McNeill & Son* (O.H.), 1917, 1 S.L.T. 89.

[3] Rules of Court 1965, r. 189 (a) (xxii).

[4] *Campbell* v. *Grant* (1869) 8 M. 227 at p. 232; *Innes, Chambers & Co.* v. *T. D. McNeill & Son* (O.H.), 1917, 1 S.L.T. 89; *Carmont*, 1922 S.C. 686 at p. 688. See *Wemyss* (1860) 22 D. 556, and *Leslie's J.F.*, 1925 S.C. 464 at p. 469.

[5] Administration of Justice (Scotland) Act 1933, s. 39 and Sched.

[6] *Brown*, 1936 S.C. 689; *Smith's Trustees*, 1939 S.C. 489.

[7] 1948 Rules, r. 207 (a), and 1965 Rules, r. 189 (a), in contrast with 1936 Rules, Chap. IV, r. 1 (a).

[8] 1948 Rules, r. 208 (vii), and 1965 Rules, r. 190 (vii), in contrast with 1936 Rules, Chap. IV, r. 2 (vii).

[9] Act of Sederunt of January 30, 1970.

[10] *Accountant of Court* v. *Jaffray* (1851) 14 D. 292.

to pupils or minors,[11] or aliment agreed to be paid to pupils or minors on the divorce of their parents,[12] or by the Inner House in the course of a litigation pending before it,[13] but in most cases the appointment is applied for by petition. The statement in Thoms [14] that a factor may be appointed under a conclusion in a summons is not supported by the decisions which he cites and is inconsistent both with principle [15] and with practice. A petition for the appointment of a factor on a partnership estate raised issues which could be decided only in an action, and the Lord Ordinary sisted the petition pending the raising and decision of the action.[16] This was unnecessary if the petitioners could have included in their summons a conclusion for the appointment of a factor.

Inner or Outer House

As the result of legislation and practice nearly all petitions for appointment go to the Outer House. The Rules of Court specifically assign to the Outer House petitions for the appointment of factors *loco tutoris* and *loco absentis*, factors pending litigation and curators *bonis* to a minor or *incapax* and factors on the estates of partnerships or joint adventures,[17] and under the Bankruptcy (Scotland) Act 1913.[18] Since petitions for an appointment on property in dispute, although there was no pending litigation, were presented in the Bill Chamber,[19] these also go to the Outer House.[20] Rule 189 (*a*), however, prefixes to the list of specific appointments the general words " judicial factors." Section 4 of the Distribution of Business Act 1857 was similarly framed, and it was soon held that some limitation must be placed on the general words.[21] Otherwise the entire *nobile officium* in this matter would be committed to the Lord Ordinary, and, it may be added, the specific enumeration would be otiose, either wholly or partly.[22] Sixty years later Lord Anderson observed that the jurisdiction of the Outer House had been extended by practice beyond the specific cases mentioned in section 4 [23] and recently Lord Fraser made a similar observation.[24] A Lord Ordinary has jurisdiction to appoint in the following cases not mentioned specifically in either section 4 or rule 189 (*a*): on intestate estates,[25] on executries,[26] on the estate of a building

---

[11] Rules of Court 1965, rr. 131–134. In this case the factory is part of the original process: *McIntosh* v. *Wood*, 1970 S.C. 179.
[12] See Succession (Scotland) Act 1964, s. 26 (2). *Kynynmound* v. *Kynynmound*, May 27, 1965 (unreported).
[13] *Simpson's Executor* v. *Simpson's Trustees*, 1912 S.C. 418.
[14] (2nd ed.) p. 445, repeated in more absolute terms by Irons, p. 486.
[15] *Tomkins* v. *Cohen*, 1951 S.C. 22 at p. 23.
[16] *Blake's Trustees* v. *Jolly*, 1920, 1 S.L.T. 304, 57 S.L.R. 431.
[17] Rules of Court 1965, r. 189 (*a*) (i), (ii).
[18] r. 189 (*a*) (vii).
[19] *Padwick* v. *Steuart* (1871) 9 M. 793; *Thoms* v. *Thoms* (1865) 3 M. 776.
[20] r. 189 (*a*) (xxii).
[21] *Dixon's Tutor* (1867) 5 M. 1052.
[22] See r. 199.
[23] *Innes, Chambers & Co.* v. *T.D. McNeill & Son* (O.H.), 1917, 1 S.L.T. 89.
[24] *Fraser* (O.H.) 1971 S.L.T.(Notes) 18.
[25] *Rutherford* v. *Lord Advocate*, 1932 S.C. 674, and cases there overruled.
[26] *Birnie* v. *Christie* (1891) 19 R. 334; *Rhind* v. *Sheach* (O.H.) (1875) 2 R. 1002.

society which was unable to dissolve itself under the statute,[27] on the surplus left in the hands of a trustee in bankruptcy after he had paid all creditors [28] and *ad interim* on the estates of a limited company.[29] Rule 189 (*a*) does not expressly mention the appointment of a factor on a trust estate and the effect of subhead (iii) is limited,[30] but a petition for sequestration and appointment goes to the Outer House,[31] as it did under the 1857 Act,[32] and since under subhead (iv) a Lord Ordinary has jurisdiction to remove trustees he probably has jurisdiction also to appoint a factor, if necessary, in their place.

A petition wrongly presented to the Inner House has been remitted to the Outer House,[33] and the Inner House has given judgment in petitions wrongly presented to the Outer House and coming before it on reclaiming motion [34] or report.[35] Where a petition contains a crave proper to the Outer House and one proper to the Inner House the Inner House deals with both.[36]

Pleadings and procedure

The Rules of Court 1965 prescribe the general requisites of all petitions.[37] The additional requisites of petitions under section 163 of the Bankruptcy (Scotland) Act 1913 are dealt with separately.[38] In petitions for the appointment of factors there must be specified as far as possible the property forming the estate [39] and the names of all persons interested,[40] also, where the ground is the nonage of the proposed ward, his age and, where it is mental incapacity, the duration of the malady and the person who has had control over him and his estate.[41] The name and qualifications of the proposed factor should be stated.[42] The prayer is first for intimation and service.[43] The usual *induciae* is seven days if the person is on the mainland of Scotland: otherwise it is fourteen days.[44] But in great emergency an *interim* appointment may be made before service.[45] Intimation in the *Edinburgh Gazette* is required under section 163 of the Bank-

---

[27] *Gaff* (1893) 20 R. 825.
[28] *Divers*, 1966 S.L.T. 181 (narrative).
[29] *Fraser* (O.H.), 1971 S.L.T.(Notes) 18.
[30] *Cockburn's Trs.*, 1935 S.C. 670; *Smith's Trs.*, 1939 S.C. 489.
[31] *Courage* v. *Ballantine*, 1946 S.C. 351.
[32] *Rhind* v. *Sheach* (O.H.) (1875) 2 R. 1002.
[33] *Smith's Trustees*, 1939 S.C. 489.
[34] *Carmont*, 1922 S.C. 686.
[35] *Viscountess Ossington's Trustees*, 1965 S.C. 410.
[36] *Prime Gilt Box Society*, 1920 S.C. 534; *Anderson's Trustees*, 1921 S.C. 315; *Craig's Trustees*, 1934 S.C. 34; *Viscountess Ossington's Trustees*, 1965 S.C. 410.
[37] r. 191. See Thomson and Middleton, *Manual of Court of Session Procedure*, pp. 200 *et seq.*
[38] r. 201. See Chap. VII.
[39] *Allan* (1852) 14 D. 486; *A.B.* (1852) 14 D. 849; *Mathew* (1851) 14 D. 312.
[40] *Russell* (1855) 17 D. 1005.
[41] *Mathew* (1851) 14 D. 312.
[42] *Anderson* (1854) 17 D. 97.
[43] Rules of Court 1965, r. 191 (*b*), (*c*). Any specialities of service are mentioned in particular chapters.
[44] Rules of Court 1965, r. 192. It may be shortened or extended.
[45] *Dobson* (O.H.) (1903) 11 S.L.T. 44; *Goold* (1856) 18 D. 1318; *Kirk* (1827) 5 S. 564.

ruptcy (Scotland) Act 1913 [46] and advertisement may be necessary of a petition for appointment, for example, of a factor *loco absentis*. There follows a crave for sequestration of the estate, if necessary,[47] and for the appointment of the nominee " or such other person as to your Lordships shall seem proper." It should be unnecessary to suggest an alternative nominee since the petitioner ought to make sure that his nominee is willing to accept office. Where an alternative nominee was proposed and the first named was appointed, but declined office, the court ordered intimation of new before considering the alternative nominee.[48] But this was not done where the court with consent of the parties appearing made an appointment under the general alternative.[49] The court will not appoint A, whom failing, B.[50] The prayer should include all that may be required and be competently granted. Part may be abandoned, but if the prayer has to be added to by amendment, further intimation and service may be ordered.[51] Expenses should be craved out of the estate. Petitions under section 14 of the Bankruptcy (Scotland) Act 1913 may be signed by the petitioner's solicitor. All others must be signed by counsel.[52] The petition is lodged in the Petition Department [53] and a copy of it, of the answers, if any, and of papers lodged must be supplied to the accountant.[54] If no answers are lodged, the Lord Ordinary, after any necessary inquiry, disposes of the petition.[55] The court has proceeded on affidavits.[56]

Answers may be lodged at any time within the *induciae*, provided that the court may, on cause shewn, prorogate the time for lodging answers and allow the same to be received though not lodged within the *induciae*.[57] If the proviso conferred two separate powers on the court (1) to prorogate the time for lodging answers and (2) to allow answers to be received though not lodged within the *induciae*, they would naturally have been connected by the word " or," not " and," [58] and the first power would have been unnecessary. Accordingly, the second phrase appears to be exegetical of the first, and the court exercises its power to prorogate the time by allowing the answers to be received. But since there is no need to exercise this power unless the answers are late, it follows that the power to prorogate may be exercised after the *induciae* have expired.[59] This view is supported by the fact that rule 196 (*a*), unlike other Rules allowing prorogation,[60]

[46] r. 201 (*b*).
[47] See pp. 4, 33.
[48] *Thomson* (1851) 14 D. 311; *Scouller* (1834) 13 S. 101.
[49] *Hay* v. *Boreland* (1837) 15 S. 850; *Davidson* v. *Bogle* (1837) 15 S. 421.
[50] *Dow* (1847) 9 D. 616.
[51] See general observations of Lord President McNeill; (1855) 18 D. 33.
[52] Rules of Court 1965, r. 193.
[53] *Ibid*. r. 189 (*a*).
[54] *Ibid*. r. 200 (*a*).
[55] *Ibid*. r. 197. The grounds for appointing are discussed in the particular chapters.
[56] *Wishart* (O.H.) 1910 2 S.L.T. 229.
[57] Rules of Court, 1965, r. 196 (*a*).
[58] The context does not require " and " to be read as " or "; *D. & J. McCallum* v. *Doughty*, 1915 S.C. (J.) 69.
[59] See *Macnab* v. *Nelson*, 1909 S.C. 1102, where a similar result was reached on a construction of the Sheriff Courts (Scotland) Act 1907.
[60] rr. 27, 200 (*c*), 206 (*f*).

does not require that a motion be lodged before the expiry of the period. Answers should normally be signed by counsel.[61]

Disputes as to the capacity of an alleged *incapax* are settled by a remit to a specialist,[62] and arithmetical disputes by a remit to the accountant.[63] In many cases there is sufficient material in the averments, documents, and statements at the bar, but a proof may be necessary when the issue depends on the conduct of individuals.[64]

Expenses

Where the application is granted without opposition the petitioner is entitled to expenses from the estate,[65] taxed as between solicitor and client. If there is opposition, the court has a discretion, and where the award follows the result there is often to be found, even when it is not expressed, some special consideration. Unsuccessful petitioners or respondents were found liable in expenses where their legal ground was unsound,[66] where the conduct of a trustee had been irregular, but beneficial to the estate and his removal, not sequestration of the estate, was craved,[67] where the allegations against the father of a pupil were wholly insufficient to justify the appointment of a factor *loco tutoris*,[68] and where the court were from the first doubtful of the petitioner's claim on the merits.[69] The conduct of trustees or other respondents suggests why they were found liable in the expenses of unsuccessful opposition, either *simpliciter* [70] or *quoad* the expenses caused by their opposition.[71] But where the necessity for the appointment of a factor on a trust estate arose from circumstances rather than from the conduct of the trustees, in two cases both petitioner and respondent trustee were allowed expenses from the estate,[72] and in another, where no expenses were found due to or by either party,[73] the trustee's expenses were subsequently recovered from the estate.[74] On refusing an application for an appointment the court found no expenses due to or by either party, possibly because the respondent had created unnecessary difficulties.[75] Where an appointment was made, two respondent trustees, who had acted reasonably, were awarded expenses from the

---

[61] *Denny* v. *Macnish* (1863) 1 M. 268.

[62] Chap. IV.

[63] *Allan* v. *Gronmeyer* (1891) 18 R. 784, at p. 788.

[64] *Collins* v. *Young* (1853) 1 Macq. 385; *McWhirter* v. *Latta* (1889) 17 R. 68; *Allan* v. *Gronmeyer* (1891) 18 R. 784, at p. 788; *Booth* v. *Mackinnon* (O.H.) (1908) 15 S.L.T. 848.

[65] *Macqueen* (O.H.) 1910, 2 S.L.T. 445, where decree passed in name of the agent disburser; *Hill* v. *Piercy* (1854) 16 D. 425.

[66] *Collins* v. *Young* (1853) 1 Macq. 385; *Primrose* v. *Caledonian Railway Co.* (1851) 13 D. 464. See also *Baird* v. *Caledonian Railway Co.* (1851) 13 D. 795.

[67] *Gilchrist's Trustees* v. *Dick* (1883) 11 R. 22.

[68] *Wardrop* v. *Gossling* (1869) 7 M. 532.

[69] *Padwick* v. *Steuart* (1871) 9 M. 793.

[70] *Thomson* v. *Dalrymple* (1865) 3 M. 336, where the trustees were held personally liable; *Bailey* v. *Scott* (1860) 22 D. 1105. In *Maxwell's Trustees* v. *Maxwell* (1874) 2 R. 71, the award was in substance against the respondents.

[71] *McNab* v. *McNab* (1871) 10 M. 248.

[72] *Henderson* v. *Henderson* (1893) 20 R. 536; *Thomson* v. *McNicol* (1871) 8 S.L.R. 623.

[73] *Smith* v. *Smith* (1862) 24 D. 838.

[74] *Baxter & Mitchell* v. *Wood* (1864) 2 M. 915.

[75] *Hope* v. *Hope* (1884) 12 R. 27.

estate and two, who had acted unreasonably, were found personally liable in expenses.[76]

When an *incapax* has unsuccessfully opposed the appointment of a curator *bonis* to himself he can no longer intromit with his estate and cannot pay his solicitor's account. The question then arises whether it should be paid from the estate. This turns largely on whether the condition of the *incapax* justified the solicitor in taking instructions from him or indeed whether the *incapax* had given instructions at all. At one time the question was decided in the petition proceedings. In one case all the expenses were allowed out of the estate [77] and in another the solicitor who had appeared for the *incapax* was found liable in the petitioner's expenses.[78] The more modern practice appears to be in such circumstances to make no award of expenses when the appointment is made.[79] The curator *bonis* has then two courses open to him. If he is satisfied that the solicitors received instructions and acted reasonably in accepting them he may apply for authority to pay the account.[80] If he is not so satisfied, he may refuse payment and defend an action.[81] The court is more likely to authorise, or decern for, payment of Outer House expenses than for those of an unsuccessful reclaiming motion.[82] In *Mitchell & Baxter* v. *Cheyne*, however, the House of Lords in refusing an appeal brought by an *incapax* described by Lord Watson as " most groundless ",[83] disregarded the Court of Session practice and found the appellant's solicitors entitled to expenses there. The Court of Session therefore felt obliged to authorise the curator *bonis* to pay the solicitors' accounts not only for the Outer, but also for the Inner House. If the only dispute is as to who shall be appointed factor and the opposition to the petitioner's nominee has been successful both parties may be allowed expenses from the estate.[84]

Application for Special Powers

Procedure

The court has occasionally entertained applications by third parties, who, under the guise of craving special powers for the factor, seek to compel him to do some act. The competency of this procedure is discussed elsewhere.[85] In certain circumstances special powers have been granted at

---

[76] *Stewart* v. *Morrison* (1892) 19 R. 1009.
[77] *Taylor* v. *Macfarlane* (1847) 10 D. 38.
[78] *McCall* v. *Sharp and Bayne* (1862) 24 D. 393.
[79] *Mitchell & Baxter* v. *Cheyne* (1891) 19 R. 324, Lord Adam at p. 328; *Mitchell & Thomson* v. *McGregor*, 1951 S.L.T. (Sh. Ct.) 80 (narrative).
[80] *Mitchell & Baxter* v. *Cheyne* (1891) 19 R. 324.
[81] *Mitchell & Thomson* v. *McGregor*, 1951 S.L.T. (Sh. Ct.) 80; *Baxter & Mitchell* v. *Wood* (1864) 2 M. 915, an action by solicitors against the factor on a trust estate for payment of the account incurred to them by the trustee in opposing the factor's appointment.
[82] *Mitchell & Baxter* v. *Cheyne* (1891) 19 R. 324 at p. 329.
[83] *C B* v. *A B* (1891) 18 R. (H.L.) at p. 46.
[84] *Raeburn* (1851) 14 D. 310; *Cochrane* v. *Macaslan* (1849) 12 D. 147. See also *Brown* v. *Brown* (1852) 14 D. 856.
[85] See p. 111.

appointment on the crave of the petitioner.[86] Normally the application is by the factor.

Until 1849 the application was by petition,[87] but the Pupils Protection Act [88] introduced a new procedure, which applied specifically to two cases, estate management and the purchase of an annuity for a lunatic or other person incapable of managing his own affairs. A factor desiring special power in such cases " shall report " to the accountant, who states his opinion in writing, and the report and opinion are submitted to the Lord Ordinary with a note praying for sanction of the court to the measure proposed. The Lord Ordinary reported to the court, which granted or refused the application.[89] In these two cases therefore the new procedure became obligatory.[90] Section 7 finally provides that " in all other matters in which special powers are . . . in use to be granted by the court, the court shall have power to grant the same in like manner and form as is above provided." This is permissive, so that procedure in the other matters may be either by petition or by note,[91] and the alternative is express in the Titles to Land Consolidation (Scotland) Act 1868.[92] A note is now the usual procedure.[93] The Distribution of Business Act 1857 [94] altered the procedure by transferring to the Junior Lord Ordinary applications, including applications by factors for special powers.[95] Section 4 was repealed in 1933, and the application may be made to any Lord Ordinary.[96] Where a factor presented a note for special powers without having obtained the accountant's opinion the Lord Ordinary remitted to the accountant, holding that without his opinion he could not entertain the note.[97]

The factor in his report to the accountant should mention " the circumstances and his own views " and state " the exact powers he wishes the court to grant to him." [93] The circumstances include the name of the original petitioner, the dates of presenting the petition and of the factor's appointment,[98] a general narrative of the course of management and the reasons for the application,[99] which may be supported by opinions from men of skill.[1] The accountant may order any necessary inquiry, e.g. by remit to a man of skill,[2] and then gives his opinion. The accountant

---

[86] See p. 78.

[87] *Mackenzie* (1862) 24 D. 844 at pp. 845, 846 (report presumably framed or at least revised by Sheriff Thoms himself).

[88] s. 7.

[89] See *Paisley* (1857) 19 D. 653.

[90] *Mackenzie* (1862) 24 D. 844, Sheriff Thoms' argument, but the point did not arise for decision and opinions were reserved.

[91] *Mackenzie* (1862) 24 D. 844.

[92] s. 24.

[93] Notes for Guidance of Judicial Factors, note 25.

[94] s. 4.

[95] See *Macqueen* v. *Tod* (1899) 1 F. 1069.

[96] *Mitchell*, 1939 S.L.T. 91.

[97] *Gillespie's Factor* (O.H.) (1902) 9 S.L.T. 421. This point was not mentioned in *Tennent's Judicial Factor* v. *Tennent*, 1954 S.C. 215. See p. 133.

[98] *Scott* (1856) 18 D. 323.

[99] *Grant's Curator* (1880) 7 R. 1014.

[1] *Macqueen* v. *Tod* (1899) 1 F. 1069.   [2] *Macqueen* v. *Tod* (1899) 1 F. 1069.

cannot form a satisfactory opinion unless he knows the precise power the court is to be asked to grant. Further, the court, unless in very exceptional circumstances,[3] will grant only a specific power, so that even if a vague description of the power passed the accountant, a further remit to him would probably be necessary when the crave in the note was, or by amendment became, sufficiently precise. The note, which is presented along with the factor's report and the accountant's opinion, should narrate the circumstances briefly and in particular should specify the name and date of the original petition,[4] the persons on whom service is craved, including the cautioner,[5] and crave intimation and service,[6] the special power desired, and expenses out of the estate. Whether answers are lodged or not, the report, the accountant's opinion and the averments will usually provide sufficient material for a decision, but it may be necessary to make a remit to a man of skill [7] or to the accountant.[8]

Expenses

If the special power is granted the expenses will naturally come from the estate. Even when it was refused, but the accountant's opinion was in favour of granting, it may be inferred from the opinions that expenses were allowed from the estate [9] and, where the procedure was by petition even the expenses of amendment of an incompetent crave were allowed.[10] In fact there does not seem to be any reported case where the factor was not allowed his expenses out of the estate.[11] Possibly the accountant's opinion is sufficient to prevent hopeless applications from reaching the court.

Applications under section 5 of the Trusts
(Scotland) Act 1921

Section 5 empowers the court to grant authority " on the petition of the trustees," and consequently of a judicial factor, and section 26 provides that applications to the court under the authority of the Act shall be brought in the first instance before one of the Lords Ordinary. But the distinction between this procedure and that for obtaining special powers has not been rigidly adhered to in practice. A curator *bonis*, having submitted a report to the accountant and obtained an opinion from him, presented a note craving authority to feu. The note " came before " the

---

3 *Grant's Curator* (1880) 7 R. 1014; *Carmichael's Judicial Factor*, 1971 S.L.T. 336.
4 *Scott* (1856) 18 D. 323.
5 *Rutherford* (1845) 17 Scot. Jur. 152.
6 See *Cameron's Curator Bonis* (O.H.) 1961 S.L.T. (notes) 21, where service on an *incapax* was held unnecessary.
7 *Grant's Curator* (1880) 7 R. 1014 (unopposed). See Distribution of Business Act 1857, s. 5.
8 *Gilligan's Factor* v. *Fraser* (1898) 25 R. 876 (opposed), where the accountant had presumably given an opinion at an earlier stage.
9 *Gilligan's Factor* v. *Fraser* (1898) 25 R. 876.
10 *Watson* v. *Crawcour* (1856) 19 D. 70.
11 *Mitchell*, 1939 S.L.T. 91, where the note was refused, but both factor and concurring minuters were allowed expenses from the estate. See *Cruickshank* v. *Ewing* (1864) 3 M. 302.

Junior Lord Ordinary. This was the normal procedure for obtaining special powers under section 7 of the Pupils Protection Act 1849 and section 4 of the Distribution of Business Act 1857, which remained in force until 1933, but the case was dealt with as if it had been a petition under section 5.[12] A factor presented a note craving authority to compromise an action, founding not on section 5, but on common law. As he had not reported to the accountant and laid his opinion before the Lord Ordinary the note was incompetent under either of the procedures recognised in section 7 of the Pupils Protection Act 1849.[13] The Lord Ordinary, however, entertained it and dismissed it as unnecessary. The respondents reclaimed, and the Division allowed the noter to amend so as to found both on common law and on section 5. Since most of the expenses would probably come out of the estate, it was not in the interest of any party to object to the competency of the amendment on the ground that section 5 requires the application to be made by petition. The Division held that they could entertain the application only under section 5, but, at p. 227, the Lord President considered that a report from the accountant was " imperative under the statutes, regulations and practice governing applications by factors for special powers." [14]

Interim Audits

The annual audit required by the Pupils Protection Act 1849 has rendered interim audits unnecessary except in special circumstances, *e.g.* the death of a cautioner. The factor applies to the court by petition, now usually by note, to order intimation and service, to remit his accounts to the accountant, on his report to declare the balance due and to find the petitioner entitled to expenses from the estate.[15] Such an application was formerly made to the Junior Lord Ordinary [16] and therefore is now made in the Outer House.[17]

Reports by the Accountant

The accountant is required to make all such requisitions and orders on a factor as he may consider necessary, and if the requisition or order is disobeyed or neglected, to report this to the Lord Ordinary, giving previous notice to the factor or his agent, who may lodge objections in writing within forty-eight hours. The Lord Ordinary, with or without objections, may recall, vary, confirm or repeat the requisition or order, and his decision is final against the accountant and also against the factor,

---

12 *Marquess of Lothian's Curator Bonis*, 1927 S.C. 579.
13 *Mackenzie* (1862) 24 D. 844.
14 *Tennent's Judicial Factor* v. *Tennent*, 1954 S.C. 215. On 29th June 1954 the Lord Ordinary granted authority under s. 5. Applications under s. 5 by note are entertained without comment: *Telfer's Judicial Factor*, March 18, 1971 (unreported).
15 See *Morison* (1856) 19 D. 132.
16 Distribution of Business Act 1857, s. 4 (5); *Miller* (O.H.) (1895) 2 S.L.T. 520.
17 Rules of Court 1965, r. 189 (*a*) (xxii).

unless he at judgment gives notice of his intention to bring the judgment under review, in which case the Lord Ordinary disposes of expenses and makes any interim order necessary.[18] The section does not give the factor a right of appeal against the requisition or order; it obliges the accountant to report every disobedience or neglect, even if the factor does not object to the requisition or order.

Section 20 also requires the accountant " at all times when requisite " to report to the Lord Ordinary, *inter alia*, any disobedience of any requisition or order, and empowers the Lord Ordinary to deal with the matter as accords of law. It does not appear to have been considered how far this particular provision and section 19 are alternatives or whether a report under section 19 is a necessary preliminary to a report as to disobedience under section 20, but proceedings which began with a report under section 19 developed into proceedings under section 20, without any further report by the accountant, and resulted in the removal of the factor and a report to the Lord Advocate.[19] Unlike section 19, section 20 makes no provision for notice to the factor, but the direction to proceed " as accords of law " implies that notice is essential. The report is also served on the cautioner.

The accountant has made requisitions on factors to consign the estate or part of it,[20] and to realise investments of which he did not approve.[21] For long it was the accountant's practice to make requisitions on factors to lodge overdue annual accounts [22] and to report to the court only in extreme cases. But he has now intimated, with the concurrence of the court, that it is his duty to report all defaults.[23] Such default falls under section 20, which empowers the accountant to report any misconduct or failure in duty on the part of a factor. These reports have ranged from cases of malversation or near malversation [24] to difficulties arising from excess of caution.[25] When the accountant reasonably suspects malversation he may report to the Lord Advocate.[26] The court has also entertained reports by the accountant craving a ruling on the propriety of investments,[27] on the factor's right to commission,[28] on the regularity of the factor's appointment,[29] and on diversities of procedure in the Sheriff Court.[30]

---

[18] Pupils Protection Act 1849, s. 19.

[19] *Accountant of Court* v. *Jaffray* (1851) 14 D. 292. No criminal proceedings followed: (1854) 17 D. 71. *Cf. Accountant of Court* v. *Baird* (1858) 20 D. 1176, which was wholly under s. 19.

[20] *Accountant of Court* v. *Dewar* (1854) 16 D. 163, 489; *Accountant of Court* v. *Baird* (1858) 20 D. 1176, where the court remitted to the accountant to recall his order *in hoc statu*.

[21] *Grainger's Curator* (1876) 3 R. 479, where the court instructed the accountant to withdraw the requisition. See also *Lloyd's Curator* (1877) 5 R. 289.

[22] See *Marshall* v. *Chisholm* (1901) 3 F. 642.　　　　　　　[23] 1947 S.L.T. (News) 55.

[24] *Accountant of Court* v. *Wilkie* (1856) 18 D. 793; *Accountant of Court* v. *McAllister* (1853) 16 D. 301.

[25] *Accountant of Court* v. *Geddes* (1858) 20 D. 1174.

[26] s. 21.

[27] *Accountant of Court* v. *Crumpton's Curator Bonis* (1886) 14 R. 55.

[28] *Accountant of Court* v. *Watt* (1866) 4 M. 772; *Accountant of Court* v. *Gilray* (1872) 10 M. 715.

[29] *Accountant of Court* v. *Morrison* (1857) 19 D. 504; *Accountant of Court* v. *Buchanan* (1854) 16 D. 717.

[30] Judicial Factors (Scotland) Act 1880, s. 4 (7); *Accountant of Court*, 1907 S.C. 909; *Accountant of Court* (1893) 20 R. 573.

Review

Competency of reclaiming motion

No question of review arose until power to deal with petitions and applications for the appointment of factors, for special powers and for discharge, and with reports under the Pupils Protection Act 1849 was in 1857 transferred from the Inner House to the Junior Lord Ordinary.[31] Section 6 of the Act of 1857 provided that it should not be competent to bring under the review of the court any interlocutor pronounced by the Lord Ordinary on any such petition, application or report with a view to investigation and inquiry merely and which did not finally dispose thereof on the merits; but that any judgment pronounced by the Lord Ordinary on the merits might be reclaimed against by any party having lawful interest to reclaim, provided that a reclaiming note should be boxed within eight days, after which the judgment of the Lord Ordinary, if not so reclaimed against, should be final. Section 6 thus treated each petition, application and report as a separate process for purposes of review, and sections 4 to 6 were described as " a short but complete and well-considered code for the disposal of summary petitions." [32]

It was settled by a uniform series of decisions that section 6 provided a complete code of review in cases to which it applied, that it was unaffected by the provisions for review contained in the Court of Session Act 1868, in particular the provision of section 52 that a reclaiming note brought prior interlocutors under review, and that a judgment on the merits meant, not a final judgment in the technical sense that it disposed of the whole merits of the cause, but one which decided the point at issue on any petition, application or report.[33] Judges stressed the advantage in a judicial administration of having each such point finally determined, and the inconvenience which might arise from applying the rules as to review prescribed for an action.[34]

The effect on these provisions of the Administration of Justice (Scotland) Act 1933 and of the Acts of Sederunt and Rules of Court which followed it has not been considered in any reported case. The only express mention of section 6 in the legislation is that the 1933 Act [35] repeals the proviso to the second part of the section to the effect that interlocutors on the merits should be final unless reclaimed against within eight days. The Acts of Sederunt repeal earlier legislation so far as inconsistent with the Rules.[36] It was held by Lord McLaren,[37] with whom the other judges

[31] Distribution of Business Act 1857, s. 4.
[32] *Macqueen* v. *Tod* (1899) 1 F. 859 at p. 861.
[33] *McNab* v. *McNab* (1871) 10 M. 248; *Macqueen* v. *Tod* (1899) 1 F. 859; *Clark* v. *Barr's Trustees* (1903) 5 F. 856; *McCardle* v. *McCardle's Judicial Factor* (1906) 8 F. 416; *Marquis of Queensberry's Trustees* v. *Douglas*, 1907 S.C. 924. See also *Wallace* v. *Whitelaw* (1900) 2 F. 675.
[34] *Marquis of Queensberry's Trustees* v. *Douglas*, 1907 S.C. 924, Lord McLaren at p. 926; *Clark* v. *Barr's Trustees* (1903) 5 F. 856, Lord Kinnear at p. 858. See also *Tomkins* v. *Cohen*, 1951 S.C. 22, Lord Keith at p. 23.
[35] s. 38 and Sched.
[36] Act of Sederunt (Rules of Court, consolidation and amendment) 1965, para. (1).
[37] *Macqueen* v. *Tod* (1899) 1 F. 859 at p. 860.

concurred, that section 107 of the Court of Session Act 1868, which repealed all statutes in so far as inconsistent with the provisions of the Act, did not affect sections 4 and 6 of the 1857 Act, and this formed the basis of that and the subsequent decisions before 1933. His reason was that the jurisdiction of the Junior Lord Ordinary to deal with the enumerated petitions created by the 1857 Act was not altered by the 1868 Act, which moreover provided no new machinery for the disposal of such petitions. But the office of Junior Lord Ordinary has now been abolished and his jurisdiction conferred on any judge sitting in the Outer House,[38] all petitions (with certain exceptions irrelevant here) are presented in the Outer House,[39] and the Rules provide machinery to deal with them. The reasons for Lord McLaren's opinion are thus no longer applicable, and there seems to be no other for not giving full effect to the Act of Sederunt of 1965.

The apparent absence for forty years of any practical difficulty in applying the new provisions suggests that it is unnecessary to consider their effect in terms of the actual legislation. Broadly speaking, the Rules, have been applied. But this does not carry one the whole way. The reports, with one exception,[40] do not disclose whether paragraph (a) or (b) or (c) of what is now rule 264 was applied, nor is there any reported case which could have raised the meaning of rule 262 (c) *quoad* the effect of a reclaiming motion on prior interlocutors. Accordingly it may be useful to consider these points, even if some of the solutions suggested seem fanciful.

The express repeal of the proviso to the second part of section 6 of the 1857 Act renders that part unworkable. Either the appropriate number of reclaiming days must be ascertained from the Rules or the Rules supersede the remnant of this part of the section, the result being the same either way. Accordingly, an interlocutor granting or refusing a petition for appointment falls under rule 264 (a), since it disposes of the whole subject-matter of the cause (at least so far as this has then emerged).

But, as Lord Kinnear pointed out,[41] a petition for the appointment of a judicial factor is " merely a process for instituting a judicial administration and in the course of such administration there may be disputed questions of right, each of which must be determined on its merits." Section 6 of the 1857 Act dealt with each of these disputed questions in the same way as petitions, whether it was raised by application for special powers or by report.[42] But this is now impossible. Section 6 (1) of the 1933 Act enacts: " Save as hereinafter provided all causes initiated in the court shall be initiated . . . either by summons or by petition. . . ." The words " save as hereinafter provided " are satisfied by subsection (3), and the definition of " cause " [43] cannot affect the peremptory provision of

---

[38] 1933 Act, s. 3 (1).
[39] 1933 Act, s. 6 (1) and (3); Rules of Court 1965, rr. 189 and 190, both as amended by A.S. January 30, 1970.
[40] *Brower's Executor*, 1938 S.C. 451.
[41] *Clark* v. *Barr's Trustees* (1903) 5 F. 856 at p. 858.
[42] As in *McCardle* v. *McCardle's Judicial Factor* (1906) 8 F. 416.
[43] s. 40.

section 6 (1). Accordingly, a note for special powers or a report does not itself initiate a cause, or at least a competent cause, and to fall under rule 264 (*a*) or (*b*) an interlocutor disposing of it must be either an interlocutor which, taken along with previous interlocutors, disposes of the whole subject-matter of the cause initiated by the petition for appointment, in which case it falls under paragraph (*a*), or an interlocutor which disposes of part of the merits of that cause and falls under paragraph (*b*). It does not appear from the report in *Tennent's Judicial Factor* v. *Tennent* [44] whether the reclaiming motion was presented under what is now paragraph (*a*) or paragraph (*b*). No leave to reclaim seems to have been given. If it falls under both, the reclaimer may rely on the alternative more favourable to him.[45] If it is neither, rule 264 (*c*) might apply on the very doubtful ground that neither the Rules giving the right to reclaim [46] nor paragraph (*c*) refer expressly to an interlocutor in a " cause."

The first part of section 6 of the 1857 Act provides that it shall not be competent to bring under review any interlocutor which does not finally dispose of the merits. This is inconsistent with the Rules, which provide that, subject to procedural rules, any interlocutor may be reclaimed against,[47] and is repealed, at least in so far as it makes it incompetent to bring such an interlocutor under review by reclaiming against it,[48] and it is reclaimable under rule 264 (*c*). The opposite view has been taken,[49] but no reasons are given and it was contradicted by the procedure followed in a case decided the following year.[50] In a petition for the appointment of a factor and for authority to him to complete title to stock the Lord Ordinary made the appointment, refused *in hoc statu* the crave for authority to complete title and granted leave to reclaim. He therefore did not dispose finally of the merits, a fact emphasised by the Lord President. In granting leave to reclaim the Lord Ordinary was clearly proceeding under the Rules of Court,[51] which provide that such an interlocutor may be reclaimed against with leave. The Division did not question the competency of the reclaiming motion.

Title to reclaim

Under the Rules of Court any party to a cause may reclaim.[52] Nevertheless, where the Lord Ordinary sequestrated a trust estate and appointed a factor, it was held that beneficiaries who were called as respondents and opposed the petition in the Outer House had no title to reclaim.[53] The

---

[44] 1954 S.C. 215.
[45] *Reavis* v. *Clan Line Steamers*, 1925 S.C. 725.
[46] rr. 261, 262 (*a*).
[47] rr. 261, 262 (*a*).
[48] s. 6 was probably not intended to apply to review by reclaiming against a subsequent interlocutor, which first became competent in 1868. But even if in terms it covers that situation it is inconsistent with r. 262 (*c*) and so repealed.
[49] Thomson and Middleton, *Manual of Court of Session Procedure*, p. 312.
[50] *Brower's Executor*, 1938 S.C. 451.
[51] Rules of Court 1936, Chap. V, rule 4 (*c*), now Rules of Court 1965, rule 264 (*c*).
[52] r. 262 (*a*).
[53] *Courage* v. *Ballantine*, 1946 S.C. 351.

ground of decision was that as the interlocutor had relieved the trustees of
the burden of administration, only they had a title to crave its recall. The
objection was taken by the court *ex proprio motu*, and counsel for the
reclaimers seem to have been taken by surprise, for they did not refer to
the relevant rule [54] or to *Maxwell's Trustees* v. *Maxwell*,[55] where in similar
circumstances a reclaiming note at the instance of beneficiaries was entertained without objection. A beneficiary has an interest to oppose such an
appointment at least on the ground of expense.[56] In a subsequent case it
was held that a respondent who had not appeared in the Outer House was
entitled to reclaim against an interlocutor appointing a factor on a partnership estate,[57] a decision in accordance both with the Rules and with
section 6.[58]

Effect on prior interlocutors

Until 1868 the only method of bringing any interlocutor under review
was by reclaiming against it.[59] Section 52 of the Court of Session Act
1868 introduced a second method, by providing that a reclaiming note
should have the effect of submitting to review the whole of the prior
interlocutors of the Lord Ordinary. This gave the party dissatisfied with
an interlocutor an option. He could bring it under review either by reclaiming within the reclaiming days or (subject to limitations) by reclaiming against a subsequent interlocutor.[60]

The earlier Rules of Court provided that a reclaiming motion should
have the same effect as a reclaiming note under the law and practice as
defined in section 52.[61] Under that law and practice, as already pointed
out,[62] section 52 did not apply to the proceedings specified in section 4 of
the Distribution of Business Act 1857, which included proceedings relating
to judicial factories. The effect of this appears to be that this provision
of the Rules did not apply to such proceedings and that no interlocutor,
whether on the original petition or on an application in the course of the
administration could be brought under review by a reclaiming note against
a subsequent interlocutor.

The Rules of Court 1965 abandoned the reference to section 52, but
re-enacted it in substance.[63] This may make no difference, on an application of the principle that when an expression which has been judicially
construed is repeated in a subsequent enactment the same meaning should
be attached to it.[64] But even if the rule is construed without reference to

---

[54] Rules of Court 1936, Chap. V, r. 2 (*a*), now Rules of Court 1965, r. 262 (*a*).
[55] (1874) 2 R. 71.
[56] *Yuill* v. *Ross* (1900) 3 F. 96 at pp. 98, 99.
[57] *Tomkins* v. *Cohen*, 1951 S.C. 22.
[58] *Sharp* v. *McCall* (1860) 23 D. 38; *Ewing* v. *Barclay* (1864) 3 M. 127.
[59] Court of Session Act 1825, s. 18, Court of Session Act 1850, s. 11, both repealed: Administration of Justice (Scotland) Act, 1933, s. 39 and Sched. See *Macqueen* v. *Tod* (1899)
1 F. 859 at p. 861.
[60] *Inglis* v. *National Bank of Scotland*, 1911 S.C. 6 at p. 9.
[61] *Macaskill* v. *Nicol*, 1943 S.C. 17, particularly Lord Mackay at p. 21.
[62] See p. 135.
[63] r. 262 (*c*).
[64] *Barras* v. *Aberdeen Steam Trawling and Fishing Co.*, 1933 S.C. (H.L.) 21.

the law and practice under section 52 the result may not be very different. The rule is qualified expressly by the words " to the effect of enabling the court to do complete justice " [65] and implicitly by the general principle that a prior interlocutor is not brought under review if it has been acted on as the basis of subsequent proceedings.[66] For either or both of these reasons the court will probably hesitate, except in unusual circumstances, to review a prior interlocutor on the basis of which the factor has been administering the estate. Further, just as the proceedings for settling the fund *in medio* and for deciding the competition have been treated as independent processes within a multiplepoinding for the purposes of section 52,[67] so the proceedings for disposing of a note or report might be treated as a separate process within a process of judicial factory. There is no place for the well established principle that a reclaiming motion does not bring under review a prior interlocutor which is expressly or by implication final.[68] The finality provisions of section 6 of the 1857 Act have been repealed, that in the first part of the section as inconsistent with the Rules and that in the second part expressly, and there is none in the Rules. At least it would require a most intricate argument on statutory construction to support the proposition that section 28 of the Court of Session Act 1868 now applies to a process of judicial factory.

---

[65] *Winning* v. *Napier, Son & Company Ltd.*, 1963 S.C. 293 at p. 300.

[66] *North British Railway Co.* v. *Gledden* (1872) 10 M. 870; *Ferguson's Trustee* v. *Reid*, 1931 S.C. 714; *Macaskill* v. *Nicol*, 1943 S.C. 17 (second ground of judgment); *Spencer* v. *Macmillan*, 1857 S.L.T. (notes) 32.

[67] *Walker's Trustee* v. *Walker* (1878) 5 R. 678; *Duncan's Factor* v. *Duncan* (1874) 1 R. 964.

[68] Thomson and Middleton, *Manual of Court of Session Procedure*, p. 312; *Macaskill* v. *Nicol*, 1943 S.C. 17 (first ground of judgment).

Chapter XX

SHERIFF COURT

Introductory

General

A sheriff may appoint a commissary factor, or an interim manager at the instance of a landlord to look after a farm which the tenant is neglecting,[1] or to take charge of property during a litigation before him,[2] or he may take that method of regulating possession pending appeal.[3] But his only power to appoint a judicial factor is statutory.[4] Under the Judicial Factors (Scotland) Act 1880 he may appoint a factor *loco tutoris* or a curator *bonis*, and under the Bankruptcy (Scotland) Act 1913 he may appoint a factor on the estate of a deceased person [5] or an interim factor where a petition for sequestration or summary sequestration has been presented to him.[6] Unless the contrary intention appears, the term " sheriff " includes both sheriff principal and sheriff.[7] The grounds for making appointments, granting special powers, etc. are similar to those in the Court of Session, and reference is made to the appropriate chapters. This chapter is concerned with jurisdiction, competency, procedure and appeal in the sheriff court. Under the 1880 Act jurisdiction depends, and under the 1913 Act may depend, on residence.

Residence

Residence within the jurisdiction of the sheriff is one of the grounds of jurisdiction under the Sheriff Courts (Scotland) Act 1907, its meaning there is, subject to one reservation, settled, and there is no reason to give it any different meaning as a ground of jurisdiction either in the Act of 1880 or in the Act of 1913. To found jurisdiction under the Sheriff Courts (Scotland) Act residence must be for not less than forty days,[8] and it must be actual, not constructive,[9] that is to say the defender must live within the jurisdiction, though he may be temporarily absent for short periods.[10] A soldier serving abroad does not reside at his civilian home.[11]

---

[1] *Gibson* v. *Clark* (1895) 23 R. 294.
[2] *Affleck* v. *Affleck* (1862) 24 D. 291; *Drysdale* v. *Lawson* (1842) 4 D. 1061.
[3] Sheriff Courts (Scotland) Act 1907, r. 91.
[4] *Rowe* v. *Rowe* (1872) 9 S.L.R. 493. In *Muir* v. *More Nisbett* (1881) 19 S.L.R. 59, it does not seem to have been argued that the sheriff-substitute had no power to appoint a judicial factor. A sheriff has no jurisdiction to appoint a factor under the Partnership Act 1890; *Pollock* v. *Campbell*, 1962 S.L.T. (Sh. Ct.) 89.
[5] ss. 163, 164. [6] s. 14.
[7] Sheriff Courts (Scotland) Act 1971, s. 4.
[8] *McNeill* v. *McNeill*, 1960 S.C. 30.
[9] *Carter* v. *Allison*, 1966 S.C. 257 at p. 274.
[10] *Ibid.* at p. 267.
[11] *Findlay* v. *Donachie*, 1944 S.C. 306; *McCord* v. *McCord*, 1946 S.C. 198.

A decision [12] that a minor student living in lodgings in Glasgow with no definite intention of returning to his father's house in Renfrewshire was properly cited at his father's house has been doubted,[13] and the view apparently taken in that case that events after the date of citation are irrelevant has been negatived.[14] Whether compulsory residence always founds jurisdiction is not clear. A soldier " resides " where he is stationed, although he has no choice,[15] but in that case opinions were reserved as to whether a person serving a term of imprisonment " resides " in the prison.[16] It has been held under the Act of 1880 that a woman confined to an asylum resided at her husband's house [17] and that an inmate of an asylum resided at his previous home.[18] But these decisions may be doubtful since the court had no hesitation in appointing a curator *bonis* on the estate of a farmer whose home was in Cumberland, but who was in an asylum in Dumfriesshire, and this was no case of emergency since the petition was presented by his wife and sons and his property was in England.[19] Under the Poor Law (Scotland) Act 1898, which may have some bearing,[20] a lunatic was held to reside in the asylum.[21]

Judicial Factors (Scotland) Act 1880

Competency and jurisdiction

The sheriff principal or the sheriff may appoint a factor *loco tutoris* or a curator *bonis* to a person suffering from mental disorder or to a minor,[22] subject to two conditions. The first is that the yearly value of the estate does not exceed £100, estimated as prescribed by the Act.[23] The Act is expressed permissively—" it shall be competent "—and does not support the view that the application must be made in the sheriff court.[24] Such an appointment has been made in the Court of Session with full expenses,[25] but the decision seems to proceed on a mistaken interpretation of section 7 of the Pupils Protection Act 1849. If subsequent acquisitions increase the yearly value above £100, the appointment stands. The second condition is that the petition " be presented to the sheriff principal or sheriff of the county in which the pupil or person suffering from mental disorder [or minor] [26] is resident." If the factor resigns or dies, the application for a

---

12 *Steel* v. *Lindsay* (1881) 9 R. 160.
13 *Findlay* v. *Donachie*, 1944 S.C. 306 at p. 310.
14 *Carter* v. *Allison*, 1966 S.C. 257.
15 *Martin* v. *Szyzka*, 1943 S.C. 203.
16 *Ibid.* at pp. 207, 215.
17 *Henry* (1896) 12 Sh.Ct.Rep. 121.
18 *McCormick* (1897) 13 Sh.Ct.Rep. 184; *Dougall* (1906) 22 Sh.Ct.Rep. 292.
19 *Watson* (O.H.) 1932 S.L.T. 434, 1932 S.N. 66. In *Harper* (O.H.) 1932 S.L.T. 496, where the ward, a foreigner, was in an Edinburgh asylum, she apparently had no home, there was an emergency, and her property was in Scotland.
20 *Carter* v. *Allison*, 1966 S.C. 257 at p. 267.
21 *Edinburgh Parish Council* v. *Local Government Board for Scotland*, 1915 S.C.(H.L.) 44.
22 *Penny* v. *Scott* (1894) 22 R. 5, commented on at p. 17.
23 s. 4 (2). See *Miss A.M.* v. *Miss B.H.M.* (1950) 66 Sh.Ct.Rep. 276.
24 Thomson and Middleton, *Manual of Court of Session Procedure*, p. 264.
25 *Fleming* (O.H.) (1910) 48 S.L.R. 8.
26 *Penny* v. *Scott* (1894) 22 R. 5.

new appointment must be presented in the sheriff court where the original
appointment was made, although the ward is residing elsewhere,[27] and
although the annual value was increased to over £100. This accords with
the principle of *Primrose* v. *Caledonian Railway Co.*,[28] where it was held
that, although a Lord Ordinary had no power under the relevant statute to
appoint a factor *ab initio*, he could competently appoint a successor on
the death of a factor appointed by the court, at least *ad interim*.

Procedure [29]

The Act provides that proceedings for appointment shall commence
by petition.[30] Otherwise, the procedure is prescribed by the Codifying
Act of Sederunt,[31] which in substance repeats the Act of Sederunt of
January 14, 1881. All applications are to be disposed of summarily,[32]
and, although the C.A.S. does to some extent define the form of the proceedings and contains provisions at variance with those of the Sheriff
Courts (Scotland) Acts 1907,[33] they are " summary applications." The
word " application " in the C.A.S. includes not only the petition for
appointment but also incidental applications such as those for special
powers and discharge.[34] While it seems to be implied that these are also
to be made by petition,[35] it is specifically provided that an application for
discharge shall be by note.[36] The title given to the document seems
unimportant, since the contents must be the same and all incidental
applications form steps in the original process.[37]

The first order in every application is for intimation, including intimation to the accountant, service, answers, and possibly advertisement.[38]
If the application is for an appointment and an application for a similar
appointment has already been intimated to the accountant, he informs
the sheriff-clerk.[39] No directions, however, are given as to the procedure

---

[27] *Accountant of Court* (1893) 20 R. 573.
[28] (1851) 13 D. 1214.
[29] A number of provisions relate procedure in the sheriff court to that in the Court of Session.
These include provisions that every sheriff principal and sheriff respectively shall have
over factors appointed in the sheriff court the same powers that under the Pupils Protection
Act 1849 a Division or the Lord Ordinary respectively have over factors appointed in the
Court of Session (1880 Act, s. 4); that for the purposes of the 1880 Act the word " sheriff "
shall be substituted for the words " Lord Ordinary " and " Court " in the 1849 Act (Act
of Sederunt, January 14, 1881, repeated in C.A.S., L, VIII, s. 13); and that all applications under the recited Acts, which include the 1880 Act, shall be dealt with in manner
directed by the Distribution of Business Act 1857 (Judicial Factors (Scotland) Act 1889,
s. 14).
[30] s. 4, 1.
[31] L. VIII.
[32] *Ibid.* s. 1. See Sheriff Courts (Scotland) Act 1907, s. 50.
[33] s. 3 (*b*). Under the Act a party is cited to appear (rule 4 (*a*)), while under the C.A.S. the
order is for answers (s. 4). But the Act recognises that there may be differences in procedure
between itself and the Act under which the summary application is brought (s. 50, proviso).
[34] s. 3.
[35] s. 4, " copy of petition on the walls."
[36] s. 12.
[37] s. 3. When a petition for removal of a factor was presented in the Court of Session, the
court ordered transmission of the whole process from the sheriff court; *Forrest* v. *Forrest's
Judicial Factor* (1898) 6 S.L.T. 68.
[38] s. 4.
[39] s. 5.

then to be followed such as are contained in section 17 of the Bankruptcy (Scotland) Act 1913, under which all sequestrations are remitted to the court which granted the first or in certain circumstances to the most expedient.

When not otherwise expressed in the interlocutor, caution must be found within three weeks of the appointment, but the sheriff may on motion made before the expiry of the period and on cause shown allow further time.[40] If the cautioner is a private person, certificates of his reputed sufficiency are required from a justice of the peace and the petitioner's solicitor. If the cautioner is an insurance company it must be taken bound to intimate non-payment of the premium to the accountant.[41] The premium, or such part thereof as the accountant deems proper, and the expense of the necessary procedure in obtaining approval of the bond or the limitation of the amount are good charges against the estate.[42] On the death or insolvency of the cautioner or non-payment of the premium the factor and the sheriff-clerk must report to the accountant so that new caution may be found or a new factor appointed.[43]

The appointment is made with only the usual powers,[44] and if the factor desires special powers he submits an application in writing to the accountant, whose opinion is laid before the sheriff. The sheriff then deals with the application after such procedure as he thinks necessary.[45]

If the factor keeps in his hands more than twenty-five pounds of money belonging to the estate for more than ten days he must be debited with interest at 20 per cent. on the excess for any period beyond the ten days.[46] This provision is imperative.[47] All outlays by the accountant and sheriff-clerk and office fees in the factory form a charge against the estate, unless the sheriff subjects the factor personally to the whole or part thereof.[48]

To obtain discharge the factor lodges a note in process, which is disposed of by the sheriff after intimation and service and a report by the accountant.[49] The Court of Session has co-ordinate jurisdiction with the sheriff to recall an appointment.[50] There is no report of such an application in the Court of Session, but an application there for the removal of a factor appointed in the sheriff court (for which there is no statutory warrant) should be presented in the Outer House, and transmission of the sheriff court process is ordered.[51] Presumably the same procedure would

---

[40] s. 6.
[41] s. 7.
[42] s. 8.
[43] s. 10.
[44] s. 6.
[45] s. 11. An Outer House decision which proceeded on the assumption that a sheriff could not grant special powers has not affected practice: *Fleming* (1910) 48 S.L.R. 8.
[46] Pupils Protection Act 1849, s. 5, as applied by C.A.S., L, VIII, s. 13.
[47] *Ballingal* (1853) 15 D. 711. The accountant has no express power to modify or remit as under Rules of Court 1965, r. 200 (*g*).
[48] C.A.S., L, VIII, s. 14.
[49] *Ibid.* s. 12. As to discharge see Chap. XVII.
[50] Judicial Factors (Scotland) Act 1880, s. 4 (9).
[51] *Forrest* v. *Forrest's J.F.* (1898) 6 S.L.T. 68.

be followed in an application for recall of an appointment, made by petition.[52] The statute does not expressly mention discharge in the Court of Session.

Appeal

As already mentioned, the petition may be presented either to the sheriff principal or to the sheriff, and if it is presented to the sheriff there is a right of appeal to the sheriff principal.

Section 4 (5) enacts: " In all cases of any . . . reclaiming note being competent from a determination of the Lord Ordinary . . . an appeal shall be competent in the like cases from a determination by a sheriff to the sheriff principal. . . ." " Lord Ordinary " meant the Lord Ordinary in the Court of Session discharging the duties of Junior Lord Ordinary,[53] and the subsection clearly referred to section 6 of the Distribution of Business Act 1857. Section 6 provided that only a judgment pronounced by the Lord Ordinary on the merits might be reclaimed against, provided that a reclaiming note was boxed within eight days. It thus defined the type of interlocutor which was reclaimable, *viz.* an interlocutor on the merits of the particular application, and (a separate matter) prescribed the procedure for reclaiming. An appeal to the sheriff principal against an interlocutor refusing an appointment *in hoc statu* and continuing the cause, lodged ten days after the interlocutor was pronounced, was held incompetent on two grounds, (first) that the interlocutor was not on the merits, and (second) that under the rules applicable in the sheriff court the appeal ought to have been taken within seven days.[54]

Although the matter is not free from doubt,[55] the effect of the Administration of Justice (Scotland) Act 1933 and the Rules of Court appears to be to extend the class of appealable interlocutor. Section 3 of the Act provides that any reference in any Act to the Junior Lord Ordinary shall be construed as a reference to a judge sitting in the Outer House. The reference in section 4 (5) of the Act of 1880 to an interlocutor pronounced by the Junior Lord Ordinary thus becomes a reference to an interlocutor pronounced by a judge sitting in the Outer House,[56] and under the Rules of Court any such interlocutor is reclaimable,[57] subject to conditions as to reclaiming days and leave.[58] It cannot be intended that the general provision should apply unconditionally in the sheriff court. Otherwise, apart from personal bar, any interlocutor would be appealable at any time. It must be implied that, as had been held under the previous law,[59] the sheriff court conditions apply. These conditions " affect " the right of

---

[52] Administration of Justice (Scotland) Act 1933, s. 6 (1).
[53] Distribution of Business Act 1857, s. 3.
[54] *Paul* v. *Logan* (1902) 18 Sh.Ct.Rep. 223.
[55] Sheriff Dobie did not refer to the Act and Rules in this connection: *Sheriff Court Practice,* p. 604.
[56] See Interpretation Act 1889, s. 38 (1) and *Cowdenbeath Gas Co. Ltd.* v. *Provost of Cowdenbeath,* 1915 S.C. 387.
[57] Rules of Court 1965, r. 262 (*a*). See Chap. XIX, Review.
[58] *Ibid.* r. 264.
[59] *Paul* v. *Logan* (1902) 18 Sh.Ct.Rep. 223.

appeal provided by the Act of 1880, as amended, in the sense that they complete it and make it workable, but not in the sense that they extend or restrict the right.[60]

A final judgment may be appealed against without leave within three months if not sooner extracted or implemented.[61] A final judgment is one which disposes of the subject-matter of the cause,[62] and, as " cause " includes a summary application,[63] there will normally be a final judgment in every application, including incidental applications. The word " implemented " points primarily to the obtempering of a decree, but it probably includes action taken on an interlocutor, e.g. paying money from the estate under a power granted by the interlocutor. So far the law appears to be unchanged. Where there has been a change is that certain judgments which are not on the merits may now be appealed. Of these the most likely to occur in a judicial factory are those sisting an application or allowing or refusing proof and those appealed with leave. The appeal in such cases must be taken within fourteen days.[64] Although rule 27 provides that " at any time before implement of a decree in absence the defender may apply to be reponed," this appears to be qualified by rule 25 to the effect that a decree in absence shall become entitled to all the privileges of a decree in foro in six months from its date. On that view the provision of the 1880 Act [65] that no decree in absence may be opened up after the elapse of twelve months cannot affect appeals.

An appeal submits to review the prior interlocutors in the cause,[66] but as each application is a cause, only the prior interlocutors in that application are affected. Probably therefore it will not be necessary to decide whether the twelve months rule has been impliedly repealed by the wide provisions of section 29. Rule 262 (c) of the Rules of Court 1965 provides that a reclaiming motion brings prior interlocutors under review " to the effect of enabling the court to do complete justice." Section 29 does not include these words, but it is subject to the same implied qualifications as rule 262 (c).[67]

Bankruptcy (Scotland) Act 1913, ss. 163, 164

Competency and jurisdiction

These sections provide for the appointment of a factor on the estate of a deceased person, and the circumstances justifying such an appointment have already been described.[68] The application is competent in the sheriff court only if the assets of the deceased are estimated not to exceed

---

[60] Sheriff Courts (Scotland) Act 1907, s. 50, second proviso.
[61] Sheriff Courts (Scotland) Act 1907, s. 27 and r. 86.
[62] Ibid. 3 (h).
[63] Ibid s. 3 (d) as amended.
[64] Ibid. s. 27 and r. 86.
[65] 1880 Act, s. 4 (8).
[66] 1907 Act, s. 29.
[67] Chap. XIX " Review: effect on prior interlocutors."
[68] Chap. VII.

£500, and it must be made " to the sheriff of the sheriffdom within which the deceased resided or carried on business during the year immediately preceding the date of the petition, or within which heritage belonging to the deceased at the time of his death is situated." The residence or carrying on of business requirement is satisfied by residence or carrying on of business for part of the year.[69] " Heritage belonging to the deceased " has not been judicially considered, but the phrase will probably be interpreted in the same way as the word " owner " in the Sheriff Courts (Scotland) Act 1907, that is to say that to constitute ownership infeftment is not necessary, but missives alone are not enough.[70]

Procedure

Rule 170 [71] of the Sheriff Courts (Scotland) Act 1907 provides that the procedure applicable to the appointment of judicial factors appointed under section 4 of the Act of 1880 shall apply to the appointment of judicial factors by the sheriff under section 163 of the 1913 Act. The rule appears to be limited to the procedure for making the appointment, including possibly that for appeal. It cannot affect jurisdiction, since the 1880 Act applies to the estate of a living person and section 163 to that of one deceased. Nor can it affect the administration since the 1880 Act provides for a continuing administration and section 163 for distribution. Reference is therefore made to what is said about the procedure for making an appointment under the 1880 Act.

Duties of factor

These, so far as special to the office are, it is thought, similar to those of a factor appointed by the Court of Session. When power to appoint was conferred on the court by the Bankruptcy (Scotland) Act 1856, the court considered it necessary to regulate the procedure of the factor, and an Act of Sederunt was passed for that purpose.[72] That Act of Sederunt was in substance repeated by the C.A.S.,[73] which was in force when the 1913 Act conferred jurisdiction also on the sheriff. Since any reference in the C.A.S to the Act of 1856 is held to import a reference to the Act of 1913 [74] and no Act of Sederunt was passed to regulate the procedure of a factor appointed by the sheriff, the inference is that the C.A.S. was regarded as a " relative Act of Sederunt " in terms of section 163 and therefore as applying, *mutatis mutandis*, to a factor appointed by the sheriff.[75] The relevant provisions of the C.A.S. have been superseded *quoad* the Court of Session by the Rules of Court,[76] but the substance is unchanged and it is immaterial whether the Act of Sederunt enacting the

---

[69] Goudy, *Bankruptcy* (4th ed.), p. 452.
[70] *Embassy Picture House (Troon) Ltd.* v. *Cammo Developments Ltd.*, 1971 S.C. 1.
[71] Added by A.S., July 16, 1936.
[72] A.S. November 25, 1857.
[73] G, ii.
[74] A.S. January 6, 1914.
[75] This view is implied in *Goudy on Bankruptcy* (4th ed.), p. 501.
[76] Rules of Court 1965, r. 201.

Rules has become, or the C.A.S. remains, *quoad* the sheriff court a "relative Act of Sederunt." Reference is therefore made to Chapter VII.

Appeal

The question of appeal depends in the first place on the true construction of rule 170 [77] of the Sheriff Courts (Scotland) Act 1907, which provides that " the procedure applicable to the appointment of judicial factors " under section 4 of the Act of 1880 " shall apply to the appointment of judicial factors by the sheriff " under section 163. As before stated,[78] this appears to be limited to procedure applicable to the making of the appointment. The next question is whether the words " procedure applicable to the appointment " include the procedure for appeal against an interlocutor making or refusing an appointment. If they do, there is an appeal from the sheriff to the sheriff principal,[79] whose decision is final.[80] If they do not, appeal to the sheriff principal is incompetent, as in the case of section 14 (considered below), and there is an appeal to the Court of Session, which is not excluded expressly or by necessary implication,[81] provided there is a *lis*.[82] There may certainly be a *lis* concerning the distribution of the estate, and one may also arise on the application for an appointment.[83] There are two reasons for holding that rule 170 does not apply to appeals. First, the jurisdiction of the Court of Session can hardly be said to be excluded by necessary implication from a rule which is open to more than one interpretation. Secondly, if rule 170 extends to appeals, there will be two kinds of appeal, one to the sheriff principal against the grant or refusal of an application for appointment and one to the Court of Session against an interlocutor disposing of objections to a scheme of division amongst the creditors or disposing of the surplus.

Bankruptcy (Scotland) Act 1913, s. 14

Jurisdiction

Section 14 empowers the court to which a petition for sequestration is presented to appoint a factor for the interim preservation of the estate. This must mean a court which prima facie could competently award sequestration, *viz.* either the Court of Session or " the sheriff of any county in which the debtor has resided or carried on business for the year [*i.e.* for the complete year [84]] preceding the date of the petition or in the case of a deceased debtor for the year preceding the date of his death." [85]

---

[77] Added by A.S., July 16, 1936.
[78] See Procedure, *supra*.
[79] Judicial Factors (Scotland) Act 1880, s. 4 (5); *Goudy on Bankruptcy* (4th ed.), p. 445.
[80] Act of 1880, s. 4 (10).
[81] *Arcari* v. *Dumbartonshire County Council*, 1948 S.C. 62 at p. 66; *Purves* v. *Groat* (1900) 2 F. 1174 (appeal against irregular procedure).
[82] *Arcari* (*supra*); *Kaye* v. *Hunter*, 1958 S.C. 208.
[83] *Macdonald, Fraser & Co.* v. *Cairns's Exrx.*, 1932 S.C. 699; *Marshall* v. *Graham* (1859) 21 D. 203.
[84] *Goudy on Bankruptcy* (4th ed.), p. 452.
[85] s. 16.

Of all the statutory provisions conferring jurisdiction on the sheriff this alone requires residence or the carrying on of business to be in a " county " for a specific period. Although the union of counties into one sheriffdom has effect as a complete union as regards the jurisdiction, powers and duties of the sheriff principal and sheriffs [86] and therefore any sheriff within the sheriffdom has jurisdiction throughout the sheriffdom,[87] subject possibly to the power to check abuses,[88] he has no power to award sequestration unless the debtor has resided or carried on business for a year within one of the counties in the sheriffdom. Accordingly, where the petitioner could make up the year only by adding together residences in two of the counties the petition was dismissed.[89] In a summary sequestration, on the other hand, all that is required is that the debtor should have resided or carried on business within the sheriffdom during the year immediately preceding the date of the petition.[90]

Appointment and duties

The circumstances justifying an appointment and the particular duties of the factor are described in Chapter X.

Appeal

It does not appear to have been considered whether there is a right of appeal to the sheriff principal. The general statement in Goudy [91] that there is no such right is not specifically applied to section 14 and is qualified by the reference to sequestration. It rests on the meaning of the words " the sheriff." In the authority cited [92] the court held it incompetent to appeal to the sheriff principal against an interlocutor by the sheriff reviewing a deliverance of a trustee in bankruptcy. The Act allowed an appeal " to the Lord Ordinary or the sheriff," and, as Lord Gillies put it, " ' the sheriff ' in the statute means either the sheriff principal or the sheriff, but not both." This dictum was founded on by a sheriff principal in refusing as incompetent an appeal against an interlocutor designating a burial ground, and his opinion was expressly approved by Lord Kinnear.[93] The rule was restated by Lord Sands with the qualification that it may appear from the terms of the relevant statute that " sheriff " means the sheriff court as distinct from the individual sheriff.[94] Section 14 confers the right to appoint, not expressly on the sheriff, but on " the court to which a petition for sequestration is presented." These

---

[86] Administration of Justice (Scotland) Act 1933, s. 31 (3), repeating in substance the provision of the Sheriff Courts (Scotland) Act 1870, s. 12.

[87] Sheriff Courts (Scotland) Act 1971, s. 7.

[88] *Tait* v. *Johnston* (1891) 18 R. 606.

[89] *Burness & Son* v. *Anderson*, 1959 S.L.T. (Sh. Ct.) 47.

[90] Bankruptcy (Scotland) Act 1913, s. 175 (1).

[91] *Bankruptcy* (4th ed.), p. 444.

[92] *Balderston* v. *Richardson* (1841) 3 D. 597.

[93] *Strichen Parish Council* v. *Goodwillie*, 1908 S.C. 835; *Areari* v. *Dumbartonshire County Council*, 1948 S.C. 62 at p. 67.

[94] *Ross-shire County Council* v. *Macrae-Gilstrap*, 1930 S.C. 808 at p. 812. *Bain* v. *Ormiston*, 1928 S.C. 764, is an example of the qualification.

words, however, are defined in section 16 as the Court of Session or the
sheriff of the county, and the provision for appeal to the Court of Session
within eight days [95] is inconsistent with the existence of normal rights of
appeal.[96] It appears therefore that the general statement in Goudy applies
to section 14, and that there is no right of appeal to the sheriff principal.

Although the section gives a right of appeal to the Court of Session
only against the making of an appointment, an appeal against refusal
was entertained without objection,[97] no doubt on the ground that the
jurisdiction of the Court of Session was not excluded,[98] at least where the
sheriff's interlocutor was incompetent.[99]

---

[95] s. 166. A factor may be appointed after sequestration; *Partridge* v. *Baillie* (1873) 1 R. 253
[96] *Purves* v. *Groat* (1900) 2 F. 1174 at p. 1176.
[97] *Partridge* v. *Baillie* (1873) 1 R. 253.
[98] *Marr & Sons* v. *Lindsay* (1881) 8 R. 784.
[99] *Purves* v. *Groat* (1900) 2 F. 1174.

APPENDIX

1. Distribution of Business Act 1857*

Extract from an Act to Regulate the Distribution of Business in the Court of Session in Scotland (20 and 21 Vict. cap. 56).—[25th August 1857.]

Summary Petitions, etc.

4. All summary petitions and applications to the Lords of Council and Session which are not incident to actions or causes actually depending at the time of presenting the same, shall be brought before the Junior Lord Ordinary officiating in the Outer House, who shall deal therewith and dispose thereof as to him shall seem just; and in particular, all petitions and applications falling under any of the descriptions following shall be so enrolled before, and dealt with and disposed of by, the Junior Lord Ordinary, and shall not be taken in the first instance before either of the two Divisions of the Court, viz.:—

1. Petitions and applications under any of the various statutes now in force relative to entails.
2. Petitions and applications under any of the General Railway Acts, or under the Lands Clauses Consolidation (Scotland) Act, 1845, or under any local or personal Act.
3. Petitions and applications relative to money consigned under any statute or law subject to the order, disposal, or direction of the Court of Session.
4. Petitions and applications for the appointment of judicial factors, factors *loco tutoris* or *loco absentis*, or curators *bonis*, or by any such factors or curators for extraordinary or special powers, or for exoneration or discharge.
5. All petitions, applications, and reports under the Act of the 12th and 13th *Victoria*, chapter 51, intituled, " An Act for the better protection of the property of pupils, absent persons, and persons under mental incapacity, in Scotland." [1]

Lord Ordinary to decide on such petitions, etc.

5. The Lord Ordinary before whom any such petition, application, or report shall be enrolled or brought, shall have full power to decide on and dispose of the same, after making such investigation and requiring such assistance from professional persons, or persons of science or of skill, as he shall judge proper, and his judgment upon the merits shall be subject to review in manner hereinafter provided; and the judgment of the Lord Ordinary granting or refusing any such petition or application, or disposing of any such report, unless the same shall be brought under review in

---

* Court of Session Act 1857. See Short Titles Act 1896.
[1] Section repealed: Administration of Justice (Scotland) Act 1933, s. 39 and Sched.

manner hereinafter provided, shall be equally valid and effectual as a judgment of either Division of the Court to the like effect, according to the present law and practice; and all laws and statutes inconsistent herewith are hereby repealed to the effect of rendering the provisions of this Act operative and effectual: Provided always, that such Lord Ordinary may, in special cases, if he see cause, report such petition or application to the Court, who may thereupon dispose of the same, or give such instructions thereanent to the Lord Ordinary as they may deem proper.

Review, etc. of judgments of the Lord Ordinary

6. It shall not be competent to bring under review of the Court any interlocutor pronounced by the Lord Ordinary upon any such petition, application, or report as aforesaid, with a view to investigation and inquiry merely, and which does not finally dispose thereof upon the merits; but any judgment pronounced by the Lord Ordinary on the merits, unless where the same, shall have been pronounced in terms of instructions by the Court on report as hereinbefore mentioned, may be reclaimed against by any party having lawful interest to reclaim to the Court, provided that a reclaiming-note shall be boxed within eight days, after which the judgment of the Lord Ordinary, if not so reclaimed against, shall be final.[2]

2. Act of Sederunt 1730

Act concerning Factors appointed by the Lords on the Estates of Pupils not having Tutors, and others.—[13th February 1730.]

The Lords of Council and Session, considering that they have been often applied to for appointing factors on the estates of pupils not having tutors, and of persons absent that have not sufficiently empowered persons to act for them, or who are under some incapacity for the time to manage their own estates, to the end that the estates of such pupils or persons may not suffer in the meantime, but be preserved for their behoof, and of all having interest therein: Therefore, that such persons may be under due regulations and security for the faithful and punctual fulfilling of their trust, the said Lords of Council and Session do hereby declare and ordain, That all such factors as aforesaid, appointed and authorised by them, shall be liable to pay and perform as follows:—

1. Such factors shall be liable for the annual rents of all rents and profits whatsoever which he shall recover or by diligence might have recovered; and that from and after the space of one year after the said rents and profits became due, or might have been recovered, as said is, and until he make due payment of the same.

2. Such factor, shall within six months after extracting the factory, make a distinct and special rental of the estate committed to his management, and lodge the same in the hands of the clerk to the act appointing and authorising him to be factor on the said estate, where it shall lie and

---

[2] Proviso repealed: Administration of Justice (Scotland) Act 1933, s. 39 and Sched.

be made forthcoming, and the inspection and perusal thereof be allowed unto all persons having interest, without fee or reward, to the end the same may be examined and the said factor charged thereby, or otherwise, as shall be found just.

3. When any alteration happens in the said rental by lowering any part of the rent (which is only to be done according to the rules of law), or by any increase of the same from improvements or discoveries or other addition, an account of such alteration shall, within three months of its happening, be by the said factor put in the hands of the said clerk, in manner, and to the ends above mentioned; and if the said rental given in by the factor shall be found deficient, or if he omit to add any increase thereof, he shall be decerned in the double of such deficiency and omission respectively.

4. Such factor shall once every year give in a scheme of his accompts, charge and discharge, to the clerk aforesaid, that all concerned may have access to see, and examine, and provide themselves with proper means of checking the same, wherein if the factor fail, he shall be liable to such a mulct as the Lords of Session shall modify, not being under an half-year's salary.

5. When bonds, bills, notes, or obligations of any sort, for money or effects, are under the factory, the said factor shall make a list or inventary thereof bearing the names of the creditor and debitor, conveyances thereof, the sum of money or the thing due, the date, the terms of payment, and the term from whence annual rent runs, and from whence it is then resting, so far as he can discover; which list and inventary, and an accompt of the alterations that shall happen, therein, shall, by the said factor, be put in the clerk's hands respectively at the times, to the ends, and in the manner, and under the certifications respectively aforesaid.

6. If corns, cattle, outsight or insight plenishing, or moveables of any sort, shall be under the factory, the said factor shall make inventary thereof expressing all the particulars and the quantity and quality or condition of the same; which inventary, and an accompt of such alterations as shall happen therein, expressing whence the alterations arose and the price or value got for any of the said moveables that have been disposed of, shall likewise be put in the said clerk's hands respectively at the time, to the ends, and in manner, and under the certifications respectively aforesaid; and the said factor shall be obliged to manage such obligations for money or effects, and to manage or dispose of such moveables, according to the rules of law and as prudence requires, for the benefit of the proprietor and all having interest.

7. Where it is necessary by law that such money, or effects, or moveables should be confirmed, the said factor may confirm the same in his own name as executor-dative, and as factor appointed by the Lords of Council and Session on the estate of such a person, and for the use and behoof of the said person and of all that have or shall have interest, unless some other person having a title offer to confirm, and shall put in the

said clerk's hands a just and full copy of the said testament, and of all
eiks he may afterwards make thereto, within the space of three months
after the confirmation, and that under the penalty of such a mulct as the
said Lords shall modify.

8. Such factor shall have power to grant tacks or leases, to continue
during all the time that the estate set in tack shall remain under the
inspection of the said Lords of Session, and for one year further.

9. Such factor shall make payment of his intromissions to such person
or persons, and at such times, as the said Lords, shall in the factory or
otherwise, appoint.

10. If the factor fail in any part of the premises, it shall be a ground
of removing him, without prejudice of the several particular certifications
aforesaid.

11. In the bond of cautionry for such factor, he and his cautioner
shall be bound conjunctly and severally, and be obliged for the said
factor's observing the rules and instructions appointed and ordained by
this Act, or that he shall be otherwise liable to in law.

12. This Act shall extend to all factors to be henceforth appointed
and authorised by the said Lords, except such factors as are regulated by
former Acts of Sederunt.

And the Lords ordain this Act of Sederunt to be recorded in the
Books of Sederunt, and printed and published in the ordinary manner.

---

3. Form of Bond of Caution

I, —— considering that a Petition having been presented to the Lords of
Council and Session for and in name of ——, praying their Lordships,
for the reasons therein stated, *inter alia*, to appoint a ——, Lord ——
Lord Ordinary, by Interlocutor dated the —— day of —— Nineteen
hundred and ——, nominated and appointed me to be —— foresaid with
the usual powers, I always finding caution before extract: Further considering that the caution to be found by me has been fixed at —— Pounds sterling, and that THE NATIONAL GUARANTEE AND SURETYSHIP ASSOCIATION,
LIMITED, hereinafter called " the said Association," have agreed to become
Cautioners for me to the amount of the said sum under the conditions
and in consideration of the annual premium after mentioned: Therefore,
I, the said —— as principal, bind and oblige myself, my heirs, executors,
and successors whomsoever, and we THE NATIONAL GUARANTEE AND
SURETYSHIP ASSOCIATION, LIMITED, as Cautioners, Sureties, and full
debtors for and with the said —— bind and oblige ourselves, and the
whole funds and property of the said Association, and we, the whole parties
hereto, bind and oblige ourselves and our foresaids, all conjunctly and
severally, that I, the said —— shall do exact diligence in performing my
duty as —— foresaid, and shall render just and regular accounts of my
intromissions and management in relation to the premises, and make

payment of whatever sum or sums of money shall be justly due by me as —— foresaid, and that to such person or persons as shall be found to have best right thereto; and that I shall observe and perform every duty incumbent on me as foresaid, in conformity to the rules and instructions prescribed, or to be prescribed, for the discharge of my said office, or to which I shall be otherwise subject in law: Providing and declaring always, as it is hereby expressly provided and declared, that the guarantee of the said Association is limited to, and shall not in any case exceed, the foresaid sum of —— Pounds sterling: And it is hereby agreed that the Court of Session, after having ascertained by a certificate under the hand of the Accountant of Court, the balance due by the said —— shall have power by an order or interlocutor to be pronounced in the said application, or otherwise, to find the said Association liable, as Cautioners foresaid, for the said sum of —— Pounds sterling, or for any smaller sum, and to decern therefor, which finding and decree shall be final and conclusive against the said Association: And it is hereby provided that if at any time the said Association shall desire to be relieved of the guarantee hereby undertaken by them, it shall be in their power to put an end thereto by serving on the said —— or his representatives, and lodging with the Accountant of the Court of Session at his office, a notice in writing setting forth their desire to be relieved of and intention to terminate the said guarantee; and on such notice being duly served and lodged as aforesaid, then the guarantee hereby undertaken by the said Association, and all liability on the part of the said Association, shall, on the elapse of thirty days of the lodging of the said notice, without objection stated thereto, cease and determine, and the said Association shall not be liable to make good any loss, damage, or expenses which may be occasioned or incurred by or through any default of the said —— or his representatives subsequent to the elapse of the said thirty days; but providing always that such notice shall not apply to or affect any liability under these presents incurred by the said Association prior to the elapse of the said thirty days, which liability shall remain as binding as if such notice had not been given: And further declaring that when any claim in respect of such liability shall have been satisfied by the said Association, an endorsement and discharge in satisfaction thereof shall be made hereon, and signed by all the persons for whose protection these presents are granted; and when such claim or claims shall in all amount to the sum of —— Pounds sterling, these presents shall either be given up to and become the proper writ and evident of the said Association, or shall be recorded in the books of Council and Session, and an extract thereof, and of the said endorsement and discharge, shall, be delivered to the said Association, but all at the expense of the said Association: And I, the said —— bind and oblige myself and my foresaids to pay to the said Association, the sum of —— sterling on the —— day of —— in each year during the subsistence of the guarantee hereby undertaken, or until I shall have substituted therefor another guarantee or bond of caution, with the approval and to the satisfaction of the said Accountant of Court, and also to free and relieve the said Association of the sums which may be contained in the discharge to be endorsed hereon, or in any separate receipt or discharge to be granted by the said persons for whose protection these presents are granted, or others on their behalf or in their right, for the amount of such loss as aforesaid, and of the whole obligations hereby undertaken by them as my cautioners, and generally of all loss, damage, and expenses which they may incur in the premises, including the expenses which may be incurred by the said Association in employing an Accountant or otherwise in investigating the claim for such loss, or in resisting such claim in whole or in part, which the said Association are hereby authorised and empowered to do, either in their own name or in mine, if they shall see fit: And, we, both principals and cautioners, consent to the registration hereof for preservation and execution.—IN WITNESS WHEREOF

....

....

....

....   *Manager and Secretary.*

INDEX

157